Remember
Who The F*ck
You Are

REMEMBER WHO THE F*CK YOU ARE

CANDYSS LOVE

TABLE OF AFFIRMATIONS, POWER & REMEMBRANCE

FOREWORD

I have intentionally done my best to lose you.

I'm not sure if I should apologize for that.

Letting my identity as you go has opened so much freedom even acknowledging you right now feels confusing; almost like sacrilege. The detachment from you has grown so strong it feels like I'm going backwards in this journey of total recollection of my total being just by taking the time to think of you.

I know you are just an amalgam of ideas, moments, memories and experiences that only lasted for a fraction of time. Just like family pictures on a wall. The picture is only a symbol, a relic of a reality that has long since faded and folded from form back into nonexistence. We know the picture only represents a former reality. Its only purpose is to remind us of the respect we have for the flash of realness frozen forever through the still image.

A remembering of what the real once produced.

In this moment I feel the need to remember the imagining of you. The you that has been born, crucified and reborn throughout the dream of life.

To every incarnation that is dying yet and the new one that is on the verge of being born, I know all of you are only meant to be for a blip of eternity. I know I have chosen not to acknowledge you because of realizing how fleeting your nature truly is. I know each of you is only a granule of the quicksand of time. But I honor you still. I'm grateful for each grain. Not even sure which "I" is grateful right now. It's daunting to even try to conceptualize. But each of you have been vital fixtures in the picture of

Me

You

Us

New death is palpable. The exhaustion of each dimension of this current me is felt intensely in this moment. There isn't the faintest inclination of what the next mode I will materialize as will be. It's apparent the next me is breaking through the cocoon of the current and this version of myself will not survive the process. I can hear agendas, missions and purpose echoing through consciousness as thoughts that are not yet but soon to be my own. That version of me fells both foreign and familiar. Boomeranging backwards from futures on the horizon of being my here and now.

The current me I wear is no longer comfortable or suitable for the next shift. To all my previous selves I'm sorry for the lack of acknowledgment of you. I don't have to bind myself to you to appreciate you. I vow to stop and admire the picture more. To the next version of me I can feel downloading, I trust your judgement and I offer my being to invigorate your vessel. I hand you the keys of my being to mold into the forms you see fit. I will do my best to hear you, stay out of your way and prepare the path for you no matter how unsettling it may feel. All I ask is you express your needs to become my present clearly, compassionately and with love for all of my previous selves that have preceded you that are now the cells that comprise your creation.

Written by My Husband Brick_citi_buddha

INTRODUCTION

As spiritual beings having a human experience, Evolution is our birthright. For most humans before a person was even born they were experiencing trauma; a collection of emotional data and energy that would later shape the rest of their lives, thoughts, experiences, opportunities, decision making, emotional capabilities and psychological capacity. Most humans use a great portion of their time searching for fleeting emotions like happiness, joy, peace, motivation, etc not realizing this is a coping mechanism to avoid uncomfortable emotions or memories. An attempt to not feel heaviness and an unconscious method of forcing happiness into place without actually learning why it's such a rare emotion.

Trauma isn't any particular situation that has happened to a person. I describe it as any emotion that is so overwhelming to the body and brain they work together to find ways to help the human cope and stay alive if that person doesn't have the proper tools to immediately process that stressor. Which the average person doesn't. Trauma can be experienced at any age however trauma during childhood is typically the essence of who a person is. Why they self-sabotage, are angry, search for love, think, do, feel and believe anything. Childhood trauma is what's encoded in a person's subconscious mind as an unconscious program and a map of who a person is and why. If a person truly wants to evolve they must journey back to their childhood. Trauma is also passed down generationally through the womb and during the birthing process. This means newborns are already encoded with the trauma passed from their parents and perceptions of their environment.

This matters because the child evolves into an adult and spends the rest of their lives attempting to dissect why they feel angry, sad, depressed, burdensome, unwanted and unworthy. Most of these emotions aren't even theirs to carry. They are their parents' emotions that were handed down to the child. The average person doesn't know that much of what they feel emotionally was inherited.

This is why it's so important to answer the call to our healing journeys. We don't get to a place of peace until we give back what isn't ours to carry. Until we heal the wounds that are ours to nurture and find peace with.

In this book I share my personal journey and was able to heal my own trauma transmuting it into the wisdom of my soul. I give detailed life experiences and share those lessons. What I've realized is people don't need another self-help book to read one day and forget the next. People need a book they can relate to, see themselves in. A book that reminds a person that they are not alone.

I wrote this book to give the reader an opportunity to feel seen, heard and acknowledged because at the core, we are all the same. We want to be loved and none of us want to feel alone. I wrote this book as a reminder we're going through the exact same things just in different ways. This book is also a reminder to the reader to take you power back every single chance you get. As motivational as I may come off in some of these chapters there will also be chapters where I must put on my big sister hat and keep it real with you lol. Sometimes we know exactly what we need to do and what we can do better. We just need some fire under our butts to remind us to stop playing and get to it.

DEDICATION

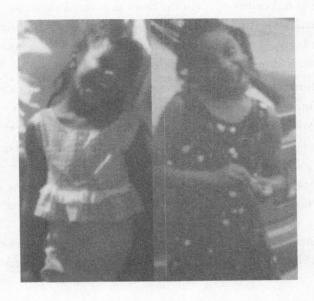

"Make sure you're writing all this down,
one day all of this will go in your book"

Dear momma,
I love you so much. I've told you every single thing since I was a little girl but the one thing I never told you is the ONLY reason I began taking my healing seriously is because I knew if something happened to you or I ever lost you; I would probably lose myself forever. So when the time comes that we do have to separate in the physical you have peace in knowing I've implemented all the lessons you've taught me. You can rest in knowing because of you & how beautifully you've raised me I will be alright. I wanted to you be able to see that all those years and even now im listening & remember every single piece of wisdom, love & guidance you've given me.

I'm on this journey because of you. Thank you for being the best momma in the world. Since I was a little girl anytime a situation would happen or id feel emotional pain the first thing you'd always say is "you're learning valuable lessons, make sure you're writing because one day this will go in your book". I honestly never thought I'd write a book however I did do what you told me & wrote everything down.

Fast forward 20+ yrs. I help guide people through their pain with my writing. You've been reminding me of who I am since I was born. You dedicated yours to making sure I had the perfect life. When I was little I'd tell kids in school we were rich lol. I didn't understand the concept of you working 3 jobs just so I could have colored tvs, 6-disc cd changers or tommy girl from head to toe. You've always provided safe spaces for me to express my emotions, be sensitive, cry, ask questions, have my own opinions & explore my open mindedness without judgment or control. Only pure compassionate guidance. Thank you for giving me the freedom to be who I Am, allowing me to explore being different as society forced others to conform.

One of the best pieces of advice you'd always tell me is "if you don't stand for something, you'll fall for anything" I didn't understand it then but that advice has guided me through the toughest situations. You're truly the best person I know. Everyone loves you & I admire that. I admire how you show up for people as you equally show up for yourself. You be quick to answer that phone so you can talk all loud lol. You lead & guide me by example.

You've never whooped or treated me anyway less than loving & nurturing. Everything I've ever wanted to do you've supported. Remember that time I randomly joined the dance team & any job I wanted to quit you reminded me you'd always take care of me until I figured myself out? I'm very aware that the average person couldn't even think up a prayer to be blessed with a momma like you.

Any issue I've ever had you allow me to then you'd ask "ok so how do we get into the solution?" I've never felt alone in any aspect of my life because I always knew I have you. I know we were sisters in other lifetimes & maybe I was your mom & you were my daughter. The fact is you & I have been exploring life together for a very long time & I could not have asked GOD for a better momma even if I tried. I love you past the understanding of infinity & ain't no way I could write my 1st book without acknowledging the woman that is the foundation for who I am & what I know. I love you momma.

Below is a photo of my momma & I as young girls with the same hairstyles and same facial expressions.

DAD, I ACKNOWLEDGE YOU

I wrote this book because of my momma but also in memory of you. This book, my life and my entire being is the essence of you. You are my story. It took me years to realize, you are me and I am you. If it weren't for you much of my story wouldn't be what it is. If it weren't for you much of my healing wouldn't be what it is. You have given me the greatest gift a human could ever ask for. You did what was necessary to ensure I would return back home to myself, my essence, my soul. All this time I vented about how you weren't there not realizing you were always there. Every moment I cried over your absence and held guilt for my anger towards you, you were there sitting right next to me in spirit. Still guiding who I am today. You've always walked me home.

You knew who I'd become, and you knew the role you'd have to play in my journey for me to evolve and fulfill my souls purpose. I'm sorry it took so long to see the brilliance in your method of being a father. Thank you for having the courage to stay away. Thank you for playing the villain in my story until now. Thank you for your absence. I thought I needed you in presence because that's what society teaches us. Both parents are supposed to be present in our lives. I now know I didn't need your presence. I needed your absence because that's what helped me find the truth of myself. You are a true guru you know that? I honor you, and I'm so very thankful for you. I take you with me everywhere I go. Thank you for walking me home dad.

A Letter to a Beautiful Soul

You may read this book however you choose but its designed to read 1 chapter a day. The reason is EGO can quickly get caught up in the process of reading. It'll allow you to feel good for completing a task, using reading as self-care, being able to brag about how quickly you read the book or skimming the book for the advice you need & never reading the rest. This is why a person can read many books & never actually implement any of it.

This is because their Ego read the book, not their soul. They'll acquire the information just enough to feel knowledgeable not enough to change their lives. This is how "self-help" authors, podcasters etc. maintain growth. The average person's Ego realizes it's time for change & begins thirsting to consume more input, but that version of ego can many times convince the person that consuming more data is healing itself. It's actually the person distracting themselves. You'll read 100 books but still be sad, depressed, confused about where to start in your healing process.

This book is designed to read 1 chapter at a time to practice spiritual patience and to become intentional about surrendering to the process. It's an invitation to only consume small amounts of information so you can consciously remember to incorporate what you've learned day by day. This design is also a subconscious reminder to you that there is no rush. Healing is a lifelong process & rushing through reading this book won't get you there faster. Anything not growing is dead, so give yourself grace & begin to practice being patient with yourself in your journey of evolving.

Each day you will read 1 chapter & journal about how that chapter made you feel and what emotions, memories or thoughts surfaced for you while reading. This is an opportunity to not just read my book, but to begin exploring your own internal book. After you read a chapter journal in full sentences and don't stop until you hear your ancestors whipster "well done'.

At the end of this book are journal prompts. You can choose to work on those at any time. Dissecting those journal prompts may give you deeper understanding of the chapters. Some journal prompts may be easy for you to write about and some may trigger trauma. Some prompts may reflect to you your emotional numbness, lapses in memory or your inability to express what you feel. All are ok. As you grow you can always return to these questions again & allow a different version of you to answer them when more self-clarity is present.

How to answer journal prompt questions?

Paint the picture. The intention behind journal prompts is to ask questions that spark thought, memory or emotions you've stored away, forgotten about, were never aware of or to highlight emotional & situational blind spots. Many people partake in my journal prompts & say "I've never thought about how this made me feel, I don't remember how this made me feel or I never thought about this situation in this way". The journal prompts are designed to invite you to see your path to healing with a broader perspective & with more clarity. So, paint the picture. Express how you feel in detail, who was present, what type of day it was, what your body felt, what lead to these events, how did you respond, how do you wish you responded etc. This is how you process emotional trauma & allow emotional residue to surface in the process. You must dissect your demons & find out what they're feeding on.

<u>Before you read this book, Answer these questions</u>

Where are you in your life & how are you feeling about it?

What are you ready to change from & into?

What are your intentions for reading this book?

What do you intend to get out of reading this book?

<u>Read this mantra out loud before starting chapter 1</u>

I have everything I need already within me.

I Am powerful enough to heal, grow & evolve through any situation or emotional pain.

I deserve to experience my best self, my truest self & my highest self.

I Am strong enough to be vulnerable.

I deserve to explore my softness.

Expressing emotion does NOT make me weak it highlights my power.

I am open to my soul revealing new perspectives & information.

I Am prepared & excited for a journey of healing, growing & evolving.

After you read & complete each chapter you will say,

THANK YOU FOR HELPING ME REMEMBER WHAT MY SOUL ALREADY KNOWS!

This is how you remind the subconscious mind that no one & no thing outside of you has the power to heal you. You take your power back when you acknowledge that ALL wisdom is already within your being, within your soul & lying dormant in your DNA. Every morsel of your being is just waiting for you to REMEMBER WHO YOU ARE to activate your divine soul level wisdom. Your body & soul is equipped with everything it needs to heal, grow & evolve. When you begin to remember who you are, you tap into your power.

This saying:

"Thank you for helping me remember what my soul already knows"

is a reminder to stop giving your power away!

Remember Who The F*Ck You Are.

THE JOURNEY OF REMEMBRANCE

My mom and dad were in the midst of their drug addiction when they found out they were pregnant with me. My mom told me that she was so afraid her entire pregnancy and that she'd constantly pray that I was healthy, could hear, see and that I'd have all my fingers and toes. As I write this, I just realized I've never asked where my dad was and what was he doing while my mom was giving birth, so I just text her to ask. She replied, "He was so proud he cried, he was a very quiet person, you brought life to him". This message certainly made me cry just now as I read it because as I write more of my story, you'll find that I don't know much about my dad so, even small messages like this are huge hugs for my inner child.

My memory begins at age 3/4ish before my mom went away to rehab. As an only child, I remember living with my mom and dad as a family in a neighborhood called acres homes, in Houston Texas. We lived on a huge property behind my grandfather's house. My grandfather had chickens but I was too afraid to go to the back of the property to see them. He used to put me on his lawn mower and drive me around while he cut the grass and I'd get glimpses of them. My dad was young at heart even before he passed away. When I was little, he had a random skateboard I would lay on my stomach and roll around on in the front yard and my momma had high heel black boots that I'd always try to wear. I remember my biggest goal was to learn how to wash dishes and one of my parents got me a stool one day so I could be tall enough to wash them.

As far as I know I was happy, I felt safe and cared for. I remember my dad loved Bob Marley and he'd always play Bob Barley's music with his posters hanging up. He would always take me next door to hang with him and his best friend named Bo-didley (yall know I had to put that country ass name in here lol) My dad would wear his socks hanging off his feet and my momma would call him trifling lol. We even had a song for his that we'd sing together "hm hm hm silly Raymonnndd". I remember this being a beautiful moment for our family. I only remember my parents arguing once, I remember crying about it and I think my mom asked him to leave. This was really confusing to me because I wasn't use to us not being together or their being tension of this magnitude that I was aware of in our home.

Childhood Trauma

After that, I only remember change. At 4 years old My mom went away to rehab. While she was only a way for a few months it felt like years. As she healed for the sake of us, I lived with my dad shortly, then my aunt who took care of me while my mom was away. I'd visit my grandparents for long stays but typically I stayed with my aunt. My dad was still in the midst of his alcohol addiction and would remain there for many years to come. It was tough not living with my mom and dad. It felt as if a part of me was missing. My chest felt a deep emptiness and achiness simultaneously.

My aunt took great care of me, made sure I had everything I needed, dressed me nicely, always did my hair and had my glistening in coco butter lol I didn't want for anything while with my aunt but I didn't understand why I was with my aunt and not my parents. I wanted someone to come save me. I was really sad, confused, and just really unclear about what was happening. Everything felt like it was moving in slow motion. Now that I'm older and wiser I know that this was trauma forming in my brain and body. Trauma occurs when a person experiences any emotion that is so overwhelming the brain doesn't know how to fully process it or understand it so it re-wires the brain to find methods to adapt and to find coping or defense mechanisms so the body can continue to survive in the environment.

One day I was playing house with my cousin that I lived with and out of nowhere she innocently said "Candyss yo momma on the phone". I remember seeing her rubber phone as she handed it to me, I just turned around and buried my face in her brown sofa and cried my eyes out. I missed my momma and I didn't know how long this would last, if this was my new life or she would come back and save me.

My aunt took us to church every Sunday and every Sunday made Sunday food. Like most black households whatever is on your plate you better finish it and be grateful "because its kids in Africa that are hungry and wishes they had this food" lol. I would always think to myself 'well can we give it to them?" lol I think as some point we all received that speech. Like most families, There was a rule that you can't get up from the table until you finish all of your food and you'd have to show your plate so the adults could make sure you ate enough before you could leave the dinner table. This was an odd transition for me because with my mom and dad they allowed me to be picky and eat the things I liked, like chicken, sandwiches and my favorite vegetables to this day, string beans.

I wasn't used to foods like Okra, black eyed peas, dressing etc. I liked string beans and corn lol Now that I was in a new environment I had to adapt and eat what they ate. Needless to say, I'd spend hours at the dinner table forcing myself to eat food I didn't want or like. Sometimes my older cousin would come save me by eating my food for me or finding a creative way to throw it away. Other times I'd have to get creative by either drinking It down with my juice or stuffing my mouth full then go to the restroom and flush it down the toilet. I dreaded dinner time because I knew I'd always be the last person at the table by myself, sometimes even falling asleep at the dinner table. I remember saying "When I get older, I'm never eating this food again".

This was the foundation to my unhealthy, unbalanced and unregulated relationship with food. To this day I still don't eat any of these types of foods and still is working on creating a healthy relationship with food. My husband pointed out to me not to long ago that when I'm introduced to new food that I'm about to taste for the first time I scrunch my face up anticipating it will be nasty almost as if I'm afraid of the food. I say this to highlight how our subtle experiences as children directly effect and manifest in our adulthood.

While my mom was away at rehab there were times I'd still get to stay with my dad. I remember one day we were at a park, and he was drinking with his friends while I was on a swing. Somehow, I fell out of the swing and landed straight on my back. I felt the air being knocked out of me and I remember the pause I had to take before I could even catch my breath for a cry to wail out of my mouth. Again everything felt as if it was moving in slow motion. My dad instantly rushed over to me to nurture me and take care of me. I knew he felt really bad. However, this was the first time I learned I didn't feel safe with him and that narrative evolved into me not feeling safe with any man and what later turned into I didn't feel safe at all in general, which later lead to me joining the military for 10 years and becoming a police officer for 7 years as an unconscious way to make myself feel safe.

This is how subconscious trauma manifests in our adult lives. The feeling of me not feeling safe allowed me to manifest a career that was literally about safety and protection. I'd walk around with weapons, m16's, m4s across my back, Glocks on my hip and ankles not even realizing my subconscious trauma manifested these careers to help me adapt with not feeling safe.

My next memory of my dad was the first time I told him he hurt my feelings lol. I had just gotten home from school, and I was about to watch barney, I think he may have been a little firm with me, more than I was use to so I cried. My dad had never yelled at me or hit me; he was truly a gentle man. At this young age 4 my momma taught me how to say "my feelings are hurt" as a way to express my emotions. Although she was away in rehab, I'd still remember this lesson. So, when I told my dad he hurt my feelings he responded by saying "What? I hurt your feelings?" I believe what I said caught him off guard and his response caught me off guard. Usually when I'd tell my mom that, I was received and nurtured but when I had just told my dad the way he responded shocked me. It made me shut down and get quiet because it was uncharted territory.

I had only been trained to express when my feelings were hurt, not how to respond when someone doesn't know how to receive that information. So I got quiet. My dad apologized but I still felt the energy of his response. This is when I first learned I wasn't safe to express how I feel, which lead to me growing up not standing up for myself, entering relationships not expressing how things were effecting me emotionally and ultimately it lead to me being an adult, silencing myself for the sake of keeping the peace as I started many wars within myself as a byproduct of my own silence and fear of acknowledging how people or situations made me feel. I became a doormat in my relationships and wouldn't say anything until I was so upset id explode with word vomit or anger. The repressed anger also led to my alcohol addiction. This emotional link is clear because the liver houses anger and resentment and is the organ directly affected by alcohol.

My mom got out of rehab a few months later and ever since that moment we've been together and best friends. We even went to an extended live in rehab facility together right after she got out of regular rehab.

When my mom and I graduated from the extended rebab facility my paw paw bought us a house. All my aunts lived in the same neighborhood, so my entire family was super close, my cousins were like my brothers/sisters. We did everything together and were always at one another's houses. Me and my mommas house had a huge back yard, and I had my own room. I grew up very privileged. Honestly growing up I thought we were rich. My momma worked many jobs, and my paw paw had a lot of money and my aunts always drove nice cars. I never went without. Shortly after my paw paw bought us a house he died. This was the first time I'd ever seen my momma cry and it was also the first time I realized how huge my family was. Everybody and they momma came out of the woodworks lol. This is also the first time I saw so many people experience grief right in front of me. I was able to see how many people handled grief differently and I was able to see how death effects people and sometimes that pain causes them to hurt others. Even though my grandfather and I were super close I didn't cry when he died. I don't think I understood what was happening. I was 6/7 years old, I knew He died, I knew he wasn't coming back, I saw his body in the casket but again things started moving in slow motion and I didn't really know how to respond, so I didn't. I was in shock because, the night that my grandfather had passed I dreamt about it. I later told my mom details, that she'd never even told me. I even knew where it had happened. So his entire funeral I was consumed with questions about my dream. How did I know this?

After my grandfather passed away my family broke apart. He had a lot of money and many people were fighting over what was left to them. I'm sure everyone in my family downloaded so much grief into their nervous systems by being in such a painful yet angry environment together.

As I grew up my mom and I remained super close. We talked about everything and truly were still best friends. She worked hard to give me everything I ever wanted including compassionate nurturing and unwavering support.

Trauma + Detachment

I had two favorite cousins growing up. They were like my sister and brother. There are truly no words that can express how much I love them. One cousin was my protector. He never let anyone mess with me. I wanted to be like his sister so bad. I couldn't wait until I got older so I could get my nails don't just like her lol. We did everything together, from going outside to play, to playing super Nintendo all day trying to beat the game and getting mad at each other if somebody made you lose lol. Like all people as you get older, everyone's life changes, they are exposed to different things and anything can change the course of a person's life. My cousins experienced a lot growing up, things they never deserved to experience, and those things greatly affected them which also effected how they showed up as young adults.

This impacted me so much, from 10-25years old no one could even mention my cousins name without me crying. I remember my mom attempting to share with me things that included my cousins and I'd instantly say "I don't want to talk about it". Not because I didn't love my cousins but I didn't know how to know what they were going through without also feeling so much deep grief and Emotional pain. I would have given my life to save them, make sure they were happy, change their lives and this was the first time I realized that I had absolutely no control over another person's life or their path. These were my best friends, my first best friends at that but I didn't know how to stay deeply connected to them without also feeling all of their pain. So, I learned how to physically and emotionally detach. Ironically detaching didn't help the situation or help me feel better, it just added a huge layer or guilt for being so distant.

I just didn't know what else to do. I felt so helpless. The love I felt for my cousins was so painful I thought it would kill me. I felt it throughout my entire body, deep love, deep pain, deep compassion, deep empathy and deep confusion. Detachment is a sign of emotional trauma. It's when the brain feels so overwhelmed with emotion and can't figure out a way to process that emotion, so it creates a defense mechanism and detaches from it. Which makes others think I don't care, I'm unbothered or I don't love them and it's the complete opposite.

When you love so hard without healthy boundaries or deep understanding it become an unhealthy attachment and it becomes unhealthy on the nervous system and because the bodies only job is to keep you alive, this also means it must keep you in comfortable environments even if the tactic and defense mechanism to do so is extremely unhealthy and detrimental to your relationships. My cousins for a long time, even at times now thought I was acting funny or just didn't love them anymore. As a young girl I didn't have the language to express to them not only do I love you, I hurt for you, as you and I don 't know how to do that and still live a normal life. The level of detachment I had to go through to get through this phase of my life numbed me emotionally, I had to learn how to shut all emotions off and I spent the rest of my young adult life and 20's detaching from people, places, things and reality itself. The level of detachment my body used to protect me, became detrimental and self-sabotaging as I got older.

Young Adult Trauma

Middle school and high school was very traumatic for me. This is the first place I learned it wasn't ok to be myself. Although I was very popular in school my whole life. I was always beautiful, had friends, my momma dressed me in tommy hilfigure or tommy girl from head to toe lol, my hair was long down my back. I grew up with role models like, Aaliyah, Brandy, Destiny's Child, so I learned how to have confidence from young adult women that looked like me. However, in school there's always a sense of not feeling good enough, not pretty enough, which ultimately exposes a child's childhood trauma of not being seen, hear, wanted, loved, or acknowledged. Even though I had all those things from my mom, there was still an energy that urged most kids to fit in. I didn't have to try to do that because I naturally fit in and still can fit in anywhere, I go.

I learned how to shapeshift. I learned how to be who I needed to be, to get the love, or acceptance I needed to feel a part of. This is a natural human instinct because the human needs to be or feel a part of a community to survive. Love and belonging are number 3 on Maslow's hierarchy of needs because the human needs to feel connection, this is why Instagram and other social platforms like it thrive, they are modern day social experiments. They expose people's traumas and create apps or movie platforms like Netflix that feed on those voids and wounds. You can thank Sigmund Freud and his nephew "Edward Bernays" For that (look them up). So, it's perfectly normal for a person to want to be a part of or feel connected, but I realize school is where I felt the most disconnected. Now don't get me wrong I had the time of my life.

I had the same friends from 6th grade up to my senior year. Even though my best friends knew the real me, I still felt like I was participating in a world that was beyond me, that I didn't belong in, that was superficial, and I dumbed myself down drastically to be a part of it. It was traumatic because daily, the environment conflicted with who I truly was. I loved my baby cats and one day I went to school and cried because one of them had just died, even though everyone comforted me, right after there was a huge fight in school. It was clear this wasn't' a safe environment and I couldn't come to school crying over no cats lol. You never really knew who would be a part of drama week to week or if your name would randomly pop up in the mix. Kids would curse out or even fight their teachers. I used to have girls randomly tell me, "I didn't like you before I met you, but you're like my sis now" and it would just confuse me and really hurt my feelings. It showed how unstable the environment was in comparison to my very stable, loving and safe life at home with my momma. School was like a mad house and anyone that graduated didn't just graduate with a diploma, they graduated from one of the toughest environments that is not conducive to healthy growth. I used to call my high school prison, but I won't go there today lol.

The most beautiful part of my school experience was my friends, I was a huge class clown honestly not even to fit it in I just enjoyed being social, laughing and having a good time. I've staged walk outs in my school for scholastic injustice haha, I'd gone to the office so many times my principal just made me an student aid lol. My friends and I did everything together. Girls and boys. We went to all the games, to the skating rink, to one another's houses, we knew everyone's parents. We literally grew up together, even got our first jobs together. A huge highlight of my teenage years was my friendships and as an only child, I treasured my friendships especially since we'd all been so close since 6th grade.

One day for me however, all my friendships ended overnight. (I'll explain with more detail later in the book) A friend in need came to live with my mom and I for what was supposed to be a couple of weeks but lasted a few months. At some point something took place with her and my mom, a very expensive item came up missing and my mom told her it was time she found another place to stay. I wasn't a part of any of that situation but the next day my friend went to school and told everyone that I was the reason she had nowhere to live. Everyone blamed me and instantly ended our relationships. Friends I'd been with since 11 years old now at 17/18 would no longer even look my way or try to ask what happened. To say I was hurt is an understatement. I felt alone, abandoned, neglected, betrayed and outcasted for something that wasn't my fault.

This sparked the deepest depression of my life. I was so depressed I could barely get out of bed to go to school and when I'd get to school, I'd just sleep through every class. I lost so much weight my teachers were calling my mom asking her if I was using any drugs because I'd become so thin. Not only did my best friends abandon me, my first real relationship had ended the exact same week with my first official boyfriend.

I didn't know what to do with myself or my life. "Coincidentally" my senior year I was taking a psychology class that usually I'd skip but she called my momma and told on me lol so now I had to go to her class even though I didn't need her class to graduate lol. One day she asked me if I had my homework, which I didn't but out of respect I still acted like I did lol. So, I looked through my junky backpack and acted like I couldn't find it. She pulled me outside the class into the hallways and said "Candyss I know you don't have your homework but are you ok?" I stood their slightly uncomfortable and confused. She told me" Your backpack is an extension of you, and it is a reflection of how you feel about yourself and what Is going on in your life so, are you ok"? I told her yes, but as I went to sit at my desk it took everything in me to not cry. It felt as if the frog in my through was about to rupture my throat so the tears could come out.

In 2019 at 30 years old, as I was driving home from work, I felt a huge sensation of grief that just hit me out of nowhere. By 2019 I was deep into my healing journey so uncovering emotional meaning had become easy for me. As I drove, I cried and soon my tears were so overwhelming I had to pull over into a sonic parking lot, just to cry and breath. I began hyperventilating because I was so emotional but still had no clue why, I just allowed the emotions to be present. As I began to catch my breath and have a small moment of relief from crying,

I said out loud "I miss my friends and I miss my childhood". In that moment I realized the grief I felt was because I never got to say goodbye to any of my friends before my life changed. That moment was stolen from me. The friends I had spent literally every day with, they all got to see each other off to college and be a part of each other's lives, I never had an opportunity to tell them I loved them or even thank them for being my friends for so many years. I wasn't able to tell them how important their friendship meant to me. I was forced to let them all go as well as all my teenage memories that were attached to them.

As I cried in the sonic parking lot I also realized this goes beyond my relationship with my ex friends, I'm an adult now and this shit is annoying af. You mean to tell me I have to work for the rest of my life? Lol and I just started crying again lol. Then I thought about my inner child who thought she was ready to grow up, that was so ready to rush her process and had no idea the amount of grief and pain that would be on the other side of adulthood waiting for her. I cried for my innocence. The part of me is native, that loves everyone and doesn't cause any harm to anyone but still didn't feel safe enough to show up as her truest self. I cried because she didn't deserve a lot of was done to her. That part of me that just wanted to ignore all responsibilities, curl up in fetal position cry and disappear.

I realized that adult Candyss was fine in that moment, but young Candyss was having a hard time coping with house fast her life had changed. I sat in the sonic parking lot and cried for my inner child, for how quickly she transitioned out of her childhood until she felt ready to drive home. That night I went home a wrote a letter to every single one of my childhood friends that had abandoned me. I forgave them, I told them thank you for the many years of laughter and connection and I wished them all the best. The ending of those friendships created space for me to meet my befriend and now brother Tim and many others that nurtured me with laughter when my old friendships ended.

The depression from high school continued up to my middle 20's. It took me years to find myself after high school. Right after high school graduation I attempted to go to college but I was so depressed I wouldn't even make it into class. I'd sit in the parking lot that was near an airport and every time I saw an airplane I'd burst into tears because airplanes represented the freedom and emotional freedom, I wish I had. A few months later I'd enlist into the ARMY and this would help temporarily heal my depression. The military helped me find true confidence, it showed me how strong I was and it showed me what I was actually capable of. The military gave me a foundation for structure, discipline and ultimately helped me become me aware of how I spoke to myself. The only way I could survive in that type of environment was to begin practicing healthy thoughts and internal conversations.

This experience helped shape my spiritual stamina, it was my reminder that I can do anything. From the military, I later joined the police force at around age 23. I hated it, I was still fighting deep depression but at the time it was a career job so I chose to be grateful and find the positives in it as much as I could.

My Journey in Relationships lol smh

"If you line up all of your ex lovers in a row you can see a flow chart of your own mental illness"

As a young girl my mom always made it clear that there was a time for everything. I recognized that a lot of girls my at middle school and high school had boyfriends, did their own hair, got their nails done or were able to wear make-up. My mom would always say, If you do everything at once you won't have anything to look forward to. So I was able to get my nails done at a certain age, wear mascara at a specific age and later on in high school I was allowed to have a boyfriend. Because my mom and I were so close she always knew who liked me in school because I would tell her. Our openness in our relationship made it easy for me to tell her everything.

In high school, at age 17 I had my first real boyfriend. Before him I'd been really close with guy friends, even those who really liked me and treated me well but no one that I could say was serious enough for deep emotional involvement. In my first relationship I truly thought I was in love but in hindsight I was emotionally sensitive, obsessive and I was in a relationship with someone who was emotionally manipulative. He'd be nice to me, super loving and attentive one day and the next be cold, annoyed by my presence and extremely mean or dismissive. Because I had never experienced a real relationship a part of me thought this was normal behavior from him as well as myself. It always felt like an emotional rollercoaster, so like all people who are experiencing an overwhelming sensation of emotion on top of daddy wounds, on top of childhood trauma I learned to adapt to the environment of my relationship. I thought silencing myself and not speaking up for myself or saying how something made me feel made me a good girlfriend because we didn't argue, and I kept the peace.

This is also where I learned how to perform to receive love. If things are easy in a relationship, you get love in return. This unhealthy logic began to plague me as I continued my future relationships. This is also my first time experiencing feeling powerless in a relationship with someone you think you really love the obsessiveness of when the person will call, if their energy is different wondering if you did or said anything wrong, if they cheat instead of holding them accountable questioning what's wrong with me? I thought this was normal behavior because my friends had the same behaviors and warped thought processes. After this relationship ended my senior year, I lost of my friends the same week and my depression began. It took me a long time to get over my first heartbreak I didn't understand that my life was just beginning and there would be plenty more relationships ahead that were just as unhealthy as this one that I'd have to learn many more lessons from.

Shortly after getting home from military boot camp, I was feeling much better and almost felt healed from my depression. I recognized that I was in a liminal phase of healing and could go either way. I could start a brand-new life going to college again or I could sink deeper into my depression. I got home started school again, and was really excited about this new space I was in. Then, I met a guy *rolls eyes. I heard my intuition say don't do it, stay focused. Actually, that was my momma lol she always told me I was the prize, and I could have any man I wanted, if I stay focused the right one will come to me. Of course, I didn't listen and spent the next 2 years trying to make a relationship work I had business being a part of. He courted me what seemed very nicely at the time. He was a gentle guy, an athlete and overall, a good person but there was one problem. He withheld very important information about his criminal background and how that affected him getting a job.

We had been together for a while before he'd finally told me that his money was from a car accident settlement and explained his background and why it was difficult for him to get a job. In the moment he told me, he also said I understand if this changes things for you and if you don't want to stay apart of this relationship. I instantly felt trapped, even with that disclaimer. I felt so much pressure to show and prove that I was loyal, supportive and good girlfriend that wouldn't leave someone because they're in a rough patch in their lives. However, I knew I should have ended things right then and there. I stayed in that relationship and spent the next 2 years supporting him emotionally and sometimes financially. I felt bad for him, and I thought I loved him.

Then one day while in class I got a text message to my phone that said "If yo man loves you so much why is he at my house" lol followed by him blowing my phone up saying don't believe her, she's crazy lol. I found out he had cheated on me with is ex-girlfriend who made it her mission to blast this information all over twitter. Instagram wasn't popping just yet lol. I wasn't that heartbroken as I was in shock. Again, everything around me began to move in slow motion. That evening after me finding out about him cheating he came over to explain himself and basically said it was true, that he did still love her but he wanted to be with me and he didn't know why these lingering feelings were still there.

I remember picking something up and throwing it across the room as he told me he loved his ex girl friend. I also remember as I threw the item I thought to myself "Candyss why did you just throw that you aren't even mad, you are hurt"? In that moment I realized that people are programmed to respond specific ways to specific situations. Society tells us that If your boyfriends cheats on you, then you should be sad, crying and angry and possibly throw things. It's as if I was able to see myself as the watcher, as a person watching a movie. So I decided I wasn't going to react how society told me I should react, I'm going to respond in a way that makes sense to me, from my heart.

I was deeply hurt but I wasn't angry. I was hurt that he loved another woman, but I was mostly hurt that I actually understood him and truthfully it made sense. Although he went about it the wrong way, the fact still stands that how you feel about someone doesn't magically go away just because you also care for another person. Both truths can exist at the same time. I wanted him to be happy and explore that happiness even if it wasn't with me. This was the first time I learned that I could be selfless in a relationship. I understood that people are not mine to possess, have, hold on to forever or control just to make myself feel loved, wanted or chosen. I also knew that if I stayed with him, I'd never be able to trust him again which would spark the obsessiveness I vowed to never allow myself to feel over a person again and I also knew that if I stayed the resentment that would settle in would make me want to emotionally hurt him so he could feel the same pain that he made me feel.

My next two relationships were with women, now you can really tell where my mental illness was setting in because the situations, I got myself into from this point forward were complete madness. However, the worse and unhealthier my relationships got the more profound my spiritual awakening became. Most times God uses pain or heartbreak to get our attention. The first woman I dated was by far the most painful and emotionally chaotic relationship I'd ever been in. For starters I entered the relationship knowing there was an ex somewhere in the picture, but I was just having fun exploring my sexuality at this stage of my life, I never actually thought it would turn into a relationship. This relationship very quickly became emotionally unhealthy, controlling, argumentative and deeply toxic. By this time in my life age 23 or so my drinking of alcohol had progressed and was out of hand but still able to be hidden. I was 50 pounds overweight because after my last break up from being cheated on I began binge eating a pint of ice cream every single day. I ate Haggen Daaz chocolate chocolate chip every single day, I knew where it was on sale, what day it would be on sale and how long the sale would last lol.

Years later as I began my healing journey, I learned that when people overeat sweet and savory foods, they have a wound of not feeling loved so they use the food to cope. In the relationship with the woman I was dating I didn't have much confidence in my appearance, I had braces and I was just in a very weird phase of my life. Truthfully, I was lost in the sauce just winging it. Unlike other relationships in this one, I spoke my mind. Much of my anger began to really surface in our arguments. I didn't allow myself to be treated any type of way because she was very controlling, jealous and had many narcissistic qualities that damaged what I did have left of my confidence. She'd say things like " you can't do anything without me" or "you're to close to your mom, you don't know how to do anything without her". As my spiritual awakening began, I was learning so much information and I was fascinated. If I'd try to share anything with her she'd either ignore me or say things like " you always care about things that don't matter none of that stuff is important". This is when I was clear, it was time to go. Like the others she also cheated with her ex. I found out because one day while at her house her ex randomly showed up at the door and went off on her for cheating and lying. All I could think was "what is wrong with me, how come no one ever chooses me?". I also couldn't help but think "how the hell did I get myself into a situation like this?"

I recognized that I was angry and honestly, I was frightened by my anger because It felt random, I wasn't sure where it came from but I knew one thing, I had absolutely no control over it. So, I began reading "Thich Nhat Hanh, Anger, Wisdom for cooling the flames". I wasn't aware that I was amid my spiritual awakening I just knew I needed help and watching Oprah Super Soul Sunday was my medicine. It taught me so much. I learned so much about myself, the world, spirituality, quantum and metaphysics and I was in love with learning more. Day in and day out I was doing more and more research. When I ended this relationship, I really began working on myself and my healing.

But yall know I had to enter one last relationship for God to finally throw me into the flames of healing, growing and evolving. I dated another woman and as soon a my momma saw a photo of her the first thing she said was, don't you date that girl she has issues that are unresolved within her. And what did I do? Date her and say "Everybody aint like that momma" *Rolls eyes lol. Like all unhealthy relationships they start off great, fun, loving and then the truth of who a person is begins to show. Like most of the people I've dated she wasn't a bad person either, but this was the first time I was able to see what triggers and trauma look like and how when you're with a person who hasn't fully acknowledged those aspects of themselves how unhealthy things can get and quickly.

I was drinking heavily once I got to this relationship and when she'd drink shed poke at me, shed bother me or create arguments that would trigger the anger I was attempting to work on. Sometimes I would argue back but afterwards I'd feel really disappointed in myself because I truly wanted to practice healthier ways. Once I started to practice stillness and not argue back, she'd do everything in her power to get me to snap, even small annoying things like messing with my ears to just get under my skin to the point I'd have to leave to maintain my composure and honor the information I was learning. At some point the relationship was so toxic and unhealthy I decided to end it.

A few days after ending the relationship my house burned down and I lost everything, I'll speak about this more in depth in the next chapter. The night my house burned down my mom went to a hotel, but I couldn't take my cat there, so she offered for me to come to her house until I figured something out. I didn't even have clothes, a tooth brush, nothing. While at her house we had a drink, and she started a conversation about the things I was learning by watching Oprah super soul Sunday and she wanted to argue about religion. Well, I don't' argue about religion because I respect everyone's beliefs, and this is when I knew it was time to go. My friends were already on their way to pick me up to take me to purchase clothes and basic things I needed.

I just remember texting them saying "PLEASE HURRY" I knew the energy that was present was not good, not healthy, I had just lost everything, I had nothing to my name and she wanted to argue religion. Before I knew it, I had lost it. We both were going off, intoxicated. My friends got there, and I just remember saying get my cat, get my cat lol They couldn't find her because she was traumatized in the fire and the bottom of her feet were burned so she was hiding somewhere in the apartment. My friends had to go through her entire apartment to look for my cat, turn over sofas, look in her closet while she and I literally screamed at one another. While in the kitchen we physically fought. I remember my nose bleeding and blacking out hitting her back as my befriend Tim attempted to break us up. Once they got my belongings I left, with blood on my shirt.

That same night I had to go home and explain to my momma what had happened with two obvious black eyes from a semi fractured nose. I was so embarrassed and ashamed. I had lost everything and on top of that I had just gotten into the first fight of my life, and I had two black eyes and a fractured nose. I was literally broken. If you look on my Instagram account in my highlights you can see photos of my black eyes, my house and my journey to rebuilding myself.

After this relationship I was single by choice for the next 4 years. I was very clear God said it was time to focus on my healing. At this point I didn't need any more signs. I didn't need any more pain to prove to me that I was neglecting clear messages from my soul to begin my process of healing and to not play with it.

The House Fire

The night my home burned down I was actually doing my first full moon ceremony. The ceremony consisted of me sageing my home, then siting in the front yard, writing in my journal to God. I acknowledged that I was ready to let go of all things that no longer served me. I acknowledged that I was angry, I was afraid of moving forward in my life, I was scared of healing, and I was scared of evolving, but I was ready. I explained to God as I journaled that I wanted to experience peace, I wanted to heal so deeply that I became unrecognizable to people.

I wanted to truly step into my purpose and never look back. After my ceremony I went' to be and A few hours later I heard my cat crying loudly and woke up out of my sleep to the smell of smoke. I ran out of my room and saw the house was full of black smoke. The first thing I thought of was to save my mom because she has asthma. I just yelled "momma we gotta go we gotta get out of the house' We quickly ran out of the house, but I had to runback in to save her dogs. I could see the fire and feel the heat as I got the dogs to bring them outside. Then I ran back into our burning house to save my cat that woke me up. Her name was "black and white". I could hear her crying, but she was so scared she was under the bed and she wouldn't come to me. I could feel myself getting dizzy from the smoke and I was afraid I was going to die so I had to leave her. I couldn't see under the bed to get her, so I ran out of the house and black smoke was everywhere. You could hear the bullets from my police weapons exploding like fireworks from the street.

POW POW POW evertime a bullet exploded in the fire. As my mom and I ran out of the house our entire neighborhood was outside. They had already called the fire department for us. They heard our fire alarms houses down yet we didn't hear anything. This is how I knew my cat was an angel because I only woke up because I heard her cry. All of the news stations reported on our housefire because they found out that we had just installed our fire alarms the day before. I was in the process of adopting a little girl and one of the safety codes was to have a fire alarm. So we installed it the day before because our home inspection for adoption was coming up. I lost everything but in the blink of an eye me and my mom's life changed for the better forever. The fire Marshall concluded that the sparks from the sage burned our house down.

I remember my mom asking what was sage and what did I do with it. After I got home from the military, I had a studio apartment built in our back yard and I told her that I cleansed my apartment of any energy that was not supposed to be there. I just said a mantra of "I release any energy that no longer serves me" and a few hours later my entire house was gone. I thought my mom would be mad, angry or disappointed she was actually intrigued to see a prayer work that fast. Insurance paid for our entire home to be rebuilt and not only that set my mom and I up for financial stability and retirement. Even though I lost everything including one of my animals that I had raised since a baby for the past 11+years, knowing that we were still taken care of financially and lowkey won the lotto gave me a tiny bit of ease. As long as my momma wasn't' disappointed me I was ok.

But I hadn't stopped drinking yet. My mom and I moved into an apartment until our house was rebuilt and my drinking got worse. Trauma on top of trauma on top of trauma and the way I was coping with it was drowning myself in alcohol. By this time I was drinking every single day as soon as I got off of work. I would drink wine, liquor, lime-aritas lol anything I could get my hands on. Also, in some way I felt like my relationship with God was deeper when I was intoxicated, I felt such a deep connection to everything around me. I'd take my germen shepherd Sasha to the park every single day and drink wine and play with her. My history of addictive behavior began at a young age with Oreos. As my mom healed from her addiction, she always took me to the AA or CA meetings with her so I could learn about alcoholism and addiction. She always taught me that I come from a background of addicts, so it was important to remember I to be mindful when I attempt to drink socially like other people. She'd also point out to me as I ate Oreos how difficult it was for me to eat the serving size. She'd inform me that these are signs of addictive behavior and to just stay mindful and to always let her know if I felt I had a problem. I began drinking at age 21 to help me get over the fear of performing and singing live. From there is just persisted from social gatherings to years later me drinking on my own away from other people and hiding how much I was drinking. No one knew I was an alcoholic because I was very good at isolating. I rarely went to clubs even though ya girl did have a club phase lol but I wasn't out and about to the point anyone could tell I was an alcoholic. I'd mastered people only knowing what I wanted them to know and what I'd shown them.

The straw that broke the camel's back during my addiction is when my best friend died. My German shepherd Sasha. She died maybe 2 weeks after my house burned down and even though my whole life was a huge expression of grief, this was the first time that I actually felt deep grief. She got sick suddenly from liver disease same as my dad which is also not a coincidence. She was everything to me. Sasha raised me and was my safe space during every single turbulent moment in my life. I got her as soon as I got home from the military and had her for 7years. I didn't know how to live without her. I felt even emptier and like I had no purpose, at least with her alive I had a reason to go outside, be in nature at the parks and take her places.

After she died suddenly it was just me by myself, and I felt so alone it was scary. I still had my cat Tithel that survived the fire, but Sasha was my baby girl. I still cry when I think about her, hell I'm crying now as I write this lol. I remember feeling lost like I didn't know what to do next. I felt empty and very fragile. I'd lost my home, 20 years of belongings, my cat and now my dog of 7 years. I instantly knew God was saying "No more" crutches.

I wasn't allowed to have anything else that could distract me or take my focus away from my own healing. Even though Sasha was my angel I was very clear that the only way I was able to get through the past 7 years was because my animals were my angels. I've always known that. I used to tell my mom "Make sure you're nice to black and white (our cat) she's the angel of the house" and she is literally the cat that saved us from dying in the house fire. Anytime I was going through a tough time emotionally a new stray animal would show up on my doorstep, something for me to nurture, nurse back to health, help find a home or take in as my own. I also knew when the animal would leave, they were only here for a season to help me get through to the next phase of my journey. When Sasha passed away, I knew that this too was the truth, her job had been complete and now it was up to me to take my healing into my own hands.

My Alcohol Addiction

No more animals, people, places or things that I could focus on or fix so I didn't have to focus on and fix myself. I realized all of my relationships I entered with people I felt I could help. That hubris wasn't just ego it was my protective mechanism. I entered relationships with broken people so I could help them heal so I didn't have to focus on how broken I was or on my own healing journey.

With all of this newfound wisdom after Sasha transitioning, I still didn't stop drinking. I used alcohol to escape my pain and to help me forget. I still continued to go even deeper down the rabbit whole of consciousness, information, anatomy, physics, science, conspiracy theories, you name it was learning about it.

Then one day a good friend and I had begun speaking in a romantic way. He and I had been friends and met in college, so we'd known each other for years at this point. After my house burned down, we explored a romantic connection that was very open and free. No rules, no expectations. I was very clear I didn't want to be in a relationship however this interaction caught me off guard and I decided to explore it. We shared very beautiful time together but nothing serious at all, we were however very honest about our feelings for one another. One day out of the blue while we were away, he told me that his ex-had come back into the picture and he'd like to explore things with her and just wanted to let me know. Of course, my only response was in support of that because I didn't want a relationship at all and I just deeply understood but I couldn't help not hear that voice that said "How come no one ever chooses me, what is wrong with me". The next few days he invited me to his event that his ex was also attending, and I was pissed lol I felt disregarded, not considered and confused as to why he wouldn't even at least give me the heads up so I could prepare myself emotionally. Long story short I started drinking Hennessey and next thing I know I was going off on him in the parking lot lol real ghetto ish smh lol. During my episode lol I remember hearing myself say "why didn't you choose me?" and that really stuck out to me like a sore thumb. Eventually a week or so later I chose to apologize to him because had I not been intoxicated, I would have never behaved that way, brought how I felt to his attention that way or embarrassed myself that way. At this point It was clear that alcohol was changing me as a person. After I apologized, I remember my mom asking me if I felt better and I responded no I don't, I just couldn't figure out why.

The next day I knew why. When I screamed to him "Why didn't you choose me?" I wasn't even talking to him; I was talking to my dad. My wounded inner child was present, and she was basically saying how come no one ever chooses me, how come every man always chooses another woman over me the same way my dad chose alcohol over me. I recognized so clearly this was the subconscious story and narrative that had been running on a loop keeping me in self sabotaging relationships for the past 7years. This pain was not about men choosing other women over me, the pain was attempting to get my attention so I could finally focus on my daddy wound. Each person I was in a relationship with was my angel. They all gave me deep profound lessens that hurt me so deeply they ultimately landed me at my dad's grave site March 27th 2018 the last day that I drank alcohol.

Growing up my dad wasn't physically present in my life. I knew that he loved and I knew that he suffered from alcohol addiction but I didn't quite understand his absence until my 13th birthday. He showed up to my birthday party drunk, crying at my front door. I knew then that my dad really loved me. However, when I saw him cry I felt bad for him, I pitied him and this kept me from being able to express my sadness, anger or resentment towards him because I didn't want to hurt his feeling and make him want to drink even more. So, my entire life I kept how I felt bottled in. Entering relationships that didn't serve me because my wounds were manifesting in the types of relationships I chose. I knew my dad was a good person, and I understood if he could stop drinking then he would have. I typically saw my dad on holidays when I went to my grandparents' house growing up. At some point he was diagnosed with liver cancer and was given a short time to live.

Suddenly I was receiving a lot of pressure from family to be a part of his life, to call him, check on him and go see him. Remember, I'd only known how to emotionally detach when I felt overwhelmed so my entire life, I emotionally detached from the fact that he wasn't present, now everyone wanted me to be present for him and not only did I not want to do that I physically and emotionally didn't know how to do that without also allowing all of those emotions that I'd stored to surface. I felt guilty for not going to see him often, but I also felt angry. I didn't understand why everyone was so vocal about me going to see him but no one was ever this vocal to tell him to come see me while I was growing up. I felt annoyed and frustrated and hurt that I, as the child was being held to a standard that he wasn't. I was being held accountable in ways he wasn't which also fueled my resentment towards him as he was getting sicker. I'd go see him on weekends but not consistently. I didn't really know much about him or what to talk about honestly. I just knew he loved me, and we had some things in common. We both joined the military. We both loved Bob Marley.

Funny story, one day a high school friend went to do electrical at my dad's apartment and saw a picture of me and was like that's candyss how do you know her? My dad told him that I was his daughter. The next day my friend came to my house and said hey I met your dad, do you know yall have the exact same Bob Marley poster hanging on the wall. I had no idea, but I love that story because it reminded me how much alike we were. When I would go spend the night at his house, he'd fall asleep watching scary movies lol and I'd wake up and cut the tv off lol and he'd wake up and cut it back on lol Little things like that I enjoyed about our experiences together. As he got sicker, I'd go to the hospital to see him.

I was at the hospital with him the day he transitioned. The doctor came out to tell us that he had died. Before I could tap into my own emotions, feel into how this news made me feel one of my family members looked at me and said "you should have been there for your daddy" and then proceeded to cry. I was in so much shock about what had just been said to me that I didn't even get the opportunity to cry or feel anything except the guilt that instantly rushed through my body. This was the first time the family gave me guilt and I picked it up and ran with it. I'd spend the next two years grappling with guilt and anger before releasing it and transmuting it.

After Apologizing to my friend, you know the one I went off on in the parking lot lol smh I recognizing I still didn't feel good about the situation, I instinctively knew that this was a conversation that was for my dad and I.

I woke up March 27th 2018 went to my dad's grave site and had a very long conversation with him. It was a hot sunny day and our first 30 minutes together I just sat there baking in the sun. Even in spirit, it was still very hard for me to tell my dad how I really felt. I was still protecting him. I had to acknowledge that by me withholding this information I was robbing his spirit and his soul from information that could potentially help his soul evolve now or even in the next lifetime. By not telling my dad how hurt or angry I was, I wasn't protecting him by shielding him from the repercussions of his own actions I was perpetuating a soul cycle that could continue to affect him if his soul chose to incarnate again.

What if my truth was the message, he needed to end his alcohol addiction in his next lifetime?

Then it dawned on me what if my dad knew all along that he wouldn't be able to participate in my life in order for me to become the woman I needed to be?

What if on a soul level his alcohol addiction was just a way to cope with knowing he'd have to leave me, so I could evolve into "Candyss Love" that can help people heal their pain, because of the pain I've been able to heal of my own?

What if my dad to some degree remembered his soul contract forbid him to interact with me because I needed the absence of my father to be so painful that it changed the course of my life, sparked an addiction and ultimately sent me on my healing journey?

What if my dad, even in his absence was my greatest teacher and angel? What if he sacrificed his time with me as a parent, just so I could become who I am today?

I had to sit with this perspective shift. Because if I truly believe in soul contracts, that means he, my mom and I all knew that we chose one another to experience in this lifetime, we knew how we'd utilize one another to experience life and to aid in our soul's evolution. This meant, my relationship with my dad had purpose and this thought made me just blurt out.

"I'm angry at you because you weren't there for me growing up, it hurt my feelings and I wish you would have chosen me over alcohol and I really need you right now and you aren't here and I'm sorry I wasn't there for you more while you were dying I just didn't know how to be and I was angry and now I feel bad and ashamed and stupid because I really want a relationship with you now".

I cried teats that felt like they would kill me. I felt pain, guilt and shame that felt like it would crush me but after 20 years of holding in my emotions I finally said it. Once I blurted this out it became much easier for me to express myself. I told him everything, as if he was next to me. I apologized to him for not being present as much as I could have while he was dying. I apologized because I chose to live in a world of anger instead of loving my dad that deeply loved me. I asked him for his forgiveness and took deep breaths in and deep breaths out to help myself release the shame and guilt I was carrying because of my absence. I held him accountable and then I asked him if we could start of and create a new relationship. I explained to him that my addiction had gotten the best of me and I was really struggling and I needed his help. I told him to earn my trust back I needed him to help me end my addiction to alcohol, to be there for me and support me. As I write this, I'm going on 5 years sober from alcohol addiction March 27th, 2023. I sat at his grave another hour and played him Bob Marley songs from my phone and cried until I began to laugh from memories is still had of him.

From that point forward I never drank alcohol ever again. The next day after leaving my dad's grave, I was sitting in the kitchen talking to my mom about something random and out of the blue she asked me "Do you have a problem with alcohol do you need any help?" and I blurted out YES!!!. I was so relieved. She had asked me before, but I wasn't ready to admit it yet. When she asked me again, I was so relieved I could finally admit it, let it out and allow myself to be nurtured. The very next day over 50 people from the AA & CA meetings that had been watching me grow up for years were there to support me. My mom is 29 years sober, and she brought her whole community to remind me I'm going to be ok. Ending my generational cycle of alcohol abuse was the best decision I've ever made in my life. I'm able to enjoy my life now and explore emotional pain without running or attempting to escape it.

The Journey to Healing

The next few years nature became my home. I was single, I was not dating, I was silent, and I was still. I had a very clear message from my soul that said get back to nature to heal and so I did. My momma told me that when you end an addiction you have to replace that time and energy with something else that's positive and healthy. So, I taught myself how use a cannon camera and I bought a bike. I lived in nature. I began to go camping, travel the world and explore life all by myself as a solo female traveler. I'd learned how to finesse my off days at work lol so I would take a month off and travel to a location and then another month in the summer to travel to another location.

After ending my cycle of drinking I went a lived in the mountains for two months in Montana, on native American reservation right outside of Glacier National Park called "Chewing Blackbone". It was a huge open field of land with tipis, warm lush green grass and a beautiful crystal clear rive with a backdrop of snowcapped mountains. I pitched my tent and lived there to connect with nature. While staying in the mountains I explored daily. I saw bears, I took photos of nature, and I even went on hikes that were 10+ miles all by myself. I pushed myself to limits I didn't know I was capable of and I was having the time of my life out in the middle of nowhere.

While on the reservation I met the native American landowner. He was about my skin complexion, with long hair plated in two ponytails. He randomly walked over to my tent, introduced himself and told me he'd like me to meet his wife. I was excited and agreed. Later that evening while speaking to his wife I asked, why do you think your husband wanted us to meet? She replied I'm not sure, let's just talk about life and I'm sure we'll find the connection at some point. In the middle of our conversation, she told me she was 25 years sober from alcohol addiction and I felt my eyes begin to water. That was it. Somehow, he knew that I was recovering from alcohol addiction and wanted me to meet his wife for support. I was in shock. How did he know? When I told his wife I was a few months sober she just laughed and said, "Yea he has a gift for that". As we talked, I became a student and listened to her journey of sobriety, but I was very eager to see her husband again. I wanted to know, how did he know that I was recovering from alcohol and how did he know that the conversation with his wife was needed?

A few days later I saw him again. I ran over to him as he was maintaining the grass, out of breath I just flat out asked him, "how did you know?" He said I saw it in your spirit, and I also saw the dark cloud that was causing you to struggle a little. He asked, did the conversation help? I replied, you have no Idea and I thanked him. This interaction was confirmation that I was on the right path and gave me the confidence to keep going. The next month I went to Mexico for the first time alone and explored new territory. This was before traveling became so popular on Instagram. There was no pressure to show my journey as a niche to grow followers. I was able to just share what the journey to peace looked like for myself and document what now gives others hope to someone day experience for themselves.

A Journey, Back Home To Self

Years ago, I heard A story that instantly made me cry. It loosely says

"There was a mother who had just given birth to a baby girl, her husband and their son were all at the hospital to support her. Once home from the hospital, the young 4yr old son asked his parents to spend time with his little sister, alone. The parents were very hesitant to leave the toddler alone with his newborn sister, so they just hoped that eventually he'd stop asking. However, the young boy was persistent and continued to ask to spend alone time with is little sister. Eventually, out of curiosity and concern the parents allowed their son to spend alone time with his little sister, just to see what he'd do. They put the newborn and their son in the same room but left the door cracked open so they could monitor what would happen. As the parents peaked through the door opening, they saw their son leaning over the baby and hear him say "Quick tell me what GOD is like, tell me where we come from and why we are here, I am starting to forget".

This story simultaneously invited me to drop to my knees in worship and remember all that I'd forgotten. It was confirmation to spirit that I wasn't trippin lol there were deep profound parts of my being that were indoctrinated into the human experience that forced me to forget who I was, what my purpose was and made me forget how to have an intimate relationship with my own intuition. As I journeyed through my healing it was clear that deep parts of my God self that were being encoded, remembered and activated. After hearing this story, I cried because I felt seen. At this time in my life, I didn't remember who I was, but I did know that I had forgotten who I was, my power and my purpose. I was clear that it wasn't a matter of me not having purpose, I just couldn't quite remember what it was, yet.

Powerful stories like this don't matter if they're real or true, all that matters is what activates within your body, when your spirit resonates as if it is true. This story was my reminder to dedicate my life to remembering who I AM. It allowed healing, self-discovery and spirituality to become my passion. From that point forward I never felt like "I lost myself" because I knew that there were just moments that I didn't remember and to give myself grace as my memory continues to download the more I heal, grow and evolve. I was now even more excited about my healing journey, Not to suddenly become healed overnight, but to truly enjoy my journey of uncovering all the messages, clues and lesson my soul and GOD have hidden in odd places like pain, relationships, death, abandonment, peace, silence, stillness and joy. My soul purpose was instantly remembered after hearing this story. I knew that my only job, my soul's purpose was to continue my journey of healing and to intentionally commit myself to my process.

My journey with GOD

I cried for hours after hearing this story, because I knew it. I knew there were things I had forgotten. I knew my connection to source, was painfully connected to my soul memory and I say painfully because isn't it painful to lose your keys, especially when you just had them in your hand. The knowing but the not remembering can physically hurt. In middle school I chose not to believe what other people believed. I remember when my thought process shifted, and I gave myself permission to not think like others. I didn't understand other religions saying if I don't believe what they believed then I was going to hell. As scary and as traumatic that type of fear-based ideology was, it was the foundation of my rebel with a cause energy. My momma always encouraged me to believe in a God of my own understanding which offered me so much freedom to explore my own beliefs, to even come to the understanding that there were multiple things I could believe in simultaneously and to know that I could also choose to believe in nothing if I wanted to. When my momma gave me permission to think how I wanted to think I was no longer in societies prison of beliefs. I could explore all of my options freely, because if my momma says I'm not going to hell, then I ain't going. *Kanye Shrugs lol

Like most people I was forced to go to church 2 or 3 times a Sunday and on Wednesdays for bible study when I was little and lived with my aunt. Do the easter speeches in my easter dress, sing in the choir, become an usher and wear a skirt and stockings lol and I hated it. I used to always say "When I get older, I ain't neva coming back to church" lol. I didn't understand why I had to wear a skirt and stockings or why I couldn't read, revelations at the back of the bible or why was God so mean? How come I couldn't think my own thoughts without him knowing and possibly getting mad for what I thought, didn't he give me this brain? Why give me a brain to think, but only allow me to think certain things lol. As a young child I intuitively knew that the church had systems and beliefs that directly conflicted with my core soul beliefs and understanding. I just didn't make sense to me, no matter how many questions I asked, I knew that the people who were attempting to answer my questions didn't know either. I was clear they were just attempting to tell me anything so I could believe what they believed to be true.

As I got older and matured, middle school I took my power back and began to explore on my own and without any fear. At this point my thought process was, God already reads my mind, he already knows I believe other things, ain't no point in hiding it, I might as well explore other religions without fear, and I did. In middle school I was fascinated with samurai culture, customs and methods. I didn't want to adopt any of their beliefs, honestly, I just loved how spiritual they were, how disciplined in their spirituality, how they honored nature but I didn't care for cutting off anyone's head as a way to show respect and honor lol However, it was refreshing just to be open and learn about other customs and traditional beliefs. I didn't understand I was naturally taking what I needed and leaving what I didn't. I was naturally only allowing myself to believe what resonated with my spirit. In middle school I was reading 1 book a week. One week it was sista soulja, the coldest winter ever. The next week, philosophy by Aristotle then the next week I was reading fly girl lol, yall know. Duality and balance lol.

As I got older in high school I saw GOD everywhere, in everything and in everyone. I understood and respected the purpose for church, religion and belief. I understood that many people needed it, but I also understood that I was allowed to hold space for their beliefs and still honor my own with no one being in the right or wrong. As a young adult my relationship with God began to become painful. I was deeply deeply angry and frustrated with God because as my spiritual awareness grew, as I began to see God in all things it became hard to have questions. When I began to really see the perfection of life even in the midst of my deepest depressions I was so deeply confused. I had so many questions and I was angry that I didn't have any answers. I didn't want answers from anyone's book because they didn't know anything for sure, they knew what they'd been taught by a book.

I had a direct connection with God, and I wanted to hear God tell me.

"Why are we here? "What is the purpose of life."

It felt as if God was playing a huge game and I wasn't laughing. I just didn't understand how so much perfection was possible. I was so tapped into my spiritual connection I could see the mechanics of how everything was connected, how nature breathed life into us all and every time I'd get a glimpse of God I'd burst into tears. Imagine seeing the most beautiful, mind blowing, life changing, abnormal event take place right in front of your eyes, then imagine seeing that every single day for years straight. At this point anytime I felt the presence of God I'd cry, then I recognized that I am the presence of God and I'd cry about that lol.

When I was a police officer, I remember one day using the restroom and looking at videos of animals on Instagram. I saw a video of a swan poking at an elephant's feet, being annoying and bothering it. Then the elephant randomly tried its best to kick the swan to leave it alone. Then, all I saw was God and I broke down crying lol in the bathroom with a gun on my side crying about a swan, an elephant and God. I couldn't escape the constant perfection of life, which was even more annoying because I was not happy in my life at all. I hated my job, I was 60 pounds overweight, love deprived, confused about what I was supposed to be doing with my life, an alcoholic but somehow, I could only see how perfect everything was.

I felt ostracized as well, like I was watching the human world and a completely different world of perfection simultaneously and I felt as if I wasn't apart of either. It felt as it I was watching a movie alone that no one else could see. This felt lonely at times because no one could see what I saw and this isn't something that I could just willfully go around explaining to people "Yea I just cried on the toilet because I saw a elephant try to kick a swan". I was clear that these spiritual moments were God's opportunities to connect deeper with me and remind me to remember who I was and what this life is.

My frustration with God grew into anger. At some point I recognized many emotions can exist simultaneously at the same time. I was deeply grateful because I was clear something big is happening and it's directly connected to God but I was angry because I didn't have any idea what the hell It was and all God kept sending were these doggon messages hidden in plain sight, angel numbers, divine aligned moments that most people would rub off as coincidences and all I could think of can you just please tell me lol I'm tired of guessing and finding clues.

There would be nights that I'd be doing deep healing work on myself, giving myself permission to work through emotional trauma and an owl would be right outside my window as I'd cry hysterically purging the pain from my past. I've never needed a miracle to happen right in front of me to know God was present. Yet still, I'd constantly question God. Not considering God he/she/it. Understanding God to be the all. Even the name God is belittling but it's the name that resonates with my spirit still. As I evolved deeper into quantum physics, metaphysics and spirituality I just couldn't understand how all this obvious perfection was even possible. When people say something is mind blowing, they mean it's inconceivable, their mind isn't equipped to understand or process the information. When a person typically feels this mind-blowing sensation, they either continue the subject by explaining the subject with intellect and passion, or they switch the subject because mentally they've hit a threshold of mentally being overstimulated or their bodies become so consumed and overwhelmed with emotion because the brain can't fathom this information and the person experiences a deep emotional release and cries.

The thought of how perfectly designed life is makes me feel like I'm going to explode. I could never fathom how I'm a part of something so perfect and then have memory lapses and forget how perfect everything is. When I remember everything is perfect, worry, stress force or confusion don't even have permission to exist within my energy because I trust the perfection of life and this trust is a natural reminder that safety and provision will always be readily available to me.

Mamma Ayahuasca

Summer of 2019, I decided to explore the plant medicine, Ayahuasca. I had known about it for year over 5years, but I didn't know how to explore it. I did so much research on all plant medicines and how they aided in the emotional and spiritual healing process. I'd investigated people like "Terence Mckenna" an author amongst many other titles, that advocated the use of psychedelic plants. He wrote many books and explained the positive neurological effects these plants have and also explained why the government has deemed them illegal in the USA. Based on much research and accounts from many doctors around the word, they feel as if the plant medicines help people heal years of emotional trauma and directly connect with the essence of God, ultimately taking away the robotic armor the average person wears. Essentially the connection to spirit that is born allows people the think freely, openly and choose a life that best benefits their soul evolution, I'm sure you all can come up you're your own reasons why this doesn't sound like good business for the government. Because I was a year sober before exploring plant medicine there was much concern by others that thought it would be an addictive drug. They didn't understand that plant medicine was not a drug, it was the medicine of the soul that only indigenous people knew how to create from a certain special tree bark.

I also studied "Bill W" The author of the Big Book and creator of Alcoholics Anonymous. During my research spree I learned that not only had Bill W partook in a plant medicine journey with Ayahuasca, during his ayahuasca ceremony is where he received the idea and soul download to create alcoholics anonymous. Many people explore the plant medicine journey to journey deeper into themselves, for more spiritual insight and clarity. I will say in hindsight, even with all of the research I'd done I was still very naïve about the medicine. In the documentaries I watched they typically only spoke about the great parts, the healing, the ability to see God, fractal images and sacred geometry. The never really spoke about the hell I'd have to travel through just to reach God and the damn sure didn't tell me that the hell I'd have to travel through would be my own.

One ceremony of Ayahuasca is considered 10 years of therapy. During my research, I saw a woman on Instagram partook in the medicine so I asked her where the location was she visited and she responded with so much love and said "When the medicine speaks to you it will guide you where you should go" That was one of the best forms of advice anyone could have given me. So I dropped the entire topic of plant medicine. I stopped looking into it, I stopped researching it, I stopped romanticizing and obsessing over an opportunity to explore it. Her message was a reminder to let go, and if it's meant for me to journey into this aspect of plant medicine then it would find me. For the next 5 years I did just that, I let go and continued doing my own work on myself and continued dedicating myself to my journey. Then suddenly after 5 years of releasing the urge to explore plant medicine, the medicine found me. I didn't have to do anything but trust. The location was right in front of me, the reviews were right in front of me and did nothing to make this happen. This is how I knew it was time, when I fully let go, the medicine found me just like the woman said it would.

Two months after reserving my space for the Ayahuasca retreat I flew to the jungles of the amazon in Peru to explore plant medicine alone and then after my plant medicine journey I'd after explore Peru for another month. Below I'll add an excerpt from my blog on my website expounding on my experience. This is my personal journal that I wrote during my ayahuasca experiences. Each night after a ceremony I'd come back to my hut and write my experiences. Below are my journal entries that I've since shared on my website blog.

"5 yrs. ago while on my journey of spiritual awakening and self-healing I learned about Ayahuasca. I asked a lady that had experienced this plant medicine for the information of the ayahuasca retreat she visited and with so much love she responded. NO,

"You don't find Ayahuasca. When your soul is ready, mother ayahuasca will find you."

After that moment I stopped searching for the plant medicine. Fast forward to today, I now know that I was nowhere near ready to receive this medicine 5 years ago. Gratefully the medicine found me this year and here is my experience. This is a very lengthy post so I will title each section appropriately just in case there is a specific story you are more interested in. I do understand many things I wrote will sound "crazy" odd or weird lol. I waited 3 years to share my experiences in this blog because I wanted to protect my experience which is very important to me, but I also know how our experiences help others so I hope that even if you all don't understand you respect my growth journey just as I would respect yours. also there aren't many pictures because this was a spiritual retreat for 10days that did not allow cell phones, only connections that took place came from within.

<u>Day 1</u>

"So far this trip has already been amazing. Meeting such beautiful like minded people, speaking about the same things & with the same intentions to grow & get better even if it's scary or hurtful.

Peru is so beautiful full of beautiful flowers, palms trees, passion fruits, star fruit, pineapple, real bananas & oranges. What's even more beautiful is the essence of this place, the history, The intention behind every action, every plant, every sunrise & sunset. The people here are called the "Shipibo People" a very intelligent shamanic people who still carry on the teachings of their ancestors from thousands of years ago.

Today we had our first flower bath ceremony which is infused with flowers & essences to clear our energies, then we had to dry ourselves in the sun. Once everyone dried, we all sat around & spoke aloud our intentions with ayahuasca & what we'd hoped it would reveal to us. Today we just got acclimated to our environment and each other.

<u>Day2 7am wake up to yoga</u>

7:30 VOMATIVO

Vomitivo is a practice used to clear out negative energy from your gut. This process clears out The gunk, bile, trauma, pain & ancestral negativity you've held within your body. They create a brown potion using plants which Tastes like tea, & then you drink the potion, wait 30 seconds & you continue to drink water until the potion forces you to VOMIT (vomitevo) Lol it SUCKS!! & It hurts. Imagine drinking a warm tasteless tea until your stomach feels like it's going to pop & your body sends a signal to your brain that it has to vomit, or you will drown!! That is what Vomitivo is Lol but it was so beautiful because usually vomiting can be embarrassing but in this case we all were yelling & routing each other on & encouraging one another to vomit on purpose, telling each other your deserve to release that pain, you deserve to release that negative energy DRINK DON'T THINK!! Is what we kept yelling as each purpose struggled, gagging & crying lol before you knew it everyone was vomiting at the exact same time lol again it sucked!! Lol we couldn't eat or even look at water after that lol Majority of us skipped lunch and because later tonight is our first ceremony we aren't allowed to eat much at all until after the ceremony or tomorrow. We have an abundance of fruit, some oatmeal and tasteless salmon caught right next to us in the amazon river. We aren't allowed any salt for the duration of the retreat., which is lame but I understand. I've grown to find that I love baby bananas which are the real banana and I love star fruit and passion fruit. I have a huge feeling I'll be living off of them for the next few days.

<u>1st Ayahuasca Ceremony</u>

At 6:30pm we go down to the Maloka for yoga & then at 8pm we will have our 1st Ayahuasca ceremony! I don't even think it's hit me yet to be honest. I'm nervous but I'm so ready!! I just want to grow, heal & get better. I'm ready!!! I've already made friends, everyone single person here is so beautiful. Today we all spoke with the shamans and expressed our intentions. I spoke about my dad and how I really wanted to forgive him. Everyone shared their deepest traumas, and that type of

intimate sharing really made us all feel close to each other. I don't feel alone at all, so that's a good thing. Ok I'll check in tomorrow.

We began at 6:30 by doing yoga which was very nice, it gave me a great opportunity to be present & soak in how incredible these moments were. The room was dark with a couple of candles. Once we finished yoga I laid back & fell asleep. Our 1st Ayahuasca ceremony was about to begin. When I woke up the guy next to me was sitting down & the facilitators were motioning for me to come over. The room was even more dark now & In a daze I got up & walked over with NO IDEA what the hell was going on, I was lost in the sauce and missed whatever instructions everybody else had received because my butt was sleep. I sat down with the two facilitators Sam & Claude & to my surprise a shaman. I didn't realize The Shamans has already entered the room while I was asleep.

Right before the mistra poured my shot glass of Ayahuasca, Sam leaned over & told me how much my story about my dad sounds like her story. She said it really touched her heart & resembles so much her relationship with her alcoholic father. After this brief whisper the mistra handed me the shot glass of red stuff & I looked at Sam & Claud like "what am I supposed to do now?" & they looked at me like girl what the hell are you doing, Drink it!! Lol mind you I just woke up so I didn't know what the hell was going on lol I couldn't even see lol so set my intention and then I drank the shot, STILL not putting 2 & 2 together that I was drinking the Ayahuasca. It tastes like Tabasco sauce lol it was weird & really caught me off guard but I took it to the head like the G that I am.

I went back to my mat & waited to see some shit lol I couldn't wait to see visions, geometrical shapes, hell I was ready to hear voices and see GOD too, but nothing happened. Now the room was pitch black with no lights & all I could think of was damn do I feel nauseous or is my stomach hurting from period cramps or do I have to pee? I was all in my head, yet still trying to stay present. 30minutes or longer passed & NOTHING!! I was like damn this sucks my stomach hurts & I have no idea why & on top of that I haven't seen not 1 doggon vision. So, I laid back down & all of a sudden, the shamans began singing. It was the most beautiful sound I'd ever heard in my life. Soothing & luring & enchanting. As soon as they began to sing, I felt everything come to life. My entire body activated. It felt like they were physically pulling me with their voices, like sucking me in with a vacuum. I instantly sat up & instantly felt nauseous.

All I could think of was ok this is it!! I'm about to see some shit, heal some traumas & grow unfortunately I ain't see a damn thing, I didn't vomit but I did spit a couple times lol annoyed I laid back down. The Shamans were working their way around the room. At our retreat we have 5 shamans that work on us during each ceremony. They take turns singing into the spirit of each person. The shamans sing songs called "Icaros" in front of you. After you take Ayahuasca, they take a bigger dosage of it to help themselves see into the spirit world.

So when they are in front of you they can see into you. Your fears, pain, blockages, energetic pains held in the body & once they see what you're holding they sing & speak to the spirit world, sending you healing energy to release those negative entities. Then the 1st mistra got to me. I had heard her voice singing to the guy next to me but when she sat right in front of me, I instantly felt an overwhelming need to cry. I wasn't sad, but I had an urge to cry. My face was frowned like I was crying but I didn't feel any tears, it was so weird & then all of a sudden it felt like rivers were flowing from my eyes uncontrollably & I had no control or idea why I was now crying & I mean boo hoo crying. But I just let go & released it all. Once I cried it all out for a few minutes I was just sitting there with my eyes closed, mouth open just in a daze, at peace, rocking back & forth with no thoughts, I was just present.

Each time the shaman finished singing to me, I'd laid down & reconnected with what I was feeling. The 2nd shaman came & when he sang, I noticed how tense my face was. It was not only tense but frowned up like I was angry. My lips were poked out my shoulders were up; my forehead was even frowned. & when I became aware I intentionally softened, while singing it felt like he was calling me to open up, to allow, to not fight it.

Visions of the past

So, I released my shoulders & unclenched my face & instantly I started to think about Sasha my German Shepherd that passed away right after my house burned down. My dad who died of liver cancer. Black and white, my cat that died in my house fire & my pawpaw who passed away when I was 6yrs old. Right when I tapped into those emotions the shaman was done & I wasn't ready for him to leave but I realized he had opened me up now it was my job to explore what had come to surface.

SASHA

I laid down & I spoke to Sasha & instantly broke down crying. Telling her how much I missed her, thanking her for always being there for me & saving my life so many times especially being there for me soaking up all my pain during the fire. I apologized for not being mentally present for her like she deserved, for leaving her to be in toxic relationships & for needing her to heal me after those relationships ended. I went back to the day I allowed her to transition gracefully (put her to sleep) she also died of liver failure like my dad & I thought about our last hug, her walking up to me & laying her head in my arms with tubes in her arm, there are photos on my Instagram.

My baby was saying goodbye & tonight I got a chance to hug her so many more times. I got to thank her for being there for me when I didn't know how to be there for myself & I let her know Cleo is doing a great job filling in her spot, I told her how proud she'd be of me being sober!! I cried so hard when I told her how hard things got when she left, how depressed & miserable I got without her how my world stopped & turned upside down, I revisited my saddest moments without her & then I released them. & I felt an INSTANT relief like that pain/guilt was no longer a part of my body, mind or spirit.

Black & White Cat

Then I spoke to black & white & apologized over & over & cried my heart out I felt so guilty not saving her from the house fire. I think subconsciously I blamed myself for her death. I cried so hard, I told her that I wanted to save her so bad, when I ran back into the house to save her, I could only hear her but I couldn't see because the smoke was so black & I was scared if I stayed in the house any longer I would die. I still remember her crying & I know she had scared & wanted me to help her & I tried, I just couldn't get her from under the bed because my eyes were burning so bad.

& then out of nowhere burst out laughing because I can't count how many times, I told my momma "You better not be mean to black

& white because she's a angel cat" "she's the Angel of this house" & literally if it wasn't for her everybody in the house would have died because it was her voice that woke me up!! My cat was crying because of the fire alarms going off, when I heard her cries, I woke up!! I spent some time thanking her for everything through the 10+years she was there for me. I Told her how much I loved her & again felt an instant relief of pain/guilt.

My Dad

Each shaman after that helped me deal with my dad & paw paw being gone. When I spoke to my dad, I apologized to him for not being present while he was dying. I told him over & over how much I thought he was a good person & he didn't deserve the life he had. I went back to each moment with him that made me feel scared, happy, traumatized, sad, pity, angry. I went to the memory of when I was super young not even 8yrs old yet, he got into a fight & had his jaw shattered & had to wear a mouth brace. Seeing that made me feel scared, pity for him & super uncomfortable to look at him, it made me feel powerless like I couldn't help or save him & also like I couldn't feel safe around him. I told him all everything.

My visions took me back to age 4 when he & I were at the park with some of his friends & he let me get on the swing & somehow, I ended up falling off the swing right on my back, that was the 1st time I felt the wind knocked out of me & the 1st I felt like he wasn't there for me because he was busy talking to his friends. I told him this also. I went to the memory of him not understanding he hurt my feelings, that being the first time I was ever shut down emotionally. But I told him I understand now he just didn't have the capacity to understand in that moment. I then went to a childhood memory of jumping off of the couch taking tic tacs as sleeping pills before I went to sleep lol I remembered my mom & I singing "mmhm mhmm mhmm silly Raymond" because my dad did some funny stuff when I was. A baby lol I recalled stories my mom told me about my dad how he tried to commit suicide one time & I began apologizing to him again, telling him I understand why you couldn't be there for me & be a part of my life even though i wish you were.

Then I went to good memories of us with the same bob Marley posters hanging in our rooms & watching the CSI shows right before bed lol I remember going to his apartment & he tried to hide smoking weed from me lol I wish he didn't feel like he had to hide. I told him I was a year & some change sober & that he would be so proud of me right now for breaking our generational curse. We had a great moment & then I felt relief of pain/guilt.

PAW PAW

And then I recalled memories of my grandfather. I went to my house behind paw paw & remembered the kitchen, the dining room table, the living room with the couch and my bedroom but I couldn't remember my mom's bedroom or a bathroom. Then my vision took me to paw paws house, his kitchen, him eating at his kitchen table biscuits (me eating the soft biscuit tops only & him getting mad) lol while my momma cooked. His living room with the tv had a whole bunch of guns & around sofa. The room with a mirrored wall & a furnace. His bathroom & his bedroom which I could only remember being in once or twice, I think one night he let me sleep in there by myself when I woke up I was so lost like lol where is this?

I remembered his shed outside which looked soooo big to me lol the black things that would fall of his tree & is step on them to hear them crunch lol I remembered his chicken coop at the back of the property which was so weird & scary to me. That time he let me ride on the back of his lawn mower while he cut the grass & I fell off the back it. My momma said he felt bad but I had fun lol

Then I remembered the time he took me on a road trip in his new Winnebago lol I had some nasty cereal and there was a bed I slept in as he drove us to St. Augustine & all I remember was I couldn't wait to go home lol I was so bored lol I remembered him coming to my house one day to watch me because I was sick while my momma was at work & he was watching a move called a rage in Harlem the whole time i was throwing up lol so I called my momma & told her. He found out and called me a little chicken or a heffa because I didn't tell him lol. Then the time I learned how to use a phone when I was little Lol I learned his number first & I'd call him & as soon as he'd answer I'd hang up on him and run from our house behind to his house in my mommas High heeled boots to see his facial expression. I did it about three times then he answered & said he was calling the police to come get me & I ran over his house crying & screaming. He thought that was funny lol I told him how proud he would be of me & my mom. How well we're doing, both breaking the family generational curse of alcoholism. and I could tell he was smiling & laughing with me.

MY MOMMA!!!!

Then I began to see my beautiful momma. I was so grateful for her & at the same time fearful of losing her. I think my visions of her were to help me confront my fear of losing her. I thought about how all we do is laugh at our own inside jokes lol I mean we cry laughing without even saying a word. I don't hug her enough, tell her I love her enough, take in our moments together enough. I just had a overwhelming sense of wanting to hug her so badly. I miss her so much, like I wonder what she's doing if she's laughing or are my cats getting on her nerves or if she's worried about me which I hope she isn't.

My momma changed her whole life JUST FOR ME!! That's crazy!! Like I'm able to be here just because of the decisions she intentionally made. I need to be more available to her & not so caught up in my own stuff, alternate realities. I want my mom to be so happy, & my fear was that she is not. I want her to be fulfilled. & I just thanked her for everything & saw visions of us being sisters & mom & daughter & just broke down crying!! Like this type of relationship, I have with my mom is unreal & I have it!! I just kept telling her thank you!!

Then the ceremony was over, the shamans stopped singing & I was so at ease, full of peace & I felt weightless. When the ceremony ended, I came to my tombolo (cabin) to rest.

<u>Trauma & Pain in my body</u>

My day was beautiful, I felt such a relief from my 1st ceremony. I felt like a ton of bricks were lifted off of me, literally that's how light my spirit and body felt. As usual before our ceremony we took our flower baths and got ready for yoga and our 2nd Ayahuasca ceremony. My 2nd round of Ayahuasca I was READY!! lol Now looking back, I was a little bit to ready lol still excited about my visions and traumatic releases of pain the night before I was too excited about what the spirit world would reveal to me this night. I couldn't wait to fly, see images, memories from my past, past life, different dimensions etc., I was ready for it all.

Long story short, I AINT SEE SHIT!! lmao. Long story short, I was in excruciating pain ALL NIGHT LONG!!! My body hurt so badly all I could do was cry. Imagine having a migraine, the worst cramps, body aches and a pulsating sensation all through your body 4-5hrs straight. It was damn near unbearable. At one point the pain got so bad I called over the facilitator Sam. I told her how much pain I was in and asked was this normal. She told me that pain in the body is very normal, it actually signifies that I may have a lot of traumas stored in my body since that is where the medicine seems to be working most.

She brought to my attention my addiction to alcohol and any other traumas my body has absorbed since I was born. She reminded me that those trapped emotions can still be lingering in my body, in the deepest part of my tissue and cells. With this information I felt a little better knowing the pain wasn't pointless, it had purpose. Then I remembered MY purpose. I remember saying my first day arriving at the retreat that I wanted to grow no matter how much it hurt lol. Well, I ate those words quickly lol. Hours past and as each shaman sang to me the pain got worse and worse, but I sat with it. At this point everyone in the room was vomiting and I was praying to vomit, I just knew that if I could vomit, I would feel better.

Each time a Shaman would finish singing I would gag uncontrollably. There was no question how powerful these shamans were, I could literally feel them cleaning out my trauma from my body. Finally, I counted my 5th and final shaman I couldn't wait for her to stop singing lol I was like giiiiiirrllllll please hurry the hell up lol I knew once she finished, I would be released from the hold they had on my body and literally the second she stopped singing I felt my stomach in knots. I immediately reached for my bucket and vomited 4-5hrs worth of trauma, which basically translates to a lifetime of stored and forgotten trauma. I was so relieved the ceremony was finally over, but because my body had just gone through so much pain, I didn't have the energy to go back to my cabin, so I slept on my mat the entire night like. a baby.

I MET MY SOUL!!!!

3rd Ayahuasca

All I can say is "WTF WAS THAT lol man!! Where do I start? I tried to go into last night's ceremony with an open heart, set intentions & humble respect for the medicine & the shamans. This time when we drank the medicine, we were allowed to choose how much based on 3 cup sizes. Claude & I agreed that the 2nd cup size was best which was maybe a tad bit more than the shot I had the day before. I took the shot & went back to my mat. I instantly felt nauseous. I was like damn body, we gotta go through this again? Lol but after a couple minutes the nausea went away & I was so happy because I felt great. I thought to myself, cool this is going to be an easy & beautiful night haha. I believe I dosed off for a little while & then the medicine hit me like a bus!!!

I instantly saw shapes, moving fractal images, geometrical shapes and beautiful colors, it was amazing. I could zoom in & out of one image to another. then my body started to tingle, this feeling was familiar because I had felt this way at the beginning of my day 2

Ayahuasca experiences. Yet this time the intensity kept getting higher & scarier. The funny thing is I wasn't in pain like the day before, I was just extremely uncomfortable. This intensity was all through my body & I'd try to move my body to shake the feeling off but that didn't work. Imagine having an orgasm but constantly second after second after second! That type of overstimulation doesn't feel good at all. It begins to feel unbearable.

Then I'd drift off into a fractal world when the intensity got too strong almost as if my body passed out from not being able to handle this intense feeling. When I'd open my eyes, I was still in a fractal world with vibrant colors, moving shapes, I was able to see everything from a cellular level even with my eyes open. I could see the insides of flowers, the cellular make up of plants. Then the intensity came back, it's so hard not to call it pain but it wasn't pain, it was just very intense stimulation. It was so unbelievably uncomfortable.

I DIDN'T KNOW HOW 2 LOVE MYSELF

The tingling was still there in my entire body, so I flashed my red light for Sam to come over. I told her I'm nauseous, & my body feels super funny, this feeling doesn't feel good at all & I'm kind of scared. Sam told me again this medicine is really working in my body, try not to resist because what you resist will persist. She told me to find the pain in my body & send love to it, be aware of how I'm speaking to myself. She told me that maybe this is my time to practice self-love, she said now it seems like that's the reason I'm here, to learn how to give that love to myself that I've been seeking through alcohol, people, places & things. Then she kissed my cheek & walked away. I broke down crying. Sam read the hell out of my ass like I was an open book test I cried because i knew she was 100% correct. I lacked so much self-love, I wasn't nice to myself, I never would send love to myself. I never spoke to myself with love, compassion or patience. So, I laid down & used the rest of my time sending love to myself.

I hyped myself all the way up. I was telling my breast how nice they were, my skin how vibrant & glamorous it is. I sent love to my nails, my butt, my liver, kidneys, eyes, spinal cord, my gut, intestines, colon, teeth, tongue, bones ear drums, vocal cords, thyroid, lymphatic system. Everything!! I then imagined myself taking out my heart & washing it over crystal clear water that sparkled so much it looked like glitter. I washed my heart, I squeezed all the gunk out it which was black & green & I kept washing, cleaning the inside of my heart, the corners & crevices. Then as a maestro came over to sing to me, I laid down in front of him & kept sending love to myself. This made me so emotional, I just kept saying My life is beautiful and I love myself. After a while I actually began to believe it, and I felt this love for myself sooo deeply I cried even more.

<u>Pain is TRAUMA leaving the body</u>

This was just the beginning of my night. My attention instantly shifted once the shaman moved to the person next to me. I took a deep breath & then I passed out. No more images, emotions or memories. Everything was just blank. The shaman started singing again & my stomach turned into knots! Twisting & turning, my body was shivering & that overwhelming intensity came back. I was miserable & I couldn't shake it. The more he sang the worse I felt. At this point I had a fever & was curled up in so many blankets in fetal position crying and shivering & all I could imagine was my great friend Titus saying, "Allow Candy Just Allow"! I literally heard his voice the entire night, as if he was there walking me through every step, I mean every step. Every time I wanted to give up, his voice was the only thing I could hear cheering me on and motivating me.

<u>MY SOUL CRIED</u>

Then another shaman came over to sing to me. It felt like he got a string & started pulling something out of my stomach & I started crying sooooooo sooooo hard!! It didn't even hurt but I was hysterically crying & I remembered thinking, wait why am I crying lol. I cried so hard I started gagging, almost vomiting. It was a deep, dark, sad, sorrowful cry full of grief & pain. It felt as if the veins in my face were going to pop. It was the deepest cry I've ever felt in my life, I couldn't stop. My face was frowned up like a baby crying. Actually, I felt just like a baby. & Then I randomly thought to myself wow, my soul has been really sad. I then realized this wasn't me crying, it was my SOUL. My soul was letting out all of the Pain, grief & sorrow she's carried around for 29 years. I was shaking uncontrollably, as if I was having a seizure. I felt like I had the worst flew of my life, I'm positive I had a fever for the next hour. I was SICK with the chills, & crying so hard my teeth would chatter together like when a person is extremely cold. I turned into a little sick infant baby with a fever. & all I could think of was Damn, my soul was really sad!! I felt bad for her & an overwhelming sense of compassion and love.

I thought to myself no one has ever comforted my soul, no one hugged her when she experienced trauma, each experience I've encountered since childhood my soul has had to deal with it all alone with no one to speak to about it. I can't even imagine how scary, hard, painful, lonely & traumatizing that was for her. While I continued to cry it all made so much sense, I've always felt a sense of deep sadness, pain, loneliness & grief in the pit of my core!! No matter how beautiful my life was, how many things were going perfect for me I just couldn't shake this sadness & I'd write about it every night. I couldn't shake the confusion & overwhelming thought of my existence, why I'm here, what does all this mean. At night sometimes I just cry my eyes out & I never had any true idea why, I just thought I was a hypersensitive person.

But seeing my soul cry made so much sense, she was yearning to purge all that toxicity she'd been holding on to for 29 years. Imagine coming to this new dimension to grow, love & evolve. Everything is new, your birth is traumatic, my environment was traumatic, my parents leaving was traumatic, all of this trauma I & my soul experienced before the age of 3 and the trauma of my entire life she'd been trying to cope with all these years. It was like my body had to physically go through all this pain with Ayahuasca to allow my soul to surface & just CRY! It was so f*cking beautiful!! Like wow, my soul deserves this, I thought to myself how I had never felt connected to my soul and when I'd speak about my soul, I'd literally picture a distant being in the sky, never within me & last night was the first time I saw my soul.

I MET MY SOUL

She literally stood over me & looked at me like she was so proud of me, as if she was saying "WELL DONE". She was very tall; she was shining so bright yellow color like the sun & felt so warm & looked rested & rejuvenated. I cried even harder knowing we had just done this together. She was a part of me now. This moment felt like it was our first time ever meeting and like we'd known each other forever. Meeting my soul has been the highlight of my life.

I was laughing because seeing her be proud of me reminded me of the scene from the movie BAPS when Niecy was dancing & showing her skills while waiting in line to audition & her friend was hyping her up like "YEA yea that's my girl, that's MY girl, WE GOT THIS!! BaybeBaybehh (BOOYOWW" this made me laugh so hard lol

The shamans continued singing & at this point I had to sit up & look at the shaman in front of me like GIRLLLL, can a sista get a break gah lee lol this night they wouldn't not let up on us. Everyone was vomiting so loudly & my body aches were still there. At this point I had the cover over my head hoping the cover could block out some of the pain as the shaman Sang in front of me but I wasn't consumed by the uncomfortableness like I was before. I think because my soul & I got a lot of pent-up energy and trauma out but my stomach was still turning the more they sang. At this point everything was so crazy, painful and mind-blowing all I could do was laugh out loud and ask how is this shit real.

Then I started repeating over & over "my life is beautiful" with a huge smile on my face. My life is beautiful, my body is beautiful, my mind is beautiful, my brain is beautiful. Then I went into my brain & cleaned it like I did my heart, I told her how smart she was, intelligent, thoughtful, creative, I empowered my memory & told my mind we could do anything. I showered my brain with love and then the shamans got louder and the intensity in my body went to each organ inside me. It was in my vagina, then my spinal cord which really hurt, inside my liver, kidneys and eyes. I felt this intensity working, clearing & cleaning my insides, it sucked but I wasn't as bothered because I could now see the bigger picture.

I laid back & let the medicine do its job while I smiled, cried & literally moaned like a baby. Finally, the shamans shut the hell up lol and my body was put to ease. I took the biggest deep breath & felt so good. Once the shamans stopped singing you could hear everyone around the room take the biggest deep breathes, I guess we were all going through hell together and all were experiencing relief together. All I could think of was "my soul cried, YES!" I knew it!! I knew there was something attached to me, a reason I could never be fully happy, a reason I always had a sense of sadness! I was so happy for my soul like girl!!! Yessss!! You deserved that cry!! I was so crunk, my soul cried & she was proud of me! Just wow. That was such an amazing experience. My soul is so beautiful I can't wait for us to thrive together for the rest of our lives!!

Lessons LEARNED : Lessons EARNED!

This was by far the most amazing experience I've ever had in my life. Ayahuasca plant medicine allowed me to heal 30yrs worth of trauma in 10days. I was able to let go of Guilt, Abandonment, fear and lack of self-love and it was all replaced with compassion, love, patience and understanding. At times It was so scary it forced me to trust myself and love myself. This medicine not only healed my trauma, but it showed the areas I still need to work on. It revealed to me that this is just the beginning of my healing journey, but it gave me tools to navigate any emotional pain. I learned true self love and how to show up confidently as my true authentic self. I have never felt more perfect than I do now. It also reminded me how important it is to stay focused on my journey! This life is mine, I can allow people to experience it with me, but I cannot allow anything, or anyone deter me from my path. I'm deeply grateful for this experience and I'm grateful to embark on my new journey of self-love, and continuous healing of my wounds. The shamans told us that after ayahuasca our spirits are fragile like we just got out of brain surgery so the ayahuasca plant medicine does part of the work, it's up to me to honor my soul and keep intentionally working on myself and growing as I journey through this beautiful life.

IM GRATEFUL

I LOVE MYSELF

MY LIFE IS BEAUTIFUL

I continued my healing journey, I remained single and dedicated my life to my emotional healing and spiritual journey. It was my passion and I enjoyed seeing myself evolve. I continued to travel and expand my awareness of life. I eventually transitioned out of being a police officer into teaching criminal justice. I recognized that I didn't need or want a career that kept me in fear and provided the false illusion that I wasn't safe. Now as I evolved, I trusted that I was safe within my own being and didn't need a gun or a job to unconsciously prove that to myself.

My Continued Journey With GRIEF

March 1st 2020 before the pandemic hit, my family got a call in the middle of the night that my favorite cousin had been killed in a night club. Initially I was in shock. I showed absolutely no emotion. I rationalized in my mind what could have happened and really didn't know how to process this level of grief, so I didn't. It took me two days to actually cry and when I did, I felt like I was going to die. Literally I've never in my entire existence felt a pain like that. I didn't understand how I could feel a pain of that magnitude and still live. My cousin had just gotten out of prison and was really doing his best to change his life around. He was on his spiritual and emotional healing journey as well. Most of the things I'm speaking about in my book he was learning, and we would talk about these things together before he was killed. I know his heart and soul where in a beautiful place and on the path to healing. But this knowledge didn't ease my pain of losing him. The images in my mind of him being shot just shattered me.

My cousin was one of the best people in the world with the most beautiful heart. He'd give anything to help anyone, and he cared about heling people to his own detriment. I was overcome by guilt because of how I had to distance myself from him growing up to protect myself emotionally. I felt so bad that I couldn't save him. Again, everything began to move in slow motion. Trauma was setting in. As I'd cry my energy of processing emotion would become more violent, hyperventilating, chocking on my tears, vomiting as I cried and crying so deeply, I'd forget to breath. Unlike in my young adult years emotional detachment wasn't an option for me anymore.

Now that I had tools to help me in my healing journey, I knew that the only way out was through, so I let it all in, every single emotion that I'd ever run from in regard to my cousin I let them all rush over me and take over my body. My cousin was my first best friend. We did everything together and he always protected me. He didn't even call me Candyss, he called me STAR because he believed in me so much and always told me one day, I'd be a star. I was so hurt I didn't understand how I'd continue life. The next few days on my way to return to work I realized that I had forgotten how to get to work. I was almost an hour late because I couldn't remember where I was, and I'd worked in the same location and drove the same route for 6 years. I also had a few days where I couldn't use my phone because I couldn't remember my passcode. I had also forgotten the passcode to the alarm in my home and on top of that I couldn't move my right shoulder or arm for the next few days. I was very clear that trauma was present, and it was manifesting in my body. When trauma Is present it does one or two things to continue to help the body function when emotional pain or stressors begin to overwhelm the body. One method is to shut down memory, this is why many people can't remember their childhood or specific moments of their lives. Lack of memory is a clear sign of emotional trauma.

Another way to identify if trauma is present is if there is pain in the body. When the brain experiences an overwhelming amount of stress, if the stress isn't processed properly, it becomes trauma, and that stress begins to manifest as pain in the body. The brain will store trauma in the body to continue to keep the human alive so it can function of a daily basis. This is why people have cancer, disease, fibromyalgia, lupus, asthma, arthritis, organs that don't function properly, chronic back pain or struggle to have children, womb trauma. These are signs and symptoms that trauma has been stored In the body. A great book to read is "The body keeps the score" and a great documentary to watch is "Emotion 2.0" Two people to know and do research on are Dr. Joe Dispenza and Dr. Bruce Lipton that better explain these scientific concepts in depth.

Because I was aware of trauma and its methods of forming, I also was clear that giving myself permission to cry every single time a wave of grief was present was healing to my body. I allowed myself to let it all out, I cried every single time I thought of my cousin, I journaled, I spoke to him, I even went to see my therapist to work through the guilt I was carrying. I did all the things I needed to do to properly process the grief, but the best and most profound thing that I did was give myself permission to feel. I felt it all. Sometimes I'd stand in my home with my arms wide open inviting grief to do its job within my body because I trust myself to not run from myself and I trust that I'd done so much work on myself and I'd cultivated so much spiritual stamina that I knew I could heal in the midst of grief. So, if I needed to be broken for a while, I welcomed it and I surrendered to not knowing how long grief would stay.

Essentially, I chose to make friends with grief and gave it permission to do what it needed to do at any time, I'd adapt. And it did. Grief came over and over again at random times, painfully burning the inside of my heart and punching me in the stomach repeatedly. Sometimes I'd even have to pull over while driving just to process the emotion and cry. As 2020 went on, I renovated a cargo van and traveled the us with my German shepherd Cleo. Because it was the pandemic everyone was home, and my mom had just bought me a cargo van for Christmas, and I decided it was time to get back to nature. I thought this would help me cope with the death of my cousin but like the quote says, "Wherever you go, there you are". As Cleo and I traveled across state lines I realized driving long distances alone gave you a lot of time to think, reflect and feel. Driving was like my therapy session and grief was always the topic. Many times, I'd intentionally drove in silence. I was clear that as beautiful as music make me feel, it was a distraction from how I really felt. So the start of my day was pure silence. As I drove, I'd visualize my cousin sitting in the passenger seat with me traveling to beautiful destinations with me. I'd visualize us as kids running in the desert that I was driving through. I'd cry until my tear ducts were depleted. This process helped ease the grief. Not because I was traveling but because I had months of alone time, in nature, silence and stillness to be present with grief without any distractions whenever it chose to surface.

Healing For Love

September 30th 2020 I had just turned 31 years young and I was in what I thought was a very beautiful place in my life. My career teaching criminal justice was going well, and my social media platforms were growing because of my vanlife experience traveling the US with Cleo. Many of my videos had gone viral on Instagram, TikTok and YouTube which was exciting. I was still in the midst of my healing and enjoying my process of showing up for myself. Even though I was traveling in my van and I knew that's what people wanted to see, I made sure to maintain photos of Cleo and the van but I also wrote captions and stories that only reflected my healing and spiritual journey. As much as everyone around me in the van life community solely focused on surface topics about Van Life, I made it a point to still remind people, if they truly focus on their healing journey, they too can experience this type of life and freedom. My inboxes were full of thousands of people sending me messages in gratitude for what I share and explaining to me how my posts had helped them get through tough times. Hundreds of messages a day began flooding in.

Little did I know I was about to cross paths with my soul mate. On my birthday a man on Instagram Dox @Brick_Citi_Buddha reposted a video of me and just sent his support. I didn't think much of it, but I was also learning how to work through detachment and respond to people who were openly supportive of me. Responding to love and thanking people in my DM's for sending me love was emotionally overwhelming for me, but I made it a daily practice to say thank you and to share my gratitude. When I responded to Dox I realized I'd seen his page before. That summer he surfaced on my explore feed. I remembered being in awe of his positive, conscious and healing messages, what he spoke about on his platform really stood out to me. I thanked him for my sharing my post and I returned the love by also resharing one of his posts.

No real communicating began until sometime after this initial reaction. He'd begin sending me meditation videos, I'd also send him educational things that I enjoyed. This was the start of slight communication with no intention attached to it. We both just enjoyed quantum mechanics and metaphysical information, spirituality and shared those things. One day our conversation about the Romeo and Juliet play caused us to have deeper conversation that lasted longer than usual via Instagram DM's lol. Eventually this became a little more consistent and we both became a little more familiar and would share personal things about one another.

I remember one of our first real conversations was us almost bragging about how we'd be perfectly fine if we never entered another relationship or ever had sex again for that matter. We were both so intentional about our emotional healing and spiritual journey that we didn't want anyone or anything to distract us from our process of connecting with God or ourselves.

One day Dox began inviting me to meditate together in a place called the ethos in a spiritual realm of visualization that all spiritual beings live that instantly connects souls and allows them to freely meet and play. He lived in new jersey so having a spiritual way to connect felt very refreshening and beautiful. After our first mediation we were clear that we had a very deep connection and something was there, we didn't know what and we didn't care to force any answers we just knew it was worth exploring.

Valentines' week of 2021 he flew to Houston to meet me in person for the first time and we knew we were official from that point on. We even survived Texas's winter storm in my van while the rest of Texas had no heat or electricity, we were playing chess in my van enjoying one another's time. Our time together was so easy, fun and loving.

This was the first relationship I didn't ask "What are we" honestly, I didn't care. I didn't have any intentions and I wasn't pressed for him to tell me his. We were so honest with one another. He encouraged me to speak how things made me feel and he was so gentle and the most loving man I'd ever experienced. I had just come off journey of being single and celibate for 4 years, so I was open to exploring something with him, but I wasn't going to force anything.

We allowed our relationship to naturally flow. One of my biggest indications that he was the one for me was how supportive he was of everything I did or felt. He guided me in a way that made me feel reparented. I couldn't help but to acknowledge how quickly time sped up for me. My healing went from consistent to rapid. One day he told me "You heal a different part of yourself every week". He would say things that would spark so much emotion that I'd go down rabbit wholes of self-discovery and highlighting blind spots within myself that needed my attention and nurturing. One of the things I loved the most was how we both honored silence and personal time to heal or reflect. Some days we'd say there's a part of me that needs my attention, so I won't use my voice today and we'd honor one anther taking personal time to focus on healing. It was so beautiful. I'd never met someone who was not just ok with not speaking to you for a couple of days but was genuinely supportive of it. When we met,

I was now 60 pounds overweight and I wore a G bra size. I was confident but not in my body.

As my healing began to speed up, I began healing my relationship with my body, my womb, my inner child and other areas that needed my attention. I realized that I hadn't looked in the mirror from my collar bone down in the past 4 years. I was so turned off and afraid of my body that I only looked at my face because my skin was popping. Dox encouraged me to get a full-length mirror that literally changed my life. He also encouraged me to begin wearing color in lingerie which I'd never done. He wasn't attempting to be sexual in his suggestions for me to wear color, he was inviting me to explore how colors made me feel. I'd only worn black; I hid behind black because I thought it made me invisible. This led to me exploring all types of clothes, things I'd always wanted to wear but was afraid to wear. Wearing colorful clothes became an adventure for me, I started to wear clothes allowed me to show up big.

When I saw my full body, I also saw all of the areas of my being I'd neglected. Imagine being so afraid to look at yourself that you neglect yourself for 4 years. The body picks up on that type of neglect and self-abandonment so now that I could see the fullness of myself, I was able to find gratitude for my feet, ankles, legs and knees for holding me up for 31 years. For literally getting to each next new phase of my life. I couldn't look at my body without gratitude, empathy, compassion and without being apologetic for the years of neglect.

I'd go to the gym maybe twice a week just to move my body because it made me feel good emotionally. Before I knew It, I had lost 40 pounds in 3 months. The same weight I'd been trying to lose for the past 6 years, I'd lost in 3 months. How Sway? I realized the weight I lost wasn't fat, it was emotional weight. It was the weight I was holding on to energetically in my body. It was emotional trauma that was stored in areas of my body that I'd refused to look at for the past 4 years. Now that I was acknowledging my body and really starting to love myself and form a deep meaningful relationship with my body the weight I was carrying just fell off. I did no diet and I only worked out at the gym twice a week for 15 mins each day. That doesn't equate to 40 pounds of weight loss in 3 months. That typically takes the average person 6 months to a year to lose.

I realized I was healing rapidly and on top of that I was being loved properly. I was with a very intentional man, that loved God and knew exactly how to show up for me, guide me, teach me and love me the way I needed and desired. I was clear that he was reparenting me in a way I'd never had an opportunity to experience from my dad. My relationship began to flourish by this point we were openly together on social media. I'd still never asked him "What are we" we just naturally progressed to a space that resonated with both of our spirits.

One day he intentionally offered me his commitment and faithfulness acknowledging and honoring that he'd only share his energy with me. Which allowed me to trust even deeper that I could allow myself to fully be open to this union. I loved that his faithfulness was an offering that came from him, out of his mouth in his own time, it wasn't an expectation from me to attempt to force myself to feel safe in a relationship. What's funny is that him offering his faithfulness is not when I knew I could trust him.

I knew I could trust him when I created my organic skincare line "Sasha Flowers" (purchase at candysslove.com) and I asked him how much he thought I should price an item and before he answered he said "Let me meditate on it and I'll let you know by the end of the day" I knew I could trust him because his first reaction and response was to consult with God before he guided me. That's the epitome of provision. He was very well informed in the business world so he could have very well rested on his wisdom, knowledge or even ego when it came to pricing a product, he asked God and then told me what resonated with is spirit. That is when I knew I could trust him because his guidance didn't come from ego if came from God.

Dox was the gentlest, loving, patient, intelligent and understanding man I'd ever met. I was in awe of him, I was excited to learn from him and his soul.

Nine Months into our relationship we traveled to St. John Virgin Islands, and I fell deeper in love with him. It's like I was so shocked that God placed someone so perfect in my life. I was truly happy, at peace, I felt sexy af, I was exploring my sensuality, I was supported by my man and for the first time in my life I felt at home in my body. He loved my journey of self-exploration. He wanted whatever would make me happy, feel safe and provided for.

While on our vacation I was adamant about wanting to listen to live music. He told me to get dressed, that he'd found a place that played the type of live music that we liked. When we got there it was pouring down raining and there was only one lady in the audience, but the band was so beautiful. Dox asked her are there any beaches around we can go to at night, she said yes, "Honeymoon Beach" after the band finished, we set out on our journey in our jeep to the beach. I was thoroughly enjoying just being young, out on the town exploring and having a great time. I felt like we were in a black "The Notebook" movie lol Once we got to the beach, we just held one another starred at the full moon. Everything around us was pitch black. We couldn't even see one another, just the moon lighting up the ocean in front of us.

As he stood behind me, he asked me

"If you could have anything, what would it be?" I replied, "To have this moment for ever".

Then I felt him shift from behind me, to in front of me. I could see parts of him on the ground in the sand. Honestly, to this day I have no idea that what man said because I blanked out, all I remember was him putting a ring on my finger, telling me how much he loved me as I cried a shook like I was miss America lol and we hugged for what felt like an hour. My soul mate had just put a ring on it. I was in shock. I honestly never thought I'd get married or commit to one person intentionally. I thought I didn't want to get married until that ring touched my fanga lol. We both cried because we could feel God's presence, our angels and ancestors in the moon light. No one else was on the beach just us, in the presence of God professing our love to one another. That night was heaven for us. All I remember was spending the rest of the evening prancing around the house, dancing and holding up my ring lol. That was by far one of the happiest moments I've ever experienced in my life.

From day 1 our love story has been a love story. We began hosting yearly emotional healing retreats in Mexico together helping people expand their awareness and teaching them how to heal emotional pain. We built our first home together, that's not just a home it's a portal to God. We named it Ajna the Cathedral because everyone that enters it says it feels like a cathedral. Most importantly we love each other so much, we support one another and our foundation for our love is God, our individual healing and then our union.

So many people on social media say things like they can't wait to find love like this and each time we correct them by saying we didn't find this love, we healed for this love. Each time we chose to intentionally heal in our past we got closer and closer to God revealing us to one another. The type of love we share is not possible if we didn't commit ourselves to our healing journey. While I was single, my husband was a year into his celibacy, meditating in the forest for hours at a time no matter how hot or cold. There was no smoking, no drinking and no escaping for him, he just focused on his relationship with God and his healing just as I did. By doing this level of deep healing work you begin to attract to you other souls that match your energy, your intention and your frequency.

The Results of My Healing

As I continued my healing journey more doors opened for me. I got a breast reduction which boosted my confidence even more. I had researched this surgery for years; I'd had consultations and even paid my deposit however the waitlist was always 3-4 years out. Once I began to truly love myself including my breasts randomly one day while sitting at a lake in vegas I received a call notifying me that a cancelation opened a spot for me, but I'd have to get the surgery the next week. I knew this was a sign that I'd honored, loved and nurtured myself so beautifully and now it was ok to allow myself to make this life changing alteration.

I'd officially lost 63 pounds in total. I was able to quit my job as a police officer and criminal justice teacher and become an entrepreneur full time. My Organic skincare business "Sasha Flowers" made over 6 figures in the first couple of months and I began guiding clients in their emotional healing journey with 1 on 1 sessions.

The life I used to pray for I was not living. I used to drive to work crying because I hated my job and I felt like it interfered with my healing process. I would be in the middle of healing deep trauma but have to stop crying to go to work. I began to pray for healing to be my life and my career. I wanted every aspect of my life to reflect emotional healing and intentional growth.

Today my only job is to heal myself and guide others in their healing journey. I can rest when I need to, I can use an entire day to express emotion and focus on healing without feeling guilty because intentional healing is my job now. I'm free enough that having a relationship with God is my only priority.

My purpose and intention for writing this book and speaking about these topics is to remind people you can do this too. You can experience the exact life you desire as well, but you have to be willing to give up this version of yourself to evolve into the new version of yourself. I've died to myself, many times. So many people say, "You don't even look like the same person". It's because I'm not the same person. When you intentionally heal, grow and evolve so does the structure of your cells and DNA. The trauma that was once stored in your body releases as you heal deeper levels of yourself. When you heal, you free your body, aura and energetic field to resemble your soul and your truest frequency. Now I look like God, I no longer look like walking trauma. If you're ready to change your life and start your process of healing, just remember who you are. Believe in yourself. Take everything one day at a time and stay intentional about your journey.

Remind yourself of all of the many things you've already overcome and grown from. You deserve to thrive, to live the life you desire and feel good doing it. Healing and experiencing a life of peace and harmony is your birthright. Take your power back. Remember who the f*ck you are.

RETURN HOME TO YOURSELF

Before & after reading this book my prayer is that you give yourself permission to return back to the truest version of you. The best version of you. The you that reflects the light of your soul before society, parents, relationships, friendships, trauma, pain & money taught you how to forget who you are & dim your light. Return to who you were before you were told that fire is hot, don't touch that or you'll burn yourself. The part of you that is a warrior, fearless, strong & not afraid of life. The part of you that saw beauty in everything before you were given A name to attach you identify to, a religion to defend or beliefs that would shape the outcome of your entire life.

Healing & Returning to the truest version of yourself means you will have to give up the version of yourself you're attached to an existing as now, so the higher version of you and the newer version of you that is forming can thrive. You may be required to give up or let go of all identities, masks, characters and personas that don't truly reflect your God self. To return home to yourself is to acknowledge your soul's essence, to commit to your souls purpose and intentionally embody your natural innate power. Operating from the powerful essence of your soul is your birthright.

This will also mean that you will be required to initiate the process of letting go of people, places, things, substances, behaviors, thoughts, emotions, relationships, job and beliefs that no longer serve you or your journey of healing. This means no longer getting angry without asking yourself where your anger stems from. No longer allowing relationships to be your medicine. No longer allowing work to be your trauma response or addiction to be escape from life.

Your job is to confront yourself over and over again until you are the clearest & stillest channel for spirit to exist within.

Remember who you are, you deserve to return back home to your safe space.

As we heal, grow and evolve

Sometimes we are required to leave our entire life behind us

Not to create a new life, but to embody the life

Your soul always intended for you to have.

Don't allow anyone to make you feel as if that's

Supposed to be easy. Move forward in divine timing and

Mourn what you need to, however you need to.

Welcome home beautiful soul.

ANSWER THE CALL

If your spirit is calling you to be still or end a sabotaging cycle, answer the call.

If your spirit is calling you to create & step into action, answer the call.

If your spirit is calling you to release people, places or things, answer the call.

If your spirit is calling you to create a self-love or self-discipline routine, answer the call.

If your spirit is calling you to be gentler, give yourself grace and practice patience, answer the call.

Evolving is about being a student of the soul, a student of your past, a student of your present and a student to your pain, lessons and emotions. Life is painful when we don't practice humbling our egos enough to listen. Only you know what your spirit is calling you to do. Only you know the shame, guilt and embarrassment that comes when you dishonor, disregard & disempower your intuitive voice. Only you will have to suffer the consequences of ignoring your internal compass.

Practice Being so in tune with yourself that you become clear when your spirit is sending you signs, to change, slow down, stop, rest, pivot, adapt, move into action or retreat to nature for further guidance.

It's extremely difficult to hear your intuition, spirit or soul guiding you if you're emotionally, mentally and spiritually clogged, unclear or overwhelmed. In my line of work, I often hear so many of my clients complain about feeling lost, stuck, confused about life, behind and out of alignment. The truth is they aren't lost AT ALL, they just aren't listening. Their entire being is attempting to get their attention but they refuse to listen to their own guidance that comes from their own soul & because of this disregard of self they also must face the consequences and suffer from experiencing Imposter Syndrome, lack of motivation, insecurity and depression.

When you listen to the voices within that are created to guide you, there will be clarity on what is next for you or what you should be doing with your life. Most people aren't supposed to be doing anything but being still, sitting in silence & meditating in nature until they are guided with further instructions. Today give yourself permission to listen to the advice of your soul. Remember Who The F*ck You Are.

Practice being so in tune with yourself,

that you become clear

when your spirit is sending you signs, to

change, slow down, stop, rest, pivot, adapt,

move into action or retreat to nature

for further guidance.

HOW MANY VERSIONS OF YOURSELF HAVE YOU EXILED?

How many versions of you exist?
How many versions of you have been left to fend for themselves, left in confusion, pain, abuse & fear? When you chose to "get over it" move on & grow up what happened to the versions of you that may not have been ready yet?

When a person experiences trauma the brain rewires to adapt to the environment and situation to keep the body alive. The dilemma here is that because a person's brain attempts to help them find coping mechanisms that doesn't mean the coping mechanisms are healthy, that the person received answers, closure, validation, support, nurturing, love or care in the midst of their trauma. However, their coping mechanisms are created to keep them going and to help them survive. As a person gets older if they don't go back and heal the wounds, trauma and voids created in their past those wounds tend to bleed into their present moment. The versions of them that experienced the trauma are still alive, still hurting and still waiting to be saved, loved, seen, heard or acknowledged. They show up in a person's daily life through triggers, habits, thoughts, wounds, voids and particular thoughts but most people avoid, bypass, neglect, abandon and ignore the parts of themselves that are still hurting, still in pain and still need nurturing because of events that took place in the past.

When healing I've found that people only want to address who they are right now. 31year old you wants to be happy, at peace and live a thriving life however you can't figure out why it's such a difficult task. The reason it's so difficult to maintain "Harmony" is because there are versions of you that are still in pain. Versions of you that haven't healed, that are looking for guidance, help, love, support and attention that was never received in the midst of trauma or developmental childhood years. You're attempting to fix 31-year-old you, but it's 13yr old you that's still stuck in her/his trauma, self-sabotaging ways, binge eating, unworthiness and woundedness. It's 10yr old you that can't figure out why your dad doesn't want you. It's 8 yr. old you that doesn't understand why she/he was molested. 16yr old you that's still attempting to fit into a group to be seen liked & wanted & accepted. 5 year old you that takes care of her mother more than she takes care of you, 9 year old you that hates that he/she missed their childhood because they had to parent their siblings. When these wounds go unacknowledged, un-nurtured and unhealed they bleed into your present reality.

You're attempting to force the adult you to feel happiness and peace, but you haven't gone back to heal and nurture the younger parts of you that are still in pain, crying and doing its best to survive. Peace isn't a consistent state of mind for you because younger versions of yourself are still in survival mode. The parts of you that are still in pain hold your foundation to joy, peace & playful happiness. How can you sustain a peaceful reality when there are unreconciled versions of you that still live in chaos, confusion & pain. Until you choose to acknowledge and heal your painful baggage all of your happiness, peace, joy, success will be short lived because the other versions of you will always find ways to beg you to come back for them, to save them, choose them and be parent them in a way your parents never did, even if they have to sabotage your happiness, relationships, peace and new opportunities just to get your attention. These past versions of yourself must begin their healing process as well, these versions of yourself don't die or evaporate into thin air because you chose to forget about your past. Yourself sabotaging behavior isn't because there's something wrong with you, it's a younger version of you crying out for help & to come rescue yourself the way you wished someone else did.

When you attempt to be happy in a relationship, but you fear them leaving, there may be a version of you that was abandoned before & needs healing. If you attempt to lose weight but you end up binge eating for emotional reasons, there may be a version of you that doesn't feel safe in some capacity, so you find comfort and security in food. These are fragmented versions of your being crying out for help and for you to come back and rescue them.

Until you nurture and heal all versions of your being you'll always show up as a fragmented version of yourself and your happiness, joy, peace and love will always be short lived because the truth of your foundational pain will always find a way to surface and get your attention. This is why when people finally experience healthy relationships their trauma surfaces. Or when a person's blessings begin to manifest, they sabotage it unconsciously. These are clear indications there are fragmented parts of their being that feel unworthy of anything good, healthy and new.

Kill The Ego

How many versions of yourself have you exiled, forgotten about, left to fend for themselves and never went back to save? How many versions of yourself have you said you had to kill?

One of the most unfortunate sayings I've heard in the healing community is "kill the ego". This makes me so sad to hear because I instantly know that when a person says this, they have no real connection any fragmented versions of their being. Meaning they are deeply disconnected from themselves. To openly choose to kill a part of yourself is such a deep level of self-betrayal. Even the versions of yourself that show up the worst are only reflecting how much pain they are in, not how bad they are. The ego isn't bad at all. It's just doing its best to protect you as a human. Yes, it's methods are dysfunctional and can be aggressive and misguided but those behaviors are always you keep you safe, make you feel important and like someone who matters. As intelligent and simultaneously unhealthy the ego is, it's only doing its best to help you out in your human experience. Why would you kill a part of your being that is only trying to help. When you see a person attempting to help but they are making things worse don't you have a conversation with them, have compassion for their efforts even though they are extremely misguided and then don't you just tell them thank you, but I have it from here I'll take over. Or do you just kill them? When a person speaks about killing their ego, I know that they are babies in their healing journey because healing, growing and evolving don't reflect the energy of killing, just natural death that is a part of transition.

I remember when i first began my healing journey. I would say things like kill the ego, but I remember always feeling so much guilt around saying I would kill a version of myself. As years went on, I had a very intense dark night of the soul and met my ego. My ego explained to me how hurt, betrayed, neglected, abandoned and abused it felt by my many attempts to kill it. I instantly felt the shame, guilt and sorrow on my own self-betrayal. I had exiled a huge part of my being that was like an aggressive, flashy, loudmouth older sister. This was my first indication that I didn't love myself, I didn't love the truth of myself, and I didn't know how to feel emotion that was uncomfortable without running from or abandoning myself. That night I apologized and made amends with my ego. I also told her little butt she'd have to get in the wayyy back seat. I thanked my ego for her efforts, her attempts and her protection and then I told her "but I have it from here". So now when my ego surfaces, I laugh because we have a relationship, I can hear my ego asking do you need my help or you good? Haha I get to decide if I need her to handle my light weight or if I have to tools to process what I'm feeling and what is happening in the present moment. I get to call on my ego when Candyss is too afraid to make certain business decisions. Only my ego is confident enough to send certain invoices lol. Sometimes I allow ego to stand up for Candyss when she becomes afraid and is nervous to set boundaries. My ego is the version of Candyss that says "Those that mind don't matter and those that matter don't mind" haha.

When you are Intune with all aspects of your being you can form healthy relationships with them and there won't be a need to kill anything. When a version of your being has served its purpose it will naturally transition. When we heal all fragmented versions of our being we can begin to form relationships with them and integrate them into our present reality. Now your whole self gets to enjoy the freedom of peace, joy and happiness because there are no longer exiled versions of yourself sabotaging your progress. This is the epitome of full self-integration.

Until you do that, happiness, joy & peace will always be a fantasy you are in awe of. When you heal, that fantasy will become your reality.

When Traumas & wounds of the past

go unacknowledged & unhealed

they bleed into your present reality

You Are Your Soulmate

"How do I heal from loneliness and find my soul mate?"

When working with my clients this is one of the most frequent questions I receive. Often people forget that they receive a reflection of what they are, so if they want a soul mate, they must first become their own.

Sometimes the wound of loneliness can be so intense that people forget that they have the power to be their own medicine and cure for loneliness.

The cure to this type of loneliness is first dissecting where does this wound and void stem from?

Why does another person need to be present when loneliness is felt?

What do those people make you feel that you can't feel on your own?

Do they make you feel seen, heard, loved, acknowledged, wanted, powerful, smart, confident?

Is there by any chance that the things you're searching for in your loneliness are the same things that you never received growing up or from your parents or family?

Loneliness is not a signal to call someone to comfort you, medicate your wounds or fill your voids. Loneliness is an signal from your inner child, your young adult self, your adult self and your soul that it is time to come back home to yourself and nurture the parts of you that feel fragile and needy without handing someone else your job of self-love.

You'll find your soulmate when you choose to become your own soulmate.

When you start showing up for yourself.

When you stop using relationships to distract you from healing.

When you stop starting Monday and choose you right now!

When you stop chasing people, places and things outside of you to make you feel, happy, whole & at peace.

That beautiful high frequency love appears the second you acknowledge it's already within you. When a person constantly searches for love, validation and happiness outside of themselves, they perpetuate the idea that they are powerless and everything outside of them is powerful. They instill the idea into their mind, body, cells and DNA that they lack what they need to be whole, feel good and be loved, and only a person outside of them can provide those things.

When I began to truly take my healing journey seriously my soul gave me a very clear message that said, "No One Else Is Allowed".

So, I intentionally gave myself permission to stay single with no interaction with men, no texting/phone calls, no sexual relationships and I chose to give what I wanted from men in a relationship, to myself. This unintentionally lasted four years. I'd become so consumed with truly working through my voids of loneliness and dissecting where they were rooted. Not having interaction that made me feel wanted in the very beginning was difficult. I remember going to the mall and buying men's cologne just to spray it on my pillow at night so I could at least feel a sense of masculine energy. As the months went on and I really began to intentionally dive deeper into my solitude even the need for that false sense of emotional safety in a bottle of cologne dissipated.

I purchased a bike and began to explore all Houston parks that I could ride in. I entered a biking club that was short lived and that's when I learned I actually didn't know how to ride a bike haha. I taught myself photography and I began to travel the world solo. I found a passion in hiking mountains and visiting national parks, alone. I did everything alone. Took myself of dates, dinner dates, movie dates and explorative dates to find new cool areas within Houston. I traveled to Mexico, Guatemala, Peru, Virgin Islands, Hawaii, Glacier National Park in Montana, Explored all of Utah, Big bend national and so much more all by myself.

The point is, instead of calling someone to spend time with me as a place holder, I began to spend quality time with myself, date myself and get to know myself.

Did I even like myself?

Was I a good enough person morally to be with another person?

Honestly, I'm an only child so I was selfish af lol. In my alone time I also recognized I was deathly afraid to ask anyone other than my momma for help. I learned that i didn't know how to let people in to actually receive the love I desired. I was pleasant but closed off and only allowed people to know what I wanted them to know about me. I also recognized that I did not speak nicely to myself, and I learned this while hiking up a mountain alone. I constantly told myself to stop, turn around, you're in so much pain, don't keep going, you're going to hurt yourself, ask for help, give up, black people don't hike 10-mile inclined mountains lol. That day doing a 10-mile hike in glacier national park I realized how horribly I spoke to myself and how I defeated myself with thought alone. I thought to myself, if this is how I speak to own self when im in discomfort, how would I speak to another person. It was clear that I had more work to do, because the love I claimed I had for myself wasn't love at all. It was tolerance at best.

I knew this was an area that needed immediate attention, so two days after hiking that first mountain I set out to hike another. This time with awareness of how I want no longer want to tear myself down, I was ready to shower myself with motivation and love. When the hike would get tough I'd play Beyonce and Jayz (I can do anything). I would remind myself and speak outloud. I can do anything, there is nothing I can't do. My body is strong, my spirit is excited for this adventure and I'm going to get some fire pictures when I make it to the top haha. This was the beginning of my relationship with owning my power, being mindful of how I treated myself and allowing my validation, love and support to come from within and no longer outside sources.

When I chose to become my own soulmate, I was able to explore myself and gain deep insight on who I really was when no one else was watching. I saw who I really was when I was alone and there was no one to perform for, wear masks for or to temporarily make me feel better.

After four years of intentionally giving myself permission to fall in love with myself, I met someone who would soon become my husband. At this time, I was so peacefully single and enjoying my freedom of self-exploration.

When my husband and I met, we bonded on the fact that neither of us wanted to be in a serious relationship, possibly ever again. We both valued our healing and spiritual journey and was very open about how no one had permission to interfere with that. He had been celibate for a year, meditating for 8+ hours in the forest of New Jersey and deeply honored with solitude and time with himself and God.

It was months before we recognized how funny God was. That our meeting was the next phase of our journey that was calling us to join as one in the presence of God. I didn't ask for a husband and my husband didn't ask for a wife. I didn't use Ciara's prayer to find a soul mate, I became my own soul mate and what was meant for me found me. What matched my frequency found me and the type of pure love I get to experience today with my husband reflects the pure loved I poured into myself those four years. The type of love I get to experience with my husband would have never manifested if I didn't first become my own soul mate and love myself first.

I didn't go on my journey of self-exploration to heal for a man, I healed for myself. I let go of all expectations to outcomes. I dissolved all desire to be married, in a relationship of any kid and I found gratitude in the one relationship that I did have, and I nurtured it every single change I got. My intention for healing was just to fulfill my soul's purpose, feel my best, look my best, evolve and nurture my relationship with God. I became my own soul mate and being given an additional soul mate was icing on the cake.

Only when we re-direct the desire to love another person & it became a passion to love ourselves are we able to attract a love that matches our frequency, intentionality, emotional and spiritual evolution.

Give yourself permission to show up for you. Begin loving, treating & honoring yourself the way you wish someone else would. Show your soul that you can even handle a relationship, marriage or spouse coming into your life without losing, neglecting or abandoning yourself, again. Show your soul that you can love the depths of yourself without the help or validation of another.

Love's Hierarchy

You open the portal of love by acknowledging all the love that is already present, around you, waiting for you to acknowledge it daily. Your family, kids, friends & strangers will randomly start pouring love into you when you cultivate the frequency that you are already in love with you. When you least expect it, the love you've been intentionally giving yourself may manifests as the man/woman of your dreams. It may even come as a new passion for life, a new best friend you get to explore life with or a kitten that brightens every moment of your day. When you release the expectation to outcomes, you begin to open yourself up to all types of love, not just the love you've romanticized.

So many people place a hierarchy on love, they romanticize romantic love and completely disregard natural, platonic love that presents itself to us daily. For example, when someone holds the door open for you to walk into a building or when someone allows you to skip them in line. When someone compliments your outfit or tells you, you look beautiful. When someone acknowledges your beautiful personality, or you both share a deep laugh together. When someone prays for you during times of difficulty or just checks on you to see how you are doing. This is all love and intimacy. These are all soulmates dropping off powerful opportunities for you to feel love and to remind you, you are loved, and love is surrounding you every second of the day. Romantic love is not the all, be all. How can you receive an abundance of love if you only acknowledge one type of love, this limits you from being able to receive the very love you desire.

It's your job to stay mindful, conscious and aware of all of the moments love presents itself to you. How can a person be blessed to find the love of their life when they refuse to see the love that is everywhere and already present in their lives in so many ways. Do the work on you first love. Become your own soul mate and everything in the universe will match your energy.

You open the portal of love by acknowledging

all the love that is already around you,

waiting for you to acknowledge it daily.

Only when we re-direct the desire to love another person

& it became a passion to love ourselves

are we able to attract a love that

matches our frequency, intentionality, emotional and spiritual evolution.

Become your own soul mate and

everything in the universe will match your energy.

RETURN BACK TO LOVE

When I was 17 in high school I had four best friends that I had been friends with since middle school. We all had the same super close group of male/female friends that we did everything with and had also know since the 6th grade. We went to one another's houses; we knew everyone's parents and for me they were like family. I grew up as an only child, so they were the friends that I'd always prayed for. We talked on the phone all of the time and did everything together I even had a nick name lol which was something I always wanted. I wanted to be so close to people that they naturally nicknamed me lol.

I also had my first real boyfriend at 17 and it was such an emotionally unhealthy relationship. I was extremely passive but subtly obsessive, I thought love meant to keep the peace, to not speak up for myself, not cause any issues or not be problematic. The guy I was dating really took advantage of how loving I was towards him and would sometimes be very loving and other times be extremely mean. I put a lot into cultivating and being a part of these connections. However, in the same week for separate reasons my relationship ended, and all of my friends abandoned me.

One of my friends was living with my mom and I because of difficulty she was having with her own family. At some point my mom and friend had a discrepancy, a few very expensive items of my mom's came up missing and my mom told her she couldn't live with us anymore. My friend went to school and told everyone that I was the reason for her having to move out even though she knew I had absolutely nothing to do with the situation nor the decision. Everyone blamed me and absolutely no one attempted to ask me what happened. They all left me. Some even tried to fight me, they wrote lies about me on myspace lol would send mean hurtful messages and I never said anything.

I never explained my side of the story, I never spoke up for myself, I just shrank, hid and stored the emotion in my body which soon morphed into my first deep depression. This was the first time I experienced the trauma of people shapeshifting in front of my eyes. One minute a person could be someone I deeply love and care for and the next they could treat me as if I'm a stranger they never knew. Someone having the capacity to turn on me and remove their love that quickly not only scared me, but it also traumatized me and caused me to learn even deeper methods of emotional and physical detachment. I experienced one of the worst depressions of my life not even realizing this was another form of abandonment. This depression lingered into the next 5 years of my life. From that point forward I've always been very cautious of who I allow into my space, and I've remained mindful of how I allow others to have access to me.

As a defense mechanism I learned how to not allow anyone to get close to me and I mastered becoming hyper aware of who people are past who they present themselves to be and show the world they are.

This is partially how I became an intuitive guide. I had to learn who a person really was past their words or facades to identify if they had the capacity to shapeshift and one day hurt me the way my friends did. This is how I cultivated my intuitive muscle to become successful with my clients, from intuition I know who they are even when they attempt to hide the truth of who they are. Many gifts are born through trauma. It took me years heal from this event and it also took me years to realize I hadn't forgiven my friend.

Years later I traveled to the amazon jungle in Peru and experienced the plant medicine of ayahuasca. As I spoke with a shaman to explain my intentions and why I chose to be a student of the medicine I spoke about my father that I wanted to forgive. He told me "As you heal forgiveness will no longer be necessary, the only thing that will be present is compassion and love". After my first night of plant medicine, I knew exactly what he meant. I was so overwhelmed with love that I no longer wanted to forgive anyone I just wanted to open my heart to them. Ironically the friend from high school and my father were a part of my first night's experience with the medicine. I felt compelled to write her a letter and apologize to her while simultaneously acknowledging, I didn't deserve how she treated me and ultimately convinced others to treat me. Apologizing to her caught me off guard but it's what my heart and soul asked me to do so I honored myself. Even though her behavior played a part in changing the course of my life in the most painful way I apologized to her for not being more compassionate for what she was experiencing as a young girl, not having anywhere to live, not having safe spaces or family to protect her.

I didn't excuse what she did to me or what actually caused my mom to make her leave, but I did understand and have compassion for how her trauma caused her to do that to me. Months later I sent her the letter via Instagram. She read it but didn't respond until months later. She eventually apologized, acknowledged her part, and said that she'd felt guilty for not telling our friends the full truth and allowing them to believe I was the villain. Her apology felt very sincere, and we both were able to put closure on A wound that effected both of us of in different ways. That moment for us would have never been possible if I didn't give myself permission to return back to love. If I didn't fight my way out of pain, resentment, trauma and anger and remind myself love is my home and nothing and no one has permission to take me away from my safe space.

Wounds of The Past

A more recent situation with my husband's son's mother also triggered this past wound. As my union evolved with my husband, we all realized that a blended family was something new for all of us and we were open to this being uncharted territory that would have its ebbs and flows as we navigate these spaces. Initially his son's mom was very cordial. We shared messages of wanting to get to know one another better, but somewhere along the line her behavior and treatment towards me changed in what felt like overnight. She became mean, spiteful at times, disrespectful and even made-up lies that weren't true and all of her behavior was unprovoked by me. Even the mention of her name sent pulses to my body to armor up and protect myself.

Leaving me to question if I had the capacity to be in a relationship that brought so much pure love with a side of baby-mama-drama to my peaceful life. I didn't realize at the time that my young adult trauma of people shapeshifting, changing and removing love overnight was being triggered. It felt like high school all over again, me excited to cultivate loving relationships & then suddenly having to energetically protect myself from that person. Just like in high school I kept the peace, I didn't say anything, I did my best to be understanding of her doing her best to navigate so many new changes that also involved her son. I just wanted everyone to be comfortable, happy and at ease so I thought not rocking the boat would help matters resolve in a healthier way. I was caught in the cross fires of her emotional trauma and the more I kept quiet the worse her behavior got, the more resentment I felt towards her, the more disdain I felt and the more I disliked her as a person.

No matter much my wisdom attempted to remind me that

"When people are unhappy, they battle themselves vicariously through you"

It was still shocking to see someone shift and treat me harmfully for no reason. If I'm honest it didn't just make me angry, it really hurt my feelings, it confuses me and it scares and frightens me to see the love a person can exude minute to then see them shift into a completely different being and target me as their issue the next. It upsets me when people treat me in undeserving ways that force me to have to protect myself or come out of my loving soft energy and embody whatever energy needed to protect and advocate for myself. The soft inner child of Candyss becomes afraid of how people can switch on and off, how they love you and treat you based on what they're experiencing in their emotional internal world. I wasn't raised that way. I grew up in a deeply loving home so the inner child of Candyss is a sensitive soul that is affected by harmful treatment.

Ironically, it's equally fascinating to adult Candyss which is why I've dedicated my life to the work of emotional healing. Outside of my love for my husband one of the most beautiful reasons I chose to stay in our union and blended family is because I recognized as much emotional chaos as his son's mom stirred, she was also an angel of chaos reminding me, return back home to love. I needed the reminder to continue to soften my heart. It's as if she and her behavior was screaming to me, remember to return back to love, fight for your safe space, don't forget who you are. For the next year I dedicated my life to praying for a softer heart, not just with her but people in general. I intentionally practiced more compassion, more patience, more understanding. I apologized to my heart for the grudges I was silently allowing it to hold for me.

For the first time in my life, I gave myself permission to explore my anger without shame, guilt or thinking it makes me a bad person. I wore pink to intentionally remind my being I choose to be soft even as I give myself permission to intentionally explore my anger. When I stopped villainizing her and saw her as an angel with a message it became easy for my compassion towards her to resurface. I also realized that I had never spoken up for myself. Like ever. Yes, there were a few times in my past that I'd recklessly gone off on people who mistreated me, disregarded me or took advantage of me but I always ended up apologizing because that wasn't the person I wanted to be. I was angry at feeling weak, soft and belittled by them, but I didn't want to become who they were to me. I didn't want to treat people how they treated me or make them feel, how they made me feel, I was ashamed of doing that. So, I learned to say nothing and made myself believe that was me being a good person and the bigger person.

This situation also showed me I can tell someone they have me f'd up and still be graceful, maintain my spiritual integrity, be extremely firm and still allow love to be present. At some point I did hold her accountable for how she treated me. I explained how harmful and unhealthy her behavior was. She did make amends, apologize and take beautiful accountability. At some point I even told her thank you for how you've shown up because it's guided me to go even deeper within myself and heal inner child wounds I didn't know still existed.

Many times, we focus so much on the person that hurt us and not the lessons or the messages they were sent here to give that has been hidden in their painful mistreatment. After us having our come to Jesus' moment lol we both let out a few thug tears and expressed how difficult our journey to that point had been, but I was very clear that the journey was still a journey. I knew that to fully accept her apology and allow it to land in my heart and for the love attached to her apology to soothe the wounded parts of my nervous system, I still had work to do.

You may forget what a person has done to you, but your body & your nervous system will never forget how they made you feel. A person can apologize to you until they are blue in the face, but if you're truly committed to your healing, every time you remember or recall what happened you have to intentionally choose, to forgive them again and remember that just because a person apologizes, and you forgive them doesn't mean that love is fully restored. You are allowed time to allow the energetic residue of pain, anger or whatever emotion was felt to naturally process out of the body and it doesn't magically process out of your system just because you said I accept your apology.

It may take time for the love that is attached to an apology to actually download into your nervous system. When you're conscious of this natural process you can continue to invite the totality of your being to intentionally return back to love. This is why in romantic relationships when one spouse cheats and the other forgives them but every time they remember they become sad, angry or hurt all over again. Confusing the spouse that cheated, they often feel like I thought you forgave me? and the truth is you did forgive them, but your nervous system hasn't caught up yet, or your wounded inner child is still processing those lingering emotions. When accepting apologies is healthier to say I accept your apology, I am also doing the inner work to allow my heart to return back to love so please hold space for me as the energetic residue naturally processes out of my system.

No matter how badly a person treats you, no matter how resentful, angry, hateful, enraged, spiteful, jealous or envious you feel. Love yourself enough to leave the door open to return back to the person you were, before you were hurt. Toxic positivity tells us that once a person apologizes for how they treated you, especially if they have a good or heartfelt reason for their behavior, you're supposed to be understanding & immediately become forgiving & loving. Well as much as I'd love for you to one day have the clarity of understanding & a soft heart to exude forgiveness reality is sometimes it takes a while before you arrive to those beautiful parts of your healing journey. Anger, resentment and explosive energy serve a beautiful purpose & deserve to be fully felt & explored before you force yourself to rush to understand & forgive.

HOWEVER, while giving yourself permission to feel your most authentic & true emotions don't forget to give yourself permission to simultaneously invite healing, clarity & ease to enter your healing journey when it's in alignment with your soul. Many times, people become so addicted to their anger, replaying what was done to them that they begin to feel empowered by their anger because they fear the vulnerability that comes with surrendering to the pain that lies dormant underneath their anger. They allow their addiction to anger to make them forget about the toxicity they're willingly choosing to spread throughout their body, heart, mind & spirit, ultimately punishing themselves the longer they hold on to anger without the intention to transmute it.

You must remember to leave the door open for healing to happen. A beautiful and easy affirmation to say is

"I am open to healing, I am open to forgiveness, I am open to releasing emotional pain & resentment".

Healing requires an invitation, want & desire. It won't just show up randomly & if it does it'll be ten years later once your anger has manifested into disease & cancer when forgiveness is your last option.

Don't be so angry, hurt and resentful that you forget to leave the door open for healing, growth & evolution to occur when the soul needs it too.

Every fall

the trees remind us

to let go of what is no longer serving us.

The smell of nature reminds me to,

Just keep growing.

MEN NEED SAFE SPACES TOO

I wouldn't be me, if I didn't take time to advocate for those who don't fully know how to advocate for themselves and their emotional needs just yet.

As a woman in a healthy relationship of any kind romantic or platonic, it's important that as we ask and advocate for our safe spaces to heal, explore ourselves and share our emotions. We must also stay mindful of the fact that men need the same safe spaced while also acknowledging how limited their resources are in comparison to women. If we want healthy long-lasting relationships, we must learn how to hold space for other emotions that aren't always our own.

This doesn't mean it our job to heal any man, just as it's not their job to heal any woman. If we want love, compassion and patience from a man at any point in our lives we must learn how to match the frequency of what we desire and learn to reciprocate intentionally. There's no spiritual integrity in only receiving but refusing to give. When we display love in balanced ways it not only benefits, we begin sending energy out into the universe to restore the health of the masculine and feminine energy as a collective.

So, Ladies, goddesses, wombmen, how do you create safe spaces for your man in your relationships or male friends in your friendships that reminds them that they are safe enough to be vulnerable & show emotion with you without being judged, shut down, given unsolicited advice or interrupted?

My husband hosts an even called "Blind Folded Speed Meeting" where he guides and teaches people how to connect from the soul and not with the eyes. At my husband's event during the open discussion segment, I asked the women this question at it was crickets. Nothing. Silence, no response & from a very vocal crowd of beautiful women who were holding men to the fire of accountability & asking overall why men don't show up in relationships the way women do.

So many men flat out said "I've never felt safe in my past relationships to be myself, because how I felt would later be used against me, & when I finally would show emotion, my feelings would be diminished & I'd be told I was overreacting, being too sensitive and belittled" this was just a few things men said they felt in relationships.

In a world where women are allowed to be emotional & men are told their masculinity depends on their ability to not show emotion, our romantic & platonic friendships should be safe spaces for our men to feel safe enough to embody their vulnerability, emotions, cry & share their feelings without fear. As a woman I had to remind myself, It's not always about me. Men are attempting to heal from the exact same trauma that we are, the only difference is they've had years of societal programming to convince them it isn't safe to show or acknowledge those emotional traumas.

Women want to be loved, but subconsciously create hostile & unsafe environments for their love to thrive in. Sometimes women lack the ability create safe, calm spaces for their men because it's a reflection of how unsafe and how chaotic their internal word is. Many women have zero idea how to embody or balance their feminine & masculine energy. They display the selfishness of wanting to be heard, seen & felt but lack the ability to hear, see & feel others, keeping themselves in cycles of blocking themselves from receiving the healthy, loving & balanced relationships they desire.

Men deserve safe spaces to feel loved, seen & heard too. So again, as a woman how do you cultivate safe spaces for men you love? & I can hear some women saying what about men, they need to create space for women too. Just know that is a very "Me too" response that comes from a place of hurt and the inability to self-reflect and take self-accountability for how you choose to show up in your unions. Yes, men should cultivate safe spaces in their unions with women as well, but we aren't advocating for women right now, we are advocating for the great men that want to be heard, felt, seen and acknowledge but have never been granted safe passage to do so. Feel into your heart not your wounds as you answer this question. Our men deserve this level of provision, too. How you love others reflects how you love yourself.

Men deserve love

that doesn't require them to

spend money first.

TELL YOUR STORIES

Embody your life story & tell it from your heart, if people wanted you to speak nicely about them in your stories, they should have treated you better.

Have you fully embodied your story? Your life experiences & what has happened to you or for you? Have you ever told your life story, or stories that have made you who you are today? Or are you someone who has allowed fear, lack of confidence, shame, guilt & anger hinder you from owning what is yours to tell?

So often people want to speak up, they want to share their experiences with the world because deep down they know what they've experienced could help someone going through the same thing or they just want to release the untold stories that have been holding them hostage. So many are silenced out of fear of sharing their own experiences, but a person takes their power back when they own the details that created the person they are today.

You can't embody and honor the truth of your story while simultaneously walking on eggshells attempting not to upset someone who played a part in your journey. When you allow fear to hinder you from owning the totality of your journey you rob yourself of your power and silence the very parts of you that are begging to be set free. Standing up for yourself, speaking up for yourself, setting healthy boundaries and embodying your power all start with strengthening your throat chakra, using your voice and reflecting on the root of when you were first silenced.

People need to hear your unique story. They need to hear your advice, they need to hear your voice say specific things that will unlock their potential to growth, healing & embody their voices as well. The one thing that cannot be replicated is, your personal life story.

Fear has kept so many from sharing their stories, holding their lessons captive & hiding them from others simultaneously robbing others from words that could potentially change their lives, give them healthier perspectives, help them find gratitude, laugh for the first time in a long time or heal damaged parts of their spirit they aren't even aware of yet.

Recently while sharing a tiny portion of my story, someone said

"I wonder what's the other person's side of the story?"

I thought to myself, what an emotionally immature and emotionally dangerous thing to say. I also thought to myself who cares what another's person's side of the story is while I'm just sharing {my truth}. It's not about a side of the story, nor is it about proving someone wrong or making another person out to be the villain in my truth. It's also not my job to shield them if that's how people perceive them as I share how they played a part in my journey. Sharing our truths isn't about the people who hurt or wronged us, it's about sharing our truths that just happened to include people who played a part in our story, and our journey to healing growing and evolving.

This response was the epitome of an improper way to hold space for someone as they speak their truth However this response was a perfect example for how some will realistically respond to you when you speak and share your truth. This very response is the reason so many people won't speak their truth or are fearful of speaking about their experiences. This made me think of the many ways people are silenced, belittled, disempowered and gaslighted when they've finally mustered enough strength and power to tell their story.

No matter how much your truth triggers others or makes them feel uncomfortable, stay in your power. You'll come to find that when you speak your truth and embody your power it triggers those that are still in their prison of silence and don't know how to embody their power just yet. Keep going because you are planting a seed within them that they may not even know needs watering and nurturing.

Your truth Is not meant to be easily digestible, make others feel comfortable and it damn sure isn't so others can agree with you. Your truth isn't about who's right or wrong and it doesn't need another person's validation to make it true or valid. Your truth is already valid because it's yours, you experienced it and you felt it. No one is allowed and no one has permission to silence you anymore, not even you have permission to silence yourself anymore.

A person choosing to embody their truth and tell their story isn't about anyone else, it's about them finally gaining the strength to come out of their own shadows and no longer allowing anything or anyone to silence them.

When we tell our stories we get to see how much alike we all are, how connected we all are & how much we share so many of the exact same experiences. When we hear other people's stories our spirits start to connect on a deeper level & this opens the heart to learn more compassion, patience & understanding. When we tell our stories it gives others the confidence to come out of their shadows, to embody the power attached to their story and to stand firm in who they are and their f experiences. When you own your story, you take your power back.

Tell your stories and own your truth.

If people wanted, you to speak nicely about them

Then they should have treated you better.

When we recover loudly,

we keep others from dying slowly

IT'S OK TO MOURN & GRIEVE YOUR PAST SELF

It's ok to mourn the version of you that you're healing & growing out of.

It's important to remember when we grow, we stretch.

When we evolve, we expand.

As we heal, our wounds may still ache.

It's ok to be extremely happy, at peace but still feel a subtle sensation of sadness.

Just because your present moments may be beautiful, and your future may look promising doesn't mean you aren't allowed to feel the heaviness that comes with change.

Shedding skin requires deep surrender.

It requires you to give up control and allow the process to take place which can be painful. Change can be very scary and uncomfortable, even when it's something you crave. Typically, we crave the outcome, not necessary the liminal phase, the in between stages of the healing, growing and evolving process. It may not feel good to shed skin, to evolve out of your old behaviors that kept you comfortable in familiarity even if those behaviors were unhealthy. As you heal emotionally there are wounds that are also healing because you've chosen to intentionally medicate them. Even after a person has had surgery years ago and their wounds have fully healed there will still be moments were those wounds randomly ache, itch or feel sensation. This is an indication that healing is a lifelong process and our duty to ourselves is to fall in love with the forever evolving process.

It's very normal to want to grow, heal & evolve but also miss the version of you that was unaware of the healing and growth that needed to take place.

It's ok to experience sadness because now that you're conscious you can't go back to ignorance.

It's ok to acknowledge that healing is difficult.

It's ok to acknowledge that to intentionally grow will be one of, it not the most difficult, painful & uncomfortable thing you have ever done in your life.

To a certain degree healing intentionally can feel just as traumatic as the initial trauma you experienced because you're required to befriend those emotions as they surface out of the mind, body, spirit and subconscious until you're on the more comfortable end of your lifelong healing journey.

There were times I hated healing, growing and evolving. I would tell God "NO" I'm not doing this today. I would literally give myself permission to pout and throw a temper tantrum with God, as dramatic as I was in those moments, it was ok. I had to learn to give myself grace in my evolving.

I'd sometimes ask questions like "How come I can't drink alcohol like everyone else? Or why do I have to feel so much emotional heaviness while everyone else is oblivious to their own healing? Why can't I eat whatever foods I want without my entire body reacting as if its going to die right after a slice of pizza?"

I mourned my state of oblivion.

Being aware of my healing journey and what I was being called to evolve from felt heavy, annoying and overwhelming. I didn't want to give up food, alcohol, or my addiction to escapism. It was painful to be so connected with my soul that I constantly heard "It's time to elevate again, this thing can't come" It's time to shed this program" right as I was getting comfortable in my process of healing, I was required to heal something else. I was exhausted, angry, frustrated, fragile, very vulnerable and deeply sad. Not only was I sad that I had a clear calling to evolve in this lifetime, but I was also sad, ashamed, and embarrassed that there were many times that I didn't want to. I didn't want to change. There was also a part of me that felt as if I was trying to self-destruct on purpose and that part of myself scared me, because not only was that part of me extremely powerful she was extremely explosive and unhealthy.

Acknowledging your darkness, your shadow and your lower self is a huge part of the healing journey and mourning your evolution as you transition out of this low vibrational state into your higher frequency Is allowed. You're intentionally leaving a version of you that you've spent years with, that has helped you cope during the most painful moments, that has protected you, gave you coping and defense mechanisms and helped you survive in environments that where traumatic. Even though these survival skills later proved to be unhealthy and unsustainable, it's still ok to love, mourn and have gratitude for the versions of yourself that did their best with what they had.

It's also ok to feel afraid and uncomfortable as you enter your new journey. This is expected because you're meeting and nurturing a new healthier version of yourself. You're making a new friend, a new life partner. Give yourself time to nurture this new and healthier relationship with yourself and watch how you fall in love with healthier perspectives, healthier behaviors and healthier coping mechanisms. When the journey of becoming gets to overwhelming and stressful, don't focus on that. Don't focus on the journey ahead, it's not real. The only thing that is real, is this moment right here and right now. Give yourself permission to take things one day at a time.

It's also imperative to remind yourself while mourning your past selves that, you were built for this sh*t. When your soul manifested you came to this realm of existence fully equipped. With the power of God. Your soul literally manifested just so you could evolve into the purest form of love.

Remind yourself daily. Every day you wake you, you already have everything you need. There is nowhere to go. There is nowhere to be. There is nothing to be and nothing to do. Wherever you're in your journey is exactly where you're supposed to be. Stand firm in your power, find strength in your vulnerability and make friends with the uncomfortable growing pains. They serve a beautiful purpose so don't dismiss them, invite them in with intention and when it's time for the growing pains to leave, open the door and allow them to exit with grace.

Stay intentional on your journey, enjoy the full experience. Pout, cry, express anger, embody gratitude, welcome happiness and no matter what, Boss up! Stand firm in your power. There is nothing you can't do. Give yourself permission to experience, the experience.

There is a version of you

waiting for you surface and thrive,

keep showing up until you are united.

DON'T MANIFEST IT, HEAL FOR IT

Before you attempt to manifest anything or anyone invite yourself to explore blind spots within your subconscious programs that may fear success, may not feel worthy of receiving love or works from a place of scarcity. The version of yourself that feels the lack will always self-sabotage you from receiving the people, situations, things & relationships you deserve and desire. This is why before focusing on acquiring more, it's always healthy to heal & medicate any wounds that could sabotage that process.

Many times, people learn how to manifest their desires from techniques taught in books, social media or manifesting coaches & gurus, but once they receive what they've manifested they have a tough time keeping it & some tend to even sabotage their way out of their manifestations. This is because there is a fine line between manifesting your desires from A healthy, energetically clear spirit & embodied power vs. manipulating energy to receive what you desire.

Many aren't manifesting from a healthy place of spiritual integrity, they are manipulating their energy to be open to receiving temporarily, quickly & from an emotionally wounded & spiritually immature spirit. This is why some people can make a lot of money, but they can never keep it. They learn how to raise their frequency to receive the desired outcome, but the issue is they don't know how to maintain the frequency & tend to lose everything they've called into their lives. This is because there are autopilot subconscious programs within us that most times go un-acknowledged & unhealed & we attempt to bring those unhealed parts of us into our "new beautiful life" but the truth is no matter how many masks you wear & how many masks fit perfectly, the real you will always surface.

The part of you that fears your own potential & success, the part of you that over works because you have a scarcity mindset & fear not having or losing what you do have so you constantly need more or better. The part of you that deeply wants love but has no idea how to receive it because of the barbed wired fence around your heart. You'll ruin every relationship the second they get good. The part of you that doesn't feel worthy enough to be loved properly. If the part of you that has deep wounds, traumas & fears goes unacknowledged & unhealed, that very part of you will sabotage anything you manifest every single time. When you begin your process to clear out this stored energy with breathwork, meditation, living foods, therapy and body movement, you won't have to manifest anything because everything you desire naturally matches your natural vibration & high frequency.

To truly manifest anything a level of deep self-honesty is required, not just setting goals. You'll be required to know the dark parts of yourself that don't want these goals to happen. The version of yourself that's fears life once those goals are met. You must heal & create a relationship with those versions of yourself so you can obtain the things you desire without ruining them after you receive them.

Self-sabotage is a coping mechanism the subconscious mind uses to help you return back to the status quo, back to normalcy and familiarity even if that means returning back to survival mode, unhealthy behaviors, thoughts, emotions & toxic ways. Until you rewrite these programs & reconcile the relationships with the older versions of yourself, you always risk ruining the things you've worked hard to obtain like Peace, possessions, opportunities and love.

It's not enough to use spiritual baths, retreats, masturbation, money rituals, full moon ceremonies and prayers just to receive what you want.

The universe is responding to who you are, not who you're pretending to be.

In essence, an attempt to manifest to get what you desire instead of healing to naturally attract what is vibrationally attracted to you is like trying to trick God into giving you blessings you know you haven't worked or healed for.

There is a karma attached to manipulating this type of energy & some even say "How you get it is how you lose it". Trust that GOD already has everything mapped out perfectly.

For most people, your expansion and blessings are on the other side of forgiveness, a deep cry, letting go of smoking/alcohol, getting serious about your spiritual practices, treating people better, leaving an unhealthy relationship or starting therapy. If you want to live the life you desire, don't manifest it. Heal for it & match the frequency of evolution. You can do it! Show up for yourself, intentionally. Remember Who The F*Ck You Are!

Your nervous system must be calm

and feel safe in order to

receive larger manifestations.

Don't Hoard Your Gifts

One beautiful fact about being human is that we are all special, perfect even. Meaning we all have something special to offer this world, those around us and ourselves. Many of us are naturally gifted with soul level talents that are clear. Others may not be able to identify exactly what their gifts are because they aren't as openly obvious as others. This does not mean their gifts are less valuable, it means society has placed a hierarchy on specific types of gifts or learned talents that don't force those individuals to have to do much soul searching to identify them. For the rest of the world who may not know what their gifts are because they may be subtle or not fully nurtured, please trust and believe that you too have a gift and A purpose that is waiting to be watered with your own validation and not the validation of society.

Sometimes your gift may be singing but your purpose may be how easily you make people feel emotion and not alone when you discuss your nervousness about singing. Other subtle gifts could be negotiating, having creative vision or have A power to make people feel motivated by the way you wield words. Not only must our gifts be used by us, but they must also be used without waiting for validation in exchange. They must be used in private or in public & intentionally cultivated to honor our soul.

When we have soul level gifts it is our duty to express them, to explore them & strengthen them. Everything in society asks us to shrink ourselves, to not show up big, to be humble, well received & do what will be liked by the masses. Honoring our gifts will require us to not even acknowledge the masses but to acknowledge & have gratitude that our soul chose us to embody such beautiful gifts.

When honoring our gifts becomes a practice of self-love, fun, creativity & a thank you to God it doesn't matter who likes it, who acknowledges it, and the need to use it for monetary gain won't have to be the sole reason for you to explore, expand & express your gift.

I've personally sang my whole life, & I'm not even gone hold yall I know I'm nice as hell and truly gifted, but the societal pressure I felt as a young 16–20-year-old girl that I had to be a famous singer crippled my ability to find freedom & gratitude in my soul level gift. It took away the spirituality in my creative expression & it took me years to get that power back. By age 23 I had to acknowledge, I don't want to care about the other things, the politics, being seen or showered with compliments about my voice, I actually want anyone to comment on my voice because it triggers insecurity within me. I gave myself permission to acknowledge, I just want to sing! I took my power back when I recognized that my freedom was in exploring my gift without outside societal pressure.

Our gifts are ours and we get to choose how we want to honor them. Not Instagram, TikTok, Society or algorithms. If you have a gift of any kind I don't care if it's pottery, gaming, herbalism etc. do it with the intention to honor the gifts of your soul. Maintain and nurture your passion. Stay in your creative spirit, explore your freedom & display them however you choose. Release any & all pressure tied to showing up perfectly or a certain way. You were chosen to embody your gift, don't allow anyone or any situation make you second guess what has been gifted to you on a soul level. Take your Power back.

Creation is your birthright.

Your creations, talents and gifts are perfect

Without validation from the outside world.

Explore your gifts because they make you feel alive.

Creating is your pathway to freedom.

LET GO OR BE DRAGGED
Life is designed to be a stress test

Not to see how well we can endure stress, but how well we can surrender when stress is present. When we give ourselves permission to truly submit to the totality of surrender the stress disappears and the essence of peace and harmony become present simply because there is no attempt to control your way out of the situation.

When we practice surrender, we build a soul level of trust and acceptance for whatever is. Our soul knows that freedom lives in that space. As we heal, grow and evolve there is spiritual capital in learning to sit with the uncomfortable without being in such a rush to fix things. When you attempt to rush past uncomfortable moments you become at thief & rob yourself from your full experience of being human because even the painful moments deserve to be cherished.

In 2022 Instagram deactivated my Instagram account & I Lost all contacts to beautiful relationships & healing messages I poured my heart into creating for my community. Even though this was a frustrating process I chose to listen to my spirit and become still and silent. I used the next few weeks to do nothing, I took no new clients I just listened to the voice that said, "be still". At some point I realized I was being urged to create a relationship with surrender, new beginnings, releasing control and expectations to outcomes.

When I finally chose to accept that it was time to begin the process of starting over, I created a new Instagram account and explained my experience and my lessons in surrender. So many of applauded that message & said they really needed to hear it,

But what I didn't share was the exact same night my Instagram was deactivated I also got a huge bill from the IRS to pay $43,000k dollars in

Taxes because my skincare business was doing so well. However, the same day I received the bill, the platform I use to make a living disappears & there was nothing I could do about either situation. I couldn't control my way out it. I instantly knew surrender had to be my medicine & I knew my spiritual stamina was being tested. I was so afraid that I went to my momma's house, got in her bed and cried like a baby. She was my only safe space that could save me from the big scarry monster that I had just come face to face with. I wasn't ready to fight this monster with my spiritual tools, I just wanted my momma to tell me it was going to be ok.

So, I allowed myself to revert into my inner child. I let "Candyss Love" the business owner and social media intuitive healer go and morphed into my younger self, intentionally and went to the person I knew could sooth her, my momma.

Who do you become when control isn't an option?

Who do you become when your only remedy is to let go and befriend surrender?

Fear, pain, sadness and frustration were all present and I gave myself permission to honor them all but I never gave them permission to stay. At some point I realized if I'm going to listen to my spirit and follow my soul's guidance of deep surrender, trust and faith, then worrying couldn't come.

Worry wasn't allowed. I recognized that worrying was the epitome of praying for what I didn't want, and it was sending out the frequency of fear and not the frequency of power. Even though I never panicked I definitely mourned for myself as I also stood firm in accepting my mission to embody my new beginning. By the second week I had completely let go of any desire of regaining my Instagram & released fear of my Tax Payment. I just accepted the path my soul was guiding me on, Trusted God, myself & found gratitude in the new soul level lessons I was being bathed in. Plus, my momma told me 'Don't worry about it, everything is going to take care of itself'. *Kanye Shrugs so yall know when my momma said don't worry, the weight of the world lifted off my shoulders instantly.

The reason surrender is so scary to many is because it forces them to instantly tap into their wounds, traumas and voids. Surrender makes people grapple with the fear of not being safe, to a certain degree surrender forces us to go against our natural human instincts and tap into our soul wisdom. Surrender forces you to shed skin, quickly. Many people view surrender as giving or as a weakness but it's quite the opposite, only a deeply powerful person can let go and give themselves permission to be free in the midst of crippling fear and uncertainty.

When you tap into your soul level power there won't be a need to surrender because true acceptance of all things will already be your best friend. This is true harmony, being able to flow with whatever is without controlling or fighting your way out of the uncomfortableness.

We Heal in Flow

Not Force

FAMILY DRAMA = FAMILY TRAUMA

You don't have to condone or accept harmful, abusive behavior or mistreatment because it's from your family. You don't have to accept disrespect, disregard of boundaries and energetic bullying because they are your family.

Those that love you, care about how they make you feel.

Period.

As you heal, grow and evolve, family trauma may play a huge part in your evolving process. I find with my clients parental and family trauma are the most difficult for them to acknowledge, set boundaries, create space and heal from. The reason is because the start of the average person's trauma, wounds, voids and emotional pain begins in the family unit, so many either see their family dynamic as normal or they see it as completely dysfunctional but have no idea how to heal, grow and evolve in that same environment.

Our Families tend to know exactly how to hurt and trigger us causing us to be forced to find ways to adapt to those emotionally harmful environments be it healthy or unhealthy methods. They also tend to play a huge part in the narratives, stories and treatment that produces emotional trauma.

In your healing process it is imperative that before you do or say anything a decision must be made.

You must decide how far do you have the capacity and are you willing to go with your family?

How angry are you willing to get?

How hurt are you willing to be?

How long will you allow yourself to be disrespected?

How often will you allow your emotional and personal boundaries to be crossed?

How long will you allow yourself to shrink?

How many times will you explain and defend yourself?

How many times will you question yourself?

How many times will you take accountability when no one else does?

How many times will you attempt to mend relationships with loved ones who have no issue with tarnishing them?

How long will you be ok with being misunderstood, unheard, unloved and unsupported when there are so many people in the world waiting to hear you with ears of love?

You get to decide how you show up in these relationships and how far you are willing to go or not go to maintain them.

The topic of familial relationships can be so difficult because society has programmed us to believe you remain loyal to family even if that means taking verbal, emotional, psychological, physical abuse and even bullying. Men and women stay in unhealthy family dynamics for their kids. Adult children never set boundaries with their verbally abusive parents because, it's their parents.

People struggle with healing wounds caused by family trauma because they know that to heal, they may have to remove themselves from the unhealthy environment all together, or the people who are causing harm will have to take accountability, acknowledge their behaviors & change which is rare. But it all comes down to what I call "the love wound".

Many people don't distance themselves from unhealthy family dynamics or set healthy boundaries because they fear love being taken away. Many who have been harmed in any capacity don't speak their truths with their parents or family because even though the connection is harmful and painful at times, it's still a connection and most people fear losing that.

You aren't a bad person for setting boundaries, teaching people how to treat you and demanding the respect you deserve. Some have never spoken up for themselves and even the thought of doing so is scary and makes them feel the need to shrink. Especially in family dynamics where children were never given permission to use their voice, speak their minds or voice how things within the family unit made them feel. However, it's a new dawn & a new day.

Today is the day you take your power back, and you make whatever decision is best for you based upon your personal family dynamic. It's ok if this new change feels uncomfortable or painful. It doesn't always feel easy implementing healthier steps to protect your peace. The journey of honoring ourselves doesn't always feel good, or even peaceful but at some point, as you continue to show up for yourself and advocate for yourself peace will be present with your decision to choose you.

In my personal familial relationships, I've had family turn on me at the drop of a dime for no reason and I've also had family require things from me that I don't have to give. The pain and shock of one day feeling super close with my family and the next day being treated like a stranger guided me into a deeper level of healthy emotional detachment. I had to learn how to love some of my family from a distance and I had to try different methods of self-protection. For me, removal of all access to me was the healthiest option. This means via social media, family visits, communication and letting go of attempts to rectify the situation. I had to accept that not every relationship should be worked out, have a clear understanding or healthy ending. Sometimes the removal of a person from your life is God's protection.

You get to decide and identify which method of healthy detachment is best to honor yourself. Some families don't require a hard break up, just for you to acknowledge your lack of firm boundaries so you can implement them.

When people are deeply unhappy, they battle themselves vicariously through you & they may never take accountability for their treatment towards you. As you continue to heal, you'll learn that your healing is never dependent upon an outside source, meaning you have everything within you to medicate the wounds that weren't caused by you. You are allowed to advocate for yourself, set boundaries, create distance while still allowing love to be present. Being family and your love for family isn't an invitation for mistreatment, it isn't a pass to have full access to you and you don't have to pour out and constantly give what you don't have to give. You take your power back when you intentionally honor yourself, even if it means setting boundaries with family.

Those who love you

Care about how they make you feel.

The end.

BOUNDARIES ARE NON-NEGOTIABLE

Every time you allow someone to disregard and disrespect your personal, emotional & energetic boundaries, you dishonor & disempower your soul.

Some people are addicted to energetic chaos. They thrive when there is energetic instability in their lives. This lack of emotional discipline and emotional immaturity may even make them feel powerful & alive just as much as it makes them feel miserable. Choosing to seek Understanding instead of being "right" requires self-reflection & accountability which also causes un-comfortability so ultimately these people create chaos in relationships to avoid their emotions & distract themselves from healing & growing.

This is why, boundaries are not optional, boundaries are a requirement. Boundaries aren't to keep people out; they are to help you protect what people and energies are being let in. It's imperative to be clear on how far you are willing to go with a person who is committed to cultivating chaos, misunderstanding and are emotionally unstable for the sake of maintaining your own peace of mind.

You don't blame the clown for being a clown, you ask yourself why you keep going to the circus?

Why do you continue to allow unacceptable behavior?

Boundaries are how we practice healthy detachment. I've had to personally detach from family that I love deeply, friends that I still love deeply and others just to maintain my personal peace. Even when it's sad or annoying and hurtful because I genuinely would like to have a healthy and pure relationship with them, but the reality is some people don't have the capacity to receive love or have healthy & emotionally mature relationships, yet. Even when things are going beautifully, they will still subconsciously battle themselves vicariously through you and as long as you allow them into your space without healthy boundaries, they will always bring their hell with them, with no regard to protecting your heaven.

Until people choose to truly self-reflect, heal & acknowledge their own emotionally driven blind spots, traumas and wounds they'll always create chaos in their relationships, have unstable emotions, and project what they are going through on to others. Sometimes the boundary is loving these people from a distance and remembering that they don't hear or see things based on reality, but from their wounds, voids and traumas they are unconscious of. Practice compassion & patience for them & then practice patience and compassion for yourself and the times you didn't love yourself enough to stand firm in your own boundaries. (see back of book for methods to set boundaries)

You don't blame a clown for being a clown,

you ask yourself

why do you keep going to the circus?

WHO'S EYES ARE YOU SEEING THROUGH?

Who do you become when you are hurt angry or afraid of being hurt. In each moment we show up as different versions of ourselves based on our needs, traumas, wounds, voids and desires. These are fragmented parts of our soul that still need nurturing.

If we know ourselves well enough and cultivate deep meaningful relationships with ourselves it becomes easier to decipher when our wounded inner child or younger self is present hindering us from having emotionally mature adult conversations or when the parts of us that have experienced abandonment are present causing us to accept what we don't deserve in exchange for attention, because to someone who is starving for love accepting crumbs feels worth it.

When you've created a relationship with all versions of yourself you can articulate "my inner child is present right now, I don't want/need to hear a solution, I just want you to hug me & tell me I am safe & everything is going to be ok".

When you're clear what eyes you're seeing through moment to moment you can quiet the adult version of you that is oblivious to why you feel, think & behave in certain ways. It becomes easier to say.

"Right now I'm not operating as my emotionally healthy adult self, the wounded part of me that is afraid of being hurt is present so how I hear you & perceive this situation maybe distorted in this moment, lets revisit this conversation when I've had time to process what I am feeling."

This type of clarity benefits the people we are encountering & are in relationships with because it gives them real time insight into you and who you are showing up as moment to moment. When understanding is present it creates room for compassion & patience. It allows them to instantly recalibrate their approach in how they hold space, speak, respond & deliver their message to you.

Knowing all versions of yourself is imperative in your healing journey. These are fragmented versions of your soul that still need nurturing & attention as you attempt to evolve. Healing becomes a lot easier when you know you.

One day my husband and I were experiencing an emotionally uncomfortable moment. He knows one of my childhood wounds and daddy wounds is "not feeling chosen" which I will speak about in depth further into this book. There was a moment each of us were expressing ourselves, but he couldn't understand why I didn't understand his point of view. It took us both a while to realize it wasn't that I didn't understand, the adult version of myself understood very well what he was saying but that also isn't what my wounded inner child wanted to hear. She just wanted to feel acknowledged, heard, understood & felt. My husband recognized this is not an ideal time to rectify this situation, just to hold space. So, he got quiet, held out his arms for me to lay on his chest and just rubbed my back and rocked me as I laid on his chest and told me everything would be ok and we'd figure it all out together.

In this situation I didn't articulate what my inner child needed because I was emotionally overwhelmed, but my partner was able to adapt and adjust for both of our sake. Later on, coming to the conclusion that my inner child had surfaced in that moment, giving us both a clear game plan for how to handle future uncomfortable moments if she surfaces again.

This happens so often in relationships of all kinds. People have an argument, and they fail to realize once a person becomes emotionally triggered. When a person becomes triggered, the brain typically reverts to the age that person was when that trigger was first formed. So, you are attempting to resolve a conflict with your 33-year-old spouse, friend or family member not aware that they are 10 years old right now, and this is the reason why they don't understand you, may be acting childishly or emotionally immature.

When you begin to explore parts of your being that are still wounded you can acknowledge them when they are triggered, and you can medicate them properly from a place of love, patience and compassion. Take time to identify these fragmented versions of your being that still show up in your life. They are attempting to get your attention for a reason.

Slowing down is medicine

Rest is medicine

IT'S NEVER TOO LATE TO HAVE A BEAUTIFUL CHILDHOOD

I t's never to late to reparent yourself.

It's never to late to be the person you needed when you were younger.

I know you want these actions to come from your parents that birthed you. I know you want your parents to snap out of it, apologize for how they treated you, love your properly, change their behaviors and take accountability but the truth is they may not have the capacity to parent you the way you desire and deserve.

The good news is you do. You have the capacity, tools, want & desire to parent yourself properly. You want to support, nurture & hold space for yourself with intentionality.

No one outside of you knows what you need or how to deliver exactly what you need perfectly the way you do and the way you can, not even your parents.

Your inner child is waiting, craving & wishing that someone would come back & save him/her. You've used so much time hoping, praying, wishing, begging & trying to convince your parents to come back & save you, while your inner child is crying out for someone, anyone, anything, any relationship, any job, any addiction, any sexual activity or any man or woman to come save them & make them feel loved.

What do you think would happen if you stopped waiting on outside sources to save you & you stepped through the door to become your one savior. How happy & relived would your inner child be to know not just anyone came back to save them, you came back to save you.

You are the only person that deeply understands your inner child. What they went through, experienced & how they suffered. Maybe you're the only one that can truly guide them back to healing. You know the words that your inner child needs to hear, you know the moments your inner child needed support, a hug & to be told everything was going to be ok.

Now you can do that. You can hug your inner child when they become reactive from lack of attention. You can find them healthy outlets to release frustration & explosive energy. You can hear their cries & rub their backs as they fall asleep.

It's never too late to have an enjoyable childhood.

<u>A practice to nurture your inner child</u>

 Pick a day weekly & do something to honor your inner child

-swing at a park

-blow bubbles

-play with playdo

-play vintage video games (mario)

-paint

-climb a tree

-ride a bike

-laser tag

-wear vibrant colors

-wear 2 ponytails

-watch your fav. Childhood movies

Cultivate time that is solely dedicated to honoring, nurturing and mending your relationship with your inner child. Most people never had an opportunity to have a childhood because it was stolen from them. They either had to take care of their siblings or be an emotional sounding board for their parents, ultimately taking care of their parents.

If this was you, what did those responsibilities hinder you from doing. Sometimes kids just wanted to go outside and play kickball with friends but couldn't because they had to watch their siblings. This means, now that you are an adult, call your friends, go buy a kickball, head to the park and play.

Maybe your inner child deserves an ice cream or a slushy after having fun at the park.

When you're done honoring your inner child, take out a journal and write about your experience. Tell you inner child,

"This was for you."

Allow your inner child to feel seen, heard, loved and acknowledged.

Even when moments arise and you feel emotionally triggered, before becoming prisoner to that trigger check on the woundedness of your inner child as ask them,

"Are you ok?

What are you feeling?

What do you need from me in this moment?

Why is this upsetting you so much?

Everything is going to be ok,

let's work on a solution together,

it's ok to cry or be angry,

don't worry, I'm here with you, you aren't alone.

You are safe.

This is how you reparent your inner child.

You become the person you needed when you were younger.

It's not to late love. You didn't miss out on your childhood.

Your inner child is ready and waiting for you to come home to yourself, watch scary movies together with popcorn and fresh baked cookies. You can choose to honor and show up for yourself anytime you get ready.

It's never too late.

Paranoia Purple

A ttachment of any kind is rooted in fear.

Fear & love cannot co-exist.

Attachment is fear of not being loved, fear of love being taken away, fear of being abandoned, neglected, not wanted or not chosen. This can be described as anxious or insecure attachment. The other end of attachment (avoidant) Is a person who deeply wants love but doesn't know how to receive it. The fear of finally receiving love becomes so overwhelming to the wounded parts of that person so they unconsciously sabotage it, push it away or shut down when someone is attempting to them in unfamiliar ways or ways that remind them of their open wounds from their past. They avoid love because it triggers love wounds of their past.

The new "Instagram trend" is acknowledging what attachment style a person has. This is only helpful if a person is committed to dissecting their demons to find out what they're feeding on. This means it's not enough to rest on knowing your attachment style, you must also learn root cause of your attachment & work towards healing the wound that has manifested in this unhealthy behavior.

When did you first download the fear of not being loved? When was love first taken away? When did you need love as a child but didn't receive it?

People often say they "love hard" as a cute acceptable way to cover up that their unhealthy attachment has led to obsessiveness, possessiveness & the display of any behavior that will convince a person to love them and never leave. Many people who suffer from the wound & trauma of attachment just want to be loved however they are so fearful of this love being taken away that they use control and force to maintain it.

Partners become controlling, not wanting their partner to have male or female friends, not going out with friends, checking text messages, obsessing about how long it took them to text or call back. These are just a few signs of someone who displays unhealthy attachment.

Attachment isn't love, it's the epitome of fear, control, trauma, wounds, obsessive and possessiveness.

True Love is freedom from fear. Love is when a person can feel safe enough in their nervous system to continue to love & simultaneously let go at the same time. Let go of expectations, fears & outcomes. To allow love to come with openness & allow it to leave with grace. Until a person heals their love wound, their fear of love & their fear of love being taken away they will use every relationship they enter as medication for their open wounds & a distraction to avoid their true fear of being hurt or abandoned, again.

When you become your own medicine, you learn to love freely without the need to use control as a method to force yourself to feel safe.

May each broken part of you

Heal from your pain and

Evolve into your peace

THE REAL

#SoftLife

W hat is your relationship with softness as it applies to your emotional wellbeing, your femininity or masculinity?

Right now, the term #SoftLife trends on social media by women who have a past of unbalanced masculine energy that are ready to embody their softness and explore a life of ease. Some have even created brands titled soft life as a way motivate women to take care of themselves. The issue I've found with the soft life movement, it that it glorifies mostly if not only external methods to feel more feminine or softer. Their definition of soft seems to be mostly about experiencing luxury, taking care of themselves externally with things like nails, hair, vacations and spoiling themselves, as they should. However, to truly be soft, balance your masculine and feminine energy requires self-exploration to be present. Softness requires a level of vulnerability, the ability to release control and soften the parts of their hearts that have hardened by pain over time.

Softness doesn't imply weakness or lack of power. On the journey to healing there will be moments softness is required, a soft approach, a gentle nurturing and gracefulness to fully allow yourself to evolve from a place of love. Vulnerability requires softness, nurturing, compassion and patience. From my perspective one of the many emotional blockages men and women face while on their healing journey is the inaccurate assumption that softness and vulnerability also equate to weakness and this unhealthy perception hinders them from exploring the emotional releases that are imperative to clear our emotional energetic debris.

So often sensuality couches on social media teach that healing the feminine wound and embodying sensuality equates to sexiness, being naked and dancing sensually. However, this level of ignorance and ego don't acknowledge that it is very difficult for a person to embody their softness, feminine sensuality or balance their masculinity if they are still forcing any part of their life, mind, body, relationships or spirit into submission. To embody softness means to stop forcing life into submission. Stop forcing weight loss through unnecessarily difficult workouts, stop forcing the body to be constrictive and dance on beat, when it's begging to be free, stop forcing yourself to enjoy sex with men/women just because you subconsciously want to feel loved. Stop forcing control when surrender is asking to be present. Embodying softness and practicing vulnerability doesn't work through forcefulness only through ease & finesse.

People can feel when a person is forcing behaviors or movements that aren't yet authentic to them. They can tell when a person's sensuality is truly an expression of the divine feminine or an attempt to feel sexy and receive outward validation driven by unhealed wounds. There's a level of scriptedness that will always appear as unnatural when a person has skipped their healing process and went straight to wearing the mask of being sexy, traveling or playing out the idea of they think being soft or feminine looks like.

Balanced feminine energy, softness and sensuality are all a byproduct of spiritual integrity, how well a person keeps their word to themselves and how often they listen to their soul when it asks them to rest. True softness and feminine energy is a reflection of a person's ability to forgive, have a soft heart, be compassionate, kind hearted & a reflection of their relationship with Source. Balanced feminine and masculine energy pours through a woman's or man's veins as they truly embody the fullness of their being with balance. When their hearts become safe spaces to heal from emotional pain and they give their bodies permission to finally release the emotional pain they've been holding on to. Before anyone can embody their softness and feminine energy, they'll have to practice humility by taking accountability & apologizing for all of the things they've done & the ways they've treated people when they thrived in their unhealed & unbalanced masculine energy.

Embodying your divine feminine means to emotionally & spiritually heal the core of your wounded ness and as you heal, the essence of who you are on a soul level will emerge. Being able to release control is a pre-requisite to embodying the feminine. Having the capacity to relax into the body is necessary to fell the essence of spirit. Healing wounds to have the ability to feel creates access to explore sensuality freely and practicing the art of self-forgiveness and self-compassion are required to have a real meaningful relationship with the body. When you give yourself permission to nurture all aspects of your being your natural sensual essence will emerge.

Remember Who The F*ck You Are.

Softness and healing

require a nervous system that has been

nurtured and feels safe.

WHEN WILL I BE HEALED?

ANYTHING NOT GROWING IS DEAD

Healing is a lifelong journey, and this also means all of the energies of this universe are conspiring to help us fall in love with the process of shedding and simultaneously becoming.

This is an unconsciously loaded question that has fear, anxiousness, confusion and desperation attached to it. People typically ask this question when they are afraid of the process and have come to the smart conclusion that they cannot control their way out of the process. This idea is scarry to people simply because most times healing doesn't feel the best. Sometimes it feels as if you're re-traumatizing yourself just to heal the past trauma.

When a person asks this question, I instantly know their minds have rushed them into attempting to find a solution to their emotional pain or discomfort. It's like when a person goes to the gym after hiring a fitness trainer and as they begin their workout, they are already looking at the clock, attempting to gauge how much longer they have to go or endure pain or discomfort. This can become very tricky to the persons progression and evolution because instead of being intentional about remaining in the present moment and focusing on what is surfacing now, they are bypassing their present moment and escaping to a future that doesn't exist.

This is the epitome of time travel. Living in future moments in attempt to escape present moments.

Just know, you are exactly where you are supposed to be. There is no need to rush to a desired outcome. Healing happens in stages on purpose, this is how the soul makes sure not to give you more than you can bare. You may think you've healed a wound today just for that same wound to resurface with more intricate nuances five years later. This is an attempt to help you practice enjoying, embodying and surrendering to your life journey.

It is true that sometimes healing, growing, evolving or changing can be scarry, emotional and uncomfortable but give yourself permission to not rush past your life simply because its uncomfortable. Practicing staying mindful and aware even in the moments the mind attempts to force you into a future that doesn't exist in hopes lighter emotions live there. When we fall in love with the totality of our journeys, we don't allow Ego to rush us into futures, realities or outcomes that don't exist. When we fall in love with the totality of our journeys and the divine timing of our experiences makes it easier to relinquish control, because trust now replaces fear. Faith now replaces uncertainty and power now replaces disempowerment.

You are exactly where you need to be and if you rush your process and life experience you may miss the lessons that are meant to be in the present moment of your process. Trust yourself, Trust your soul. Remember Who The F*ck You Are.

Relax.

Give yourself grace.

You're coming back home to yourself.

THE THIEF OF LOGIC

There is beauty in having the capacity to learn new information, but deep healing can only occur when an individual has the ability to implement the knowledge, they've learned without allowing ego to believe that the learning was the final step to their process.

Healing requires the exploration of feeling and freedom to allow emotions to surface or be present. It becomes very difficult for a person to embark on an authentic emotional healing journey if they're controlled by their use of intellect and logic. Many are addicted to logical thinking because being hyper aware was the only way their nervous system could survive unstable or uncertain environments, so using logic and intelligence provides a sense of safety because exploring emotional trauma can feel very unsafe, uncertain and unstable to the nervous system.

Many adults who were raised in unstable, unloving or emotionally confusing environments tend to overthink and overanalyze because their nervous system was forced to read energy. They had to learn how to read their parents energy before asking a question or having to guess people's intentions because they didn't know if they were safe.

Many of my clients have a hard time expressing their emotions because they can only operate from their logical mind. When I ask them how something makes them feel they attempt to use intellect to explain their answer or they'll attempt to describe what happened but struggle to acknowledge the emotions that they feel. They don't have the capacity to express things like "I feel sad, abandoned, unworthy, underserving or not wanted".

The reason the mind chooses logical intellect instead of expressing emotions, is because logic & intellect makes a person feel safe and in control. It's an unconscious method to detach from pain. Expressing vulnerability and emotions subconsciously reminds a person of their environments growing up & that makes them feels unsafe, confused &

ultimately emotionally unstable. Logic is a unconscious attempt to adapt to fear and a method to control their environment by protecting themselves from emotional spaces, expressing emotions & conversations that remind them of their traumatic childhood.

An example of how the brain adapts to keep the individual safe is, how many {empaths} may have first unconsciously acquired their skill from trauma before learning it was a form of clairvoyancy. Many empaths experienced unhealthy environments that made them hyper aware of other people's emotions, thoughts & energies. They had to quickly read the room, read their parents body language, read minds and subtleties in interactions to protect themselves. This hyper awareness morphs into the super power of being able to feel what another person feels.

To a large degree the misuse of logic and intellect is a byproduct of emotional trauma when it's unconsciously used in ways that hinder them from tapping into the very emotions they need access to, to be able to heal emotionally on deeper levels. You cannot intellectualize your healing It must be felt at the core of your being to fully process. Surrender is required to give yourself permission to not protect yourself with logic in moments you may need to feel vulnerable to heal. Resting on logic & intelligence can be the one biggest component that keeps someone from healing as deeply as their soul desires. It can be scary to allow yourself to explore these parts of your emotional body, but it'll be so worth it in the long run. Start practicing staying mindful of the moments you are replacing intellect and logic to protect yourself from feeling uncomfortable emotions.

Liars never heal

because they spend so much time avoiding the truths of their emotional health.

You cannot think your way into healing.

Don't allow your logic and intellect rob you from your ability to feel into what needs to be healed.

Radical Self Acceptance Leads to Self Love

Many times it's easy to love another person outside of yourself because they lead with only showing you the best parts of themselves and they hide the truth of who they are in distant shadows.

Even when a person does show the full spectrum of who they are including the not so good parts you typically only have to experience those versions of them sporadically. The contrast is you're required to sit with the truth and the full spectrum of who you are daily, so maybe it's difficult to love yourself because you refuse to accept the totality who you are, what you are & where you are in your life journey on a daily basis.

When I began my healing journey It took me a long time to realize it was actually very easy to love myself once I accepted, stopped judging & telling myself I needed to be, look, act or show up a certain way. When I stopped forcing myself into submission, working out at the gym like crazy, trying to lose weight, working a job I hated, not setting healthy boundaries with those who'd wronged me & didn't deserve to breath the same air as me. When I stopped trying to force myself to be someone, I wasn't and accepted I'm 50 pounds overweight & it is what it is lol I quickly shed 50 pounds in 4months. I shed the emotional weight that was ready to leave my body not from an unrealistic gym routine or diet but from genuine self-acceptance. With pure love and gratitude for my body, my life circumstances and honoring where I was in my healing journey without comparing it to others, true self love formed.

Journeying into self-acceptance shed a light on how much I was hyper aware about how I was received by others, how I wanted people to know I was a good person and feared doing anything that would give a contrasting impression. This epiphany was the invitation to begin radically accepting my truth without guilting myself on how I'd be received. So, I started checking people lol setting very clear and firm boundaries. I began holding people accountable for how they treated me without feeling guilty because how I responded wasn't considered nice or positive. I accepted that all of my responses wouldn't reflect my level of wisdom, which was also wisdom.

I gave up my brand-new Mercedes Benz because I didn't want my ego to rest on luxury things to feel good about. I acknowledged I had an alcohol addiction, accepted and loved on my large G cup breasts that sagged down to my belly button. When people asked me how I was doing, I'd responded with the truth of how I felt in that moment instead of the societal norm "I'm ok thank you". I gave myself permission to think how I wanted to think with an open mind, believe in what I wanted to believe in while also being open to learn about other people's beliefs & stopped giving a damn about what other people thought. It became easy as hell to love myself, because I accepted myself for the fullness of who I was & it was all beautiful even in my most ugly moments.

Wherever you are in your life, your healing journey and spiritual journey is exactly where you should be. It becomes easier to love ourselves at any phase of our journey when we let go of the egoic approach of obtaining perfection, chasing something more, better, different, more beautiful, more money or more success. When we acknowledge that love lives here, exactly where we are in this moment if we allow it to. When we practice gratitude for where we are in our journey, we give our universe permission to grow where we are. New worlds emerge and new realties are created when we radically accept the full spectrum of ourselves. Deep joy, peace & harmony can become your home when you befriend true self-acceptance. Remember Who The F*ck You Are.

That ugly part of your story

is going to be the most

powerful part of your testimony.

I Wish I Allowed Myself to be Happy More Often.

A study showed that before some people transition or pass on, one of their regrets is "They wish they allowed themselves to be happier". Today I hope you give yourself permission to be not to just be happy but to feel everything fully and get the most of your life experiences. So often people live in their pasts which don't exist, and they romanticize their future which also doesn't exist and they rob themselves of what it actually means to live life, which is to be fully present in the now, the present moment. I pray you give yourself permission to be free, change your mind, love & live without fear. Life is the most beautiful experience that can be dreamt of.

I hope you give yourself permission to experience your life boldly & that you don't allow fear to shrink you & convince you to limit your greatness. I hope you stop wasting your energy attempting to figure things out & you begin trusting it's already figured out & unfolding exactly as it should embodying faith that you're going to be ok.

I hope you learn to allow your mind to be the oasis that it's meant to be.

But mostly I pray you stop running from pain, struggle, uncomfortableness, your wounds & trauma.

I hope you learn to befriend your storms.

When you can tell your storm how beautiful it is, watch how quickly it turns into a rainbow reflecting heaven.

You deserve peace & you deserve to be loved, properly & intentionally.

You also deserve that apology & I hope instead of waiting for someone else to give it to you, you give it to yourself so you can finally let go of that hurt & move on with your beautiful life.

Your parents love you, even if they have the worst way of showing it.

We are all trying to figure out our own level of being human & for some people they only know how to battle themselves vicariously through others.

The sky is vibrant blue & the trees are lush green not just to be pretty, but to remind you daily that you're alive! They're reminding you to choose to thrive & show up vibrantly.

They are reminding you to remember who you are, because storms will come & that's ok. But both truths can exist at the same time, a storm may be present, but you can damn sure laugh & play & enjoy yourself simultaneously as it passes.

Give yourself permission to love and practice receiving love.

Invite every cell in your body to evolve & watch how beautifully things begin to unfold.

As I journeyed through my many years of emotional and spiritual healing my biggest aha moment was seeing God in everything. I began to own all of my life experiences and all of the emotions that came with them, not just the moments that felt good. I told myself if I'm going to be alive and truly commit to life, I want my money's worth, which means don't short change me.

If happiness is on my life receipt, I want that, if pain grief or depression is also on my life receipt, give me what I'm owed. If peace, harmony and being a successful is on my life receipt I better receive everything my soul is owed.

Yall know if you get a coupon for even 2$ yall would be excited to use it lol that's because you recognize you prefer the maximize the opportunity as much as you can. Life is such a wealthy experience you would be short changing and robing yourself if you only allowed happiness or perfect moments that don't allow any other emotions to be present. That doesn't even sound like fun.

The excitement is being able to share your experiences like yea, "I definitely got drunk and went off on him in the parking lot screaming &

crying nobody ever loves or choses me, whew that was a time" lol (that really happened I'll tell yall about it later) imagine telling someone my life was happy I felt no emotional pain vs. telling them all of the things you've lived through.

As much as we claim we want a 100% easy life, imagine how boring that would be. The unpredictable lives we have are what makes our soul feel like it's on an adventure. My husband describes this as the human going down a huge roller-coaster being super afraid while the soul is screaming "Wweeee" with a huge smile on it's face. Imagine telling your life story to another person, they would be at the edges of their seat listening to your real life story because it truly is spectacular.

These are the parts of our lives that in the moment seem like the end of the world but in hindsight the soul just went for a quick joyride in our human body lol Our painful and uncomfortable moments as humans aren't to punish us, It's God and our soul experiencing life through us, as us.

So, stop playing, make life pay you all of your experiences and remind life, Nah fam we cried yesterday but I have a coupon for happiness and peace today, balance remember lol.

I pray you give yourself permission to laugh at this experience just as much as you cry.

The birds sing you love songs.

Are you present enough to see?

The sky brings you candy.

Nature brings your flowers

The trees bring you life.

Next time you hear or see them, tell them thank you.

BOUNDARIES ARE MEANT TO BE FELT.

S ometimes it's not enough for boundaries to be heard, sometimes boundaries need to be felt.

Practice setting boundaries without laughing at the end. Practices saying what you need to say without the "Lol" at the end of your text message.

Stop attempting to water down the uncomfortable moments that occur when you begin setting boundaries, teaching people how to treat you, defending yourself or just making yourself clear with certain people who carry certain energies that make you feel uncomfortable. It's necessary for them to feel the what you're saying, to feel the seriousness of your boundaries, how you will & won't be treated or spoken to etc Allow your boundaries to be felt because sometimes them hearing you isn't enough.

Those uncomfortable moments you're attempting to bypass or water down teaches the other person

1. You don't say what you mean

2. You don't mean what you say

3. You lack authority for yourself

4. You allow yourself to be treated any way by anyone.

These are just some of the subconscious & energetic messages you're sending out. Remember you teach people how to treat you and people treat you, how you treat you. Boundaries are not about shutting people out, boundaries are how you allow people in but with healthy rules that make you feel comfortable, respected & safe.

So, stop all that damn laughing because you're afraid of having an uncomfortable moment.

If it's not funny why are you laughing? If someone is doing something that makes you feel uncomfortable, why are you struggling to say that?

"If I'm uncomfortable, we all about to be uncomfortable" and discuss my uncomfortableness with what is taking place. Many people like myself, haven't always been forward or aggressive with how we protect, stand up and speak up for ourselves. As you learn to take your power back in this area of your journey it must be acknowledged that it's no longer necessary to tiptoe over how you feel or how you deliver the message.

Those that mind don't matter and those that matter don't mind.

It is your natural birthright to feel comfortable & safe within your being & in your spaces. Setting firm boundaries can be difficult, uncomfortable & scary but this is a healthy practice that teaches people how they are allowed to show up in your spaces. Stop allowing people to walk all over you with their dirty ass feet, while you just laugh & dust yourself off, NAH try again. (Aaliyah bars) Set your boundaries & stand Firm in them. This is self-love .

Remember who the f*ck you are.

Stop putting "LOL" at the end of your sentences.

Say what you mean and mean what you say.

Those that mind don't matter and those that matter don't mind

If taking your power back, standing up for yourself and reclaiming the love and treatment you deserve makes you the bad guy or the villain.

*Oh f*ckin well.*

When you speak your truth and only allow what you deserve you may always be the villain in someone else's story. All that matters Is that you are a Hero in your own story. Saving and protecting yourself, as you should.

Do You Know How to Receive Love

The next time someone offers to love you, give yourself permission to allow it.

The next time someone asks, "do you need help carrying those bags?' give yourself permission to say yes, allow yourself to rest and for them to display love by helping you out.

The next time someone asks "if you need anything just let me know" give yourself permission to let them know.

The next time someone asks "is there any way I can help or any way I can support you" don't attempt to say no and do it all on your own allow love in.

The next time a person compliments you don't change the subject, get shy or attempt to be modest or humble, receive your compliment and allow that person to shower you with acknowledgment.

These are very small deflections but they are clear indications that a person may not know how to receive the love they desire. Help from others is a form of love. People showing up for you just to lend their support is a form of love. If a person can't allow others to love them in these small capacities, how can they practice receiving love in full blown romantic relationships.

Love is diminished when only romantic love is put on a pedestal. Doing this trains, a person to now see regular gestures from strangers, friends and family as love and ultimately programs them to not take any form of love for granted.

We play a huge part in how people love us. We take our power back when we no longer wait for people to read our minds or just know how to perfectly love u. We are allowed to guide people on ways to love us perfectly and correctly.

A beautiful practice to begin receiving the love you desire is to practice asking for it. Yes, our jobs are to first love ourselves, however there are people in our lives who are ready, waiting and willing to love us the way we deserve. Call on them, not to do your love work for you, but to play a healthy part in participating in the love you desire to create in your life. The next time you'd like to experience love, first practice giving it to yourself then,

Call your friends over to celebrate you. Many people will feel uncomfortable by this and think it's weird or odd but it's a beautiful practice that allows you to not just wait for the love you deserve and to ask for it and allow the people that want to love you an opportunity to do so. Explain to your friends or family that you TRUST and feel emotionally safe with that you are practicing allowing love in and asking for the love you need. Use your words and be specific about what you're experiencing.

Some examples are

"I'm experiencing a tough time being a mom, not really finding time for myself and when I do set time for myself I feel mom guilt, could you come over just to hang with me or maybe we go out for drinks just so I can enjoy myself, your company and let loose? I would really appreciate your support."

"I just graduated a course that I've been working really hard on for the past 2 years and I'm inviting my friends over to celebrate me, with me. I'd really like to feel seen in this moment."

When we give ourselves permission to practice the strength of vulnerability to receive the love we need, we heal the parts of ourselves that fear not being love, wanted, seen, heard or acknowledged. We create opportunities for love to show up and exist in our world. Giving ourselves permission to practice receiving love also creates new realities where all types of love show up in abundance and readily available to us at all times. There is love all around you, allow it in. You deserve to feel the love you give to others. It is your season to receive.

There are people ready, waiting and willing

to love you, see you and hear you the way you deserve. Give yourself permission to practice allowing love in, even and especially when receiving feel uncomfortable.

It is finally your season to receive the love you give to everyone else.

Don't run from the love you deserve.

Honeymoon Beach

We met on the moon. After lifetimes of gracefully letting one another go and patiently finding one another again. There we were, sitting on the edge of the moon, swinging our feet regaining our memory of one another and catching up on lost time, downloading our cosmic love from the power of the ethos.

We made love on the moon, and you told me you loved me on the first night. Going to sleep that night was damn near impossible because I was in shock. There you were but, where the hell have you been and what took you so long is what I wanted to cry out. My heart had experienced many wounds in your absence but I intentionally medicated my heart with the tears of my soul in preparation for you.

What will you teach me, this time?

How will you aid in my growth, this time?

Our dates were the best when we flew to Saturn and used its rings as a slide and allowed ourselves to play. Remember how we'd lay on our backs and watch the stars until we became them, until we evaporated into God's breath. Even a thousand miles away me in Houston, you in New Jersey, we never missed an opportunity to go home and check on God.

You proposed to me with Saturn's ring with everyone watching. You gathered our entire family to bare witness to one of the most powerful connections between soul mates. Honey Moon Beach, is where I stood before you, as you with sand in my toes, pitch black night sky with a full moon lighting up the ocean. I could see nothing, not even you but I knew everyone was there. God, our angels, our ancestors and all of the versions of ourselves that healed and evolved just to experience this moment. As you placed Saturn's ring on my finger, my tears told you, I do. Trumpets blared, angels cheered, and God smiled.

How could you be so perfect, so patient, so loving, so honorable, so honest, so humble, so strong, to charismatic and so damn sexy. I healed for you. I healed for me, but my healing granted and gifted me you.

June 20ᵗʰ, 2018

I prayed for you. Riding on a boat back to my villa in Mexico I prayed for love. I felt the warmth of the sun on my skin, the mist and splashes of water touch my face as the boat collided with the ocean and the wind. I remember thinking to myself this feels like freedom. I want love that feels like freedom. I told God, I don't care what form love comes to me in, even if it's a baby kitten I'd like to enjoy it as this newly evolved me. Two years later I had a gift at Instagram DM front door talking about "I just want to support you" lol. I opened my door, freely and boldly. I asked you very few questions because I already knew who you were. I'd written letters to throughout the years in hopes youd find me. I even wrote letters to you when I was discouraged, you'd never find me again. Don't believe me? Watch this *Usher's Voice

"September 19ᵗʰ 2018"

"I can count on 1 hand the relationships I've been in, However I'd have to use my fingers and toes to count how many times I've fallen in love because I tend to fall in love with parts of each person I meet.

Sometimes I think in my past life I loved you so much I promised I'd search for you in each lifetime. This lifetime as Candyss has proven to be a bit difficult to find you, so maybe I fall in love with fragments of others because I find small glimpses of you. Maybe this is why I love everyone, even the toxic maybe I fall in love with each person I meet because everyone has a characteristic that reminds me of you, my one true love. Maybe loving fragments of people is me clinging to a change to get to love you all over again.

I've left a lot of broken hearts; unanswered questions and many people have been collateral damage once I leave them for finally accepting that they aren't you. In 2018 its difficult to explain a promise I made with my soulmate lifetimes ago without sounding crazy. No matter how much I think I love them I always know, they aren't YOU. So I leave them and continue my search for you in each person I meet.

What a relief you must feel knowing I will always find you."

December 16th, 2018

"I thought about you today. I heard a song and instantly wanted to dance with you. I thought about all of the times we'd dance anywhere and even with no music. Today I smiled while thinking about you. I missed you. I prayed for you. I allowed space for our memories, I honored them and then I sat them down and continued my journey."

February 18th, 2019

"Sometimes I forget about you. I guess I get so caught up in my own internal world I forget about us, I forget your voice and our promises. It's difficult finding you when I'm still searching for myself. Anyways it's a full moon tonight. I'm thinking of you and I'm still waiting our parallel universes to collide so we can find one another again. But don't rush, I need a couple more months so I can lose my last 30 pounds. Then I'll be ready for you lol.

-The missing piece to your soul

May 21st, 2019

ME: Dear Mr. Moon, I heard you loved Mrs. Sun so much you died every night just to let her breath. How do you continue to love her so much even though you two will never be together?

Mr. Moon: Mrs. Sun doesn't have to be present for me to still love her. My love doesn't come from sight or touch, loves comes from the heart and that is where Mrs. Sun has lived for many many lifetimes. As long as I have her in my heart our love will live on forever."

June 17th, 2019

"Don't commit to me commit to evolving. Commit to

Your journey

Your purpose

Your emotional health

Your accountability

Your health

Your happiness

Your spirituality

Your dreams and goals

I will only commit to what aids in the evolution of my soul so if you want me, commit to your individual growth, commit to evolving, I will meet you there."

June 26th, 2019 (your birthday)

"I didn't come to heal you. I came to love you. Love will heal you."

See, I told you. You were an intentional and well thought out intention. I knew from our first conversation that you were him, the faceless love I'd written about for years. But what I didn't know is how perfect you'd be. I always feel so lucky because I didn't have the vocabulary to ask for a man/soul as perfect as you. You've reparented me, held space for me, validated, reassured and poured into me in ways I never knew was possible. You are my walking, talking and breathing prayer. You are the gift that showed up once I chose to fully love and honored myself. I take pride in learning from you, you are my teacher. I honor your wisdom and I admire your heart. No matter the lifetime, I will always search for you, heal for you.

What a relief you must feel knowing I will always find you."

I love you Baba.

VISIONS OF THE PAST

Sometimes healing emotional pain requires you to revisit traumatic experiences. As heavy & painful as this can be, don't run from yourself. This is an opportunity to reparent & nurture yourself through the uncomfortableness. Cry & feel your emotions & also Remember your power!

Healing requires uprooting & clearing years of subconscious programming, rewiring the brain, cleansing out information lying dormant in the cells & DNA. Healing requires visits to the past, to go back & save the versions of yourself that are still in pain & have been left behind It's not enough to just focus on NOW especially if your traumas of the past are bleeding in your present moments & manifesting in your present behaviors.

Revisiting the past doesn't mean you have to live or be stuck there. But the past holds messages, lessons & guidance for your present self. Just like in the movies, when the present reality is threatened or a catastrophic event is about to happen, the characters often go to the past to see if there are any clues, they missed that could possibly help them solve present day issues. Some movies even show the character going to the past to visit their past selves, to ask for guidance or get clues to help them rectify their present situation.

So many people say they've healed, when they haven't. They've found skillful ways to manipulate themselves & move on, forget about it, not dwell on it & store the memory in deep dark places. Some have even practiced regurgitating healthier perspectives that don't reflect how they actually feel. Many use their healthier perspectives to bypass the pain that hasn't been acknowledged. But the mind, body & soul remembers & this is where depression is born.

Yes, you may cry & feel emotional pain when you recount events of the past, but this time, you're doing it with the intention to heal those wounds & process those emotions properly so they can surface out of the body. Sometimes, healing your emotional pain requires you to revisit traumatic experiences. As heavy & painful as this can be, don't run from yourself. This is your opportunity to reparent, nurture & empower yourself through the uncomfortableness.

Remember your power. If unwanted or undesirable behaviors are manifesting in your life, then there are pains of the past that still need nurturing. You may think you're "over it" you may be skilled enough to manipulate yourself into thinking "it doesn't bother you anymore" but if trauma & unhealed emotions are manifesting in your relationships, heathy, opportunities, self-sabotaging ways & unrelated emotions, these are clear signs that you have open wounds from your last that are still bleeding in your present. Whether you'd like to acknowledge and admit it or not.

Every now & then I'll get a client that is resistant to go back to their past to sift through the pain & search for clues & guidance to their healing. They're so afraid of their past and ultimately afraid of getting stuck in their emotional past that they convince themselves what's happened in the past doesn't matter & strong people move on. But how can you move on when your inner child is still waiting for someone to come & save them, tell them it wasn't their fault, they aren't a burden & they are worthy of love.?

As long as open wounds still live in your past, they will always find ways to bleed into your present.

To grow from your past, you gotta face it. When you practice meditation and you become a student of the mind, emotions no longer have permission to have control over you. Your ability to revisit your past without becoming a prisoner to your emotions is based upon your willingness to commit to your meditation and mindfulness practices.

Our past lives have A huge impact on your

present day experiences.

If you don't heal the wounds of your past

They will bleed in your present reality.

PAIN IS YOUR TEACHER

P ain is one of our greatest teachers.

When it surfaces, we should practice showing deep gratitude.

Sometimes pain helps us meet deep versions of ourselves happiness doesn't have access to.

Emotional pain also doesn't always mean sadness.

We can still be at peace, harmonious & even experience happy moments when pain is present.

We show the maturity of our evolution when we allow both truths to exist at the same time.

Sadness & Happiness can both exist simultaneously. This is an unpopular truth that society has subtly subconsciously programmed us to believe that only one sensation, feeling or emotion can exist at one time, causing many to take ownership and attach to the emotion of sadness while completely disregarding that happiness, gratitude or excitement for many other things may also simultaneously be present & attempting to get your attention.

When we practice "emotional non-attachment" we can still acknowledge our emotions but also see our emotions as teachers, lessons, angels & guides rather than our emotions only being an indication of how we should feel. We can allow emotions & feelings to do their job within our bodies, to show us spaces our soul is aching for healing & nurturing rather than assuming possession over emotional uncomfortableness.

When you choose to see your emotions as a teacher you can surrender to what they're teaching you and not limit yourself to feeling only the painful emotions at one time, you can give yourself permission to acknowledge any emotion that is present. You can feel intense waves of sadness & still give yourself permission to laugh if somethings funny.

Each emotion serves a purpose to take you to different levels of your soul's healing process. Happiness is no better than sadness. They both have equal value when you choose to honor them equally as your master teachers.

Remember Who The F*ck You Are.

Discomfort is a wise teacher.

When it appears, befriend it.

SOBER LIFE + ADDICTION

People say "weed" is a gateway drug but the real gate way drug is unhealed emotional trauma.

Addiction is a thief of life. It feeds on unspoken words, unhealed wounds, unacknowledged traumas and deep emotional pain. My addiction to alcohol felt like a daily ritual of poisoning myself and having to suffer through waiting for the poison to wear off. I absolutely hated feeling drunk but I loved that first 5 minutes that felt as if my body was escaping reality.

Emotional Pain is the Root

When a person is addicted to anything, to heal we must acknowledge the root cause. Emotional pain will always be the root cause whether a person is conscious of that pain or not. All addictions will lead back to emotional trauma. Addiction is a failed attempt to resolve emotional pain. It's an attempt to find relief and to numb yourself from natural emotions that you may not have the tools to cope with, yet. The reason why so many addicts relapse on their journey to sobriety is because they've forced themselves to stop drinking, smoking, doing drugs, having sex or gambling. On the surface this is the goal to stop the addictive behavior but the reason many aren't able to maintain their sobriety is because they haven't acknowledged trauma, healed the wound or found healthy coping mechanism so now, when emotional residue surfaces it knocks them off kilter.

When emotional pain becomes so uncomfortable, and a person doesn't have any healthy tools to cope with that emotion the brain attempts to find a way to help them escape that pain. People use many things to help themselves relieve emotional pain. Work, gambling, alcohol, sex, drugs, marijuana, pills, tv and food. Many people argue that marijuana isn't a drug, it's an herb and this is true, however the way they use this herb they alter it into a drug.

Marijuana is a numbing agent, it allows a person to feel their emotions less, if feel anything at all. Many people smoke marijuana multiple times a day which means throughout their day they are emotionally numb. Not only are they numb the brain begins working overtime. When a person smokes marijuana the fire they use to light the marijuana creates toxins in the body, these toxins go directly to the brain and the brain works overtime attempting to get the toxins off of the brain, then the person feels the sensation of being high. So, their idea of being high is really the brain attempting to save itself which also means their bodies are in survival mode.

I often have clients who tell me they smoke to relax and fall asleep, and I have to remind them that they aren't falling asleep, they are passing out so the body can get rid of the toxins on the brain.

True sleep requires, rest and true rest requires peace. If you have to smoke to fall asleep this is a clear sign that the nervous system is in shock and smoking is not a solution it's a temporary fix to a deep rooted issue. Why would a person want so much relief from their lives? Why would a human get lost in so many different methods of escapism?

Emotional pain will always be the root cause of addiction. If a person feels as if they are sad, depressed or feeling any heavy emotion they have absolutely no business drinking alcohol. Because alcohol is such a widely acceptable social behavior people forget that alcohol is a depressant and directly irritates the liver which is the organ that holds anger and resentment. To heal the addictive personality a person must dissect what wounds they are consciously or unconsciously running from, attempting to avoid or are too overwhelming to their nervous system to function without a coping mechanism.

When emotional pain becomes so uncomfortable the nervous system essentially goes into shock. People aren't just addicted to alcohol, smoking, sex, drugs or food they are addicted to anything that can regulate their nervous system, to ease their anxiety and calm their internal emotional storms. This is why healing any addiction must first begin with acknowledgment of the emotional stimulus, that is causing such an intense reaction that the person looks to people, places, things or substances to escape their feelings. People are addicted to withdrawing, isolating, living in secrecy or medicating their emotional pain in secrecy.

To Give Yourself A New Life You Must Give The Other One Away

During my own addiction I read a book called "The addictive personality" by Craig Nakken. This book felt as if it held a mirror directly to my face and made it clear why addiction felt so difficult to heal and it taught me what it takes to heal an addictive personality. I realized I had to let go of what no longer served me. Shortly after I found a quote that has since been my favorite quote.

"Let go or be dragged".

Obviously at this stage of my addiction I was being dragged hard af lol. Until I chose to add a positive replacement to my life routine to take the space of the times id usually drink which was after work. So, I picked up riding bikes and I learned photography on cannon 80d camera which was no joke. I taught myself through YouTube academy how to shoot raw and edit all of my photos. I could have easily just picked up a camera and pressed the buttons to take pictures, but I knew I needed to occupy my mind with something healthy. Something that still gave me a sensation of being intoxicated to a certain degree.

The sensation I came to love was showing up for myself, spending time with myself, learning new things, exploring outdoors in nature and finding new parks to ride my bike. I became excited about the new life I was creating for myself. I would wash my bike on Sundays, add a speaker to it and go ride at the park with strangers. I met new friends that also did photography and went with them to skate parks at night time to learn different methods of photography. I gave my old life away, it wasn't serving me any longer but this new life had me glowing. I was happy, my skin was beautiful and I was doing what was best for me.

Doing The Work

Inevitably when a person stops their addictive habit who they really are and how they truly feel about themselves and their life rushes to the surface. Now all of the trauma that they were ablet to run and hide from by drinking, smoking, having sex etc has surfaced loud and clear and is waiting to be acknowledged, healed and soothed. This is where a person must continue doing the work. Doing the work doesn't mean replacing one addiction with another, which is what people typically do. They'll stop drinking alcohol and then become addicted to food.

Doing the work doesn't mean find alternate ways to escape, it means the person must continue their emotional healing journey. They must continue dissecting their demons and finding out what they are feeding on. People tend to get comfortable because they haven't drank in 1, 5 or 10yrs not realizing they may just have strong will power that allows them to stop anything, but if the subconscious trauma that causes their addictive behavior isn't healed then all it will take is an intense emotional trigger to demolish their will power and allow their addictive behavior or their wounded self to resurface and take over.

This is why a person can be sober for 20+ years and still relapse, it's because there are still emotional wounds that haven't been acknowledged, healed and nurtured. This is a sign that willpower isn't a real coping mechanism it's a temporary fix. Doing the work may require many to begin therapy, meditation, breathwork, journaling or somatic therapy, in conjunction with supportive community meetings. They must begin exploring different healthy coping mechanisms and modalities that help them express, explore and interpret their emotions in a healthy manner so when moments surface that are intense and emotionally overwhelming they will have healthier outlets that can help them cultivate relief within their own power and bodies without relying on the addictive behaviors and outside sources to find relief outside of themselves.

A person is playing with fire if they believe doing the work is just about stopping the behavior. Doing the work is about getting down to the core of who they are as a person and cultivating new paradigms that aid in living a healthy, harmonious and thriving life. If you are someone who needs help, do yourself a favor and ask for help.

You deserve to live a life that you are mentally, physically and emotionally present to experience. You deserve to feel at home in your body even when emotional discomfort is present. You deserve to explore a new and healthier way of living that doesn't force you to become the worst of who you are. Healing the emotional traumas and wounds that lead to addictive behavior and no longer entertaining things that help you escape emotional pain is how you take your power back.

Remember Who The F*ck You Are.

Even warriors become distracted with habits and addictions from time to time. Though the wise warriors learn to become aware of these distractions, realizing that when obsessions take them blindly from being present.

Addictions are thieves, stealing the present moment from you. Become mindful of your addictive habits and what emotions they intend to distract you from.

Let go or be dragged

SPIRITUAL BACKGROUND CHECKS

Stop taking healing advice from people who've never healed shit. Everyone doesn't deserve to have access to you, your spirit, or your attention. Spiritual backgrounds checks are non-negotiable.

In today's society many people are looking for opportunities to become entrepreneurs and on a deeper level many people's egos are looking for opportunities to be seen, heard, loved, acknowledged, and revered.

The past few years there has a been a spike in social media self-proclaimed spiritual healers, life coaches, emotional guides and mindfulness leaders. There is also much saturation of teachings from licensed Therapist and psychiatrist via social media as well. Many have found opportunities via social media to gain clientele, teach people how to heal and create a monetarily beneficial life doing it, myself included, and that is ok.

However, the issue comes into play when people assume such an important position in the world but practice zero spiritual integrity by actively not doing their own healing work but choose to sell healing methods. They sell their personal lessons that their soul only intended for them to have and put them in the form of a course mentorship before they even implement those lessons for themselves. They know how to guide and help other people but have no idea how to implement that same advice, guide or help themselves. Not only do they not know how to, many of them refuse to. It becomes easier for them to focus on other people's emotional dysfunction than to focus on their own.

I get so many clients that tell me horrible stories about those they have gone to for help out of desperation, hoping that person could help them heal. I personally know many self-proclaimed healing practitioners that are spiritually, energetically and psychologically harmful, but their words are pure poetry. Even I think to myself "Damn that was beautifully written" then the next day I see how they are spiteful, mean, emotionally chaotic and dysfunctional. Leaving people worse than they found them. They don't care to embody spiritual integrity and don't factor in because their ego is just wants and needs validation. They don't fully see themselves or how detrimental their malpractices are to others.

The truth is I can't hold every spiritual or emotional healing practitioner accountable, that isn't my job or my bag to carry but I can spread the message for those who are in need to begin holding themselves accountable. When my clients vent to me about their past experiences, I they didn't conduct a "Spiritual Background Check" before allowing anyone to have access to them.

Spiritual Background Checks are for and not limited to

Therapist

Life coaches

Councilors

Intuitive Guides (me)

Meditation teachers

Yoga instructors

Spiritual healers

Interview them. ASK THEM ABOUT THEIR PAST.

So often when a person is desperate for help, they unconsciously see themselves as subservient and not in a position to ask questions, but questions are necessary because you need to know who a person truly is when they aren't holding the title of therapist or intuitive guide. I have clients, especially my clients that are licensed therapist, psychiatrist and psychologist ask me all of the time what are my credentials? They ask in depth about my background and certified me to teach.

I tell them,

"My experience is my certification, my wisdom is a reflection of the work I've done on myself and I never asked or desired to teach anyone, honestly I still don't, many times my work is annoying to me, but I've been ordained by God to share what I've learned through transparency, vulnerability and honestly". I remain open to questions about my personal healing history, how I healed certain traumas and how I actively work on my personal journey today. I do this because people deserve to feel safe with the person, they are essentially allowing to have access to their most painful wounds. I also keep a timeline of photos and videos explaining in depth my emotional healing journey on Instagram so my potential clients can see the progression in my healing, this allows them to not have to just trust and rest on my pretty words. I allow my proof to be seen.

Even when people refer to themselves as healers. Inquire about that, ask what does that mean to them because no one can heal you, unless you give your healing power away and dishonor yourself in the process. People can only do what you allow them to do. People can guide you; they can be very powerful vessels that lead you back home to yourself to the point you as if they'd healed you because they've helped you uproot much dormant trauma. This is a powerful guide, only you have the power to heal you, to transmute your own energy.

I see so often many get caught up in relying on spiritual readings, paying thousands of dollars on courses, hiring priestesses to curate spiritual baths and there's nothing wrong with these things if you choose to partake in them however there is an issue if you utilize these things and you haven't don't the work to tap into your own power.

If you are a manifestation of God, meaning you are a reflection of God and host that same God like power in your body, spirit and soul, why do you need an outside source or another person to create the power of healing for you?

'What makes their spiritual baths more powerful than you curating your own spiritual bath?

What makes their tarot readings more powerful that what your soul has already conveyed to you?

Stop. Pause. Come back home to yourself. When a person is desperate to feel better, they search for many things outside of themselves to ease their emotional discomfort instead of going inward and becoming their own medicine and their own healer.

Take you power back and remember who you are. You are just as powerful if not more than any person around you. You are your own healer. There's a difference between acknowledging someone can help guide you to uncovering blind spots or help guide you to spaces within yourself you haven't been able to tap into yet, this is a guide or a mentor. Acknowledge them for being a conduit but only you can do the work, only you have the power to heal you. They look the part, they have perfect Instagram esthetics, the sound very intelligent because they are. They've managed to regurgitate information & be charismatic with their words all while raising hell in their personal lives. Causing chaos all because they refuse to practice what they preach & journey into their own healing. Instead, they rather sell you the tools they refuse use for themselves.

Theirs much karma that comes from selling and teaching the lessons a person's soul only intended for them to have. AND there's much karma in not properly vetting people you allow to have access to your spirit, this is why the outcome isn't always a desired one.

This is why when listening to any person you must discern their level of spiritual integrity. It matters because the energy they teach from is the energy you receive messages in. You honor yourself properly when you are intentionally mindful of who you allow to have access to your emotional, spiritual & energetic property.

Don't be afraid to start over

You will die many times

In this life time

Many of you are already on your 3rd life

Uncomfortable Conversations

Uncomfortable conversations are the pathway to Healthy relationships.

Avoiding uncomfortable conversation cultivate internal conflicts, that spread confusion, discontentment. Choosing silence when every cell in your body is begging to express itself causes silent internal wars that lead to resentment & uncommunicated expectations.

In my marriage although we intentionally choose not to argue we intentionally choose to cultivate safe spaces for uncomfortable conversation to occur whenever they are needed. The deeper we connect in our union the deeper we are required to journey within one another. Because you can only meet a person as deeply as you've met yourself, this means uncomfortable conversations are imperative for exploring the truth of one another's reality. Sometimes we are required to have very uncomfortable conversations about many different topics to maintain our evolution as a soul partnership. These uncomfortable moments obviously don't feel good in the process but as we breathe through the discomfort & intentionally remember,

"Love lives here."

we always come out on the other end deeply grateful because we feel even closer to one another when we can stand in our truths while simultaneously allowing love to guide us.

Uncomfortable conversations are necessary as we change, heal, grow evolve as individuals in relationships & especially as we continue to heal past trauma. What worked for you in the beginning may not work anymore & the boundaries you never set before may be necessary for you to set now. Updates on what you need in your sexual experiences must be had. You may need to express how you would prefer your partner to respond to you or hold space for you when insecurities set in, or when your trauma is exposed & the ugliest, unhealthiest and most vulnerable parts of you are exposed.

Uncomfortable conversations aren't about disagreements they are a pathway that invites your soul partner to explore & adventure through the depths of your being so you both can thrive in the truth of who you both really are, while asking for the truth of what you really need to continue playing a part in your union.

Because uncomfortable conversations cause so much discomfort the best thing to do is just to acknowledge that uncomfortable energy is present & together choose to journey into that space intentionally. Don't run, don't hide, & don't deflect. Practice Enjoying what it feels like to strengthen your union with your partner. Life is birthed in discomfort & it thrives in peace.

Remember Who The F*ck You Are.

Don't keep the peace

Just to start a war within yourself.

THE SPIRIT OF COMPARISON

When the spirit of comparison attempts to infiltrate your heart, remind yourself everyone's success isn't rooted in blessings.

Sometimes you see what others have & title it as blessings but don't realize sometimes people get everything they need, want and desire just so it can bring them to their knees & teach them hard soul level lessons that can't be fixed with money, notoriety or success. How many rich people have you seen that are deeply depressed, lonely, miserable & the only thing they have is their possessions, money & success. They're loved deprived to their core but they're successful.

The issue is the average person can only see another's success they can't see that person's wounds that are bleeding into everything they create. So many people dishonor and disregard themselves just to be successful. They have no spiritual integrity, no relationship with their intuition & chase success to fill voids, medicate wounds & temporarily numb their trauma. Most people's success is a reflection of their trauma responses. Sometimes a person is granted success just so they can learn that success will never make them feel loved or heal their wounds of the past & this level of pain tends to force people into their healing.

It's Imperative to begin practicing gratitude when comparison surfaces. It becomes easy for Ego to compare, desire & strive for things that are not intended for your soul to experience. It also becomes very easy for ego to make you feel unworthy, not capable, behind, inferior and out of place.

If you aren't careful, you'll not only ask for the success you see from another person, but you'll also ask for their karmic debt that is attached to their perceived success. When you compare yourself & strive for what others have you perpetuate the idea to your soul that everything outside of you is powerful & you are powerless and that you don't trust your soul's divine path so you admire and strive for another person's path & all they have to endure to walk that path.

When you trust your soul's guidance, nurture a healthy relationship with your intuition & your higher power there will never be a need to compare because you'll trust that what is meant for you is already present or on its way. When you stand firmly in your power & you remember who you are, you know that everything in life is unfolding for your soul's definition of success. This is soul level confidence. Find gratitude in what is meant for you so when you do receive success you can ensure its covered in love, integrity & longevity.

I trust that what is for me, is designed for me.

I trust that what is for me is also healthy for my soul.

I trust that what is for me will allow me to flourish.

May what is for me and only for me, find me

FOLLOW YOUR INTUITION?

Sometimes the worst advice is telling someone to "Follow Their Intuition".

What if your intuition is guided by trauma, wounds & voids?

What if their decision making is led by their subconscious program that keeps them in self sabotaging cycles?

Then the solution wouldn't be to follow their intuition, it would be to identify if they even have a relationship with their intuition to begin with. To examine if their intuitive relationship has been damaged & then cultivate healthy tools to rebuild this part of themselves they've betrayed dishonored, disregarded & disempowered.

The intuition is a spiritual muscle that must be strengthened, nurtured & cared for, daily. The intuition is also like the voice of God, hence why the relationship must be nurtured, cared for a strengthened to hear it. When a person doesn't trust themselves or their own decision making, this could be a sign that they've damaged their intuitive muscle or have gone a long time without nurturing this divine relationship to the point that they're now forced for rely on other people's advice, books & wisdom. This continues to subconsciously perpetuate the idea that they are power-less, untrustworthy & everyone, everything outside of them is power-full.

The damaging of the intuition happens when a person continually betrays themselves. When they say yes when they'd really like to say no. When they don't keep their word to themselves, saying things like "I'll start Monday yet Monday never comes". When they disregard that subtle voice that says "Don't enter this relationship or entertain this person" and they spend the next few months or years stuck in a repetitive cycle of unhealthy behavior, toxicity and emotional trauma, all because they didn't listen. Other ways a person can damage their intuitive relationship is by asking others for advice before they even consult with their own intuition, spirit or soul. This sends a message to the body that they don't honor their divine wisdom, their compass that lives within them, they only honor the wisdom that comes from others. This is the epitome of self- betrayal and self-betrayal is one of the hardest emotions to transmute because it's coated in shame, guilt, unworthiness and insecurity.

If the intuitive relationship has been damaged, before now jumping the gun, running back to it to listen for it. Like any relationship, when you treat someone badly, when you don't nurture that relationship, when you ignore them and act as if they don't exist, when you don't listen to their advice that you actually need and when you betray they by putting them in situations that are potentially harmful, don't you think that person deserves an apology before you all can move on in a healthy way?

Now, to truly form a relationship with your intuition, this sacred part of your being you must take accountability for all of the ways you've dishonored, disregarded and disempowered yourself. You must apologize to the most sacred part of your being and acknowledge where you fell short, why and how you plan to make healthier changes to repair the relationship. If this is what you'd do with a person you love, don't you owe yourself the same courtesy?

So often people require apologies from others, but they won't even apologize to themselves and repair their own relationship with self, still unconsciously searching for an outside source to do their work for them. If the work isn't done to repair this relationship a person will always need another person's advice because their divine advice will be tainted and even if it is pure advice from the soul, they still won't trust it or they'll second guess it.

When you repair this sacred part of your being it replenishes your self confidence in all areas of your life, your decision making, interpreting your emotions, when it's time to step away from a situation, when it's time to enter a healthy relationship or even when it's time to search for a new career. The intuitive muscle is your compass that is designed specifically to guide you through life. Your intuitive compass is your direct pathway to God.

Your intuition is God. Repair this relationship with self- accountability and an apology so you can

Remember Who The F*ck You Are.

When in war of Ego,

the loser always wins.

EGO Interrupts intuition.

CODEPENDENCY

When did you learn that you had to perform to receive love? & when did you first feel the fear of if you didn't perform correctly then love may be taken away?

If you struggle with codependency, that is an indication that emotional trauma from your past is present. These are questions you should ask yourself & they will guide you to the root & source of your people pleasing behavior. A person only assumes codependent behavior & chooses people pleasing when a wounded part of them needs and craves love in return.

Those who say yes when they really want to say no,

Those who go out of their way to give their all and deplete themselves for others,

Those who feel required to help or do for others but never help and do for themselves

Those who apologize and say they're sorry first even when they shouldn't be the one apologizing,

Those who don't say how they truly feel just to keep the peace,

all have one thing in common, they use these performative behaviors to receive love and validation to medicate their open wounds and unhealed traumas. Some may even unconsciously mask their behavior as just having a "loving heart" but the truth is their behavior has nothing to do with having a loving heart, their behavior is a reflection of the love the wish they felt in their hearts. The love they're searching for In their hearts via other people. They say yes when they really want to say to to feel an ounce of love in return, to be seen or acknowledge or even thanked. Many people weren't acknowledged for good deeds as children and received no validation, now as adults they display behaviors that will allow them to be acknowledged, wanted or appreciated in the way their parents didn't when younger.

They crave someone to be grateful not just for what they've done but on a deeper level they want someone to be grateful for them as a person. People who struggle with codependency use their performative behaviors and never saying as a transactional payment to receive love in return.

Codependent people pleasers have a hard time saying no because they believe pleasing others is their only source of receiving love and just like a drug addict, they'll do things even when they don't want to just to receive the next dopamine hit of feeling loved, seen, wanted, heard or acknowledged.

Typically, codependent performative behavior stems from a childhood of not being loved or nurtured properly by parents. When the child had to perform by receiving good grades, exceling in sports, being the "child parent" by taking care of their siblings & missing out on their own childhood,

being the good child to receive love, attention, to be seen or highlighted by their parents but the moment the child didn't "perform their best" the love from their parent was taken away.

Those who suffer from the codependent wound unconsciously allow themselves to not set boundaries to avoid love being taken away. A common theme with setting boundaries and the unconscious reason people don't set them is because they fear that when they set healthy firm boundaries with someone, that person will leave, so they maintain their lack of boundaries because in their minds crumbs of love is better than no love.

No love reminds them of not feeling worthy, wanted, chosen, nurtured, wanted, deserving or acknowledge. So, the codependent person maintains their lack of boundaries to ensure a person won't leave them and ultimately remind them of the emotional wounds of their past. This is how intelligent the subconscious mind is. It begins calculating ways to avoid emotional pain without the person even knowing, leaving them deeply confused on why they display codependent behaviors not knowing their subconscious mind is working overtime to protect them and keep them safe. This is what unconscious and conscious internal conflict looks like. This method of coherency may have worked in the past to receive love but now as a person begins their healing journey it becomes clear when behaviors were created in survival mode and are detrimental to the healing process.

When a person suffers from codependency, their need to people please and do so much for others leaves them feeling taking advantage of, not appreciated and ultimately not loved. Especially if the person they are performing for did not ask for the things the codependent person is providing. When the codependent person expresses, they feel taken advantage of or unappreciated as a result of their behaviors not being acknowledged or praised properly, Many often say "I didn't ask for that or I didn't ask you to do that" forcing the codependent person to medicate their own love wounds and need for validation.

Codependency can be a deep wounded trauma & to heal you must cultivate a relationship with the version of you that FEARS not being loved if you don't show up a certain way. By reminding yourself that you are loved even when your boundaries are strong, even when you say no, even when you don't agree, even when you don't keep the peace and even when you stand up for yourself and acknowledge yourself. When you learn to love, see, hear, want and acknowledge yourself and become the source of providing your own medicine you being to heal your own wounds of codependency.

Study you......

SHAME

Shame is one of the most toxic energies that eats away at the soul. You take your power back from shame when you no longer allow it to scare you into dark corners of silence.

Shame feeds on untold stories. It uses a person's fears & insecurities against them and convinces them to build themselves a silent, corrosive, unhealthy, dark prison to live in to avoid embarrassment of acknowledging the things they're holding on to. However, shame dies when a person has safe spaces to speak their truth. Shame dies when a person acknowledges where their inner voice of judgment stems from. Often those who suffer from shame have an inner judge that actually isn't even them, it's the voice of their parent's, society or friends judging their every thought, decision or mistake.

As I work with many clients through Shame it takes them a while to finally allow themselves to explore their own darkness. Eventually many of them acknowledge that the core of their shame isn't even theirs it was given to them. This realization becomes a pathway for them to now dissect why and how this happened. How was shame given to them or possibly even passed down to them from their parents, society or generational trauma? So many women experienced the shame of being pregnant and they unconsciously fed that shame and unworthiness to their unborn child. When a heavy emotion like shame is passed through the cells and DNA it becomes the subconscious blueprint for that child and may ultimately become a subtle lingering feeling they learn to unconsciously attach to and identify with as they get older. Shame can very well be an inherited or a learned behavior.

Many of my clients uncover that their shame stemmed from never feeling good enough for their parents, having to perform for love, always feeling unworthy, society teaching them how to compare themselves to others or by a sexual predator taking their autonomy of their bodies away from them as young children.

Even though we honor all emotions, shame is not necessary or conducive to any of our soul's evolution. Shame robs us from learning our lessons, implementing them & moving on. Shame keeps us stagnant, in fear, stuck & it's the epitome of a lack of self -love. It causes cancer, disease, memory loss & eats away at the heart & soul. Shame is a self -inflicted hell people use to punish themselves for not feeling good enough, not being perfect or living up to someone else's standard.

You cannot shame yourself into change, you can only love yourself into evolution.

You can give yourself grace & still hold yourself accountable. If you truly want to heal your shame, acknowledge what you're ashamed of. When you start running your mouth about your shame lol exposes the secrets that are holding you hostage, speaking your truth outload in safe spaces, all the power shame has over you dies.

The scary monster isn't so scary when someone else hears your story & says "me too, I feel the exact same way or the same thing happened to me". Your power is in your TRUTH! Stop hiding & running from yourself. Own your stories, no matter how ugly, sad, embarrassing, guilt full they are. Your truth is where your healing is. Own it so you can let it go! Shame don't run nothing over here. Tell shame it's stayed long enough, now its time to get your sh*t and go. Respectfully lol take your power back and

Shame dies

when stories are told in safe places.

SILENCED BY THE BIBLE

The misuse of the bible verse "Honor thy mother and father" has led to many adult children needing deep emotional therapy. This incomplete phrase silences children and guilts them out of acknowledging they can love and respect their parents and simultaneously feel angry, hurt or indifferent towards them for how their lack of parenting affected them. This phrase has programmed many children to not express how they feel out of fear of being disrespectful, coming off as ungrateful, going to hell or disappointing God. It's also sent an unconscious message that how a child feels does not matter enough to be acknowledged by their parents, leading to adult children growing up and never expressing themselves to their parents and harboring fear of setting healthy boundaries with parents.

Many parents have weaponized this phrase as an attempt to avoid accountability or acknowledging that even a child's emotions, perspectives and opinions deserve to be heard without dismissing their thoughts as disrespect or being unappreciative. When parent's use this bible verse to avoid allowing their child to exercise their birthright of using their voice it become a tactic of manipulation and ultimately leads to an adult child who has to recover from being silenced, doesn't know how to use their voice to express themselves and doesn't feel worthy of being heard. Disrespect is disrespect, voicing how something makes you feel, asking questions and setting healthy boundaries is your birthright even and especially as a child.

On my 13th Birthday my dad showed up at my doorstep drunk, in tears crying about how much he loved me. This was the 1st time I realized he couldn't help he was an alcoholic, I realized he was suffering and if he had the capacity to be a part of my life and present for me then he would. This made me feel so sorry for my dad, & I felt guilt anytime my heart wanted to judge him or be angry at him. I understood he was doing the best he could do.

When a child has to parent their parent or justify a parent's actions without fully being able to feel the capacity of their own emotions it breeds resentment and other unhealthy emotions and behaviors & it also breeds an adult who doesn't know how to own or understand their own emotional behavior and how it effects their child.

Just because you "understand why" your parents did something and you understand their painful upbringing, trauma, & past that caused them to not love you properly, mistreat, neglect you & be absent doesn't negate the pain their behavior caused & it doesn't mean you don't feel the hurt their behavior inflicted. This isn't about blame it's about fully acknowledging your truth & how their lack of parenting affected you so you can finally heal the truth of your wounds, not just the parts of your trauma you choose to acknowledge.

"I didn't ask if you understood why they treated you that way, I asked you "how does that make you feel"?

This is a phrase I often say to many of my clients to allow them to see that they can't even allow themselves to own the truth of how they actually feel without also attempting to protect and be respectful of their parents, even when their parents are nowhere around. Many of my clients say "it doesn't bother me anymore, I'm used to it, I understand, my parents loved me in other ways" but the truth is, if you had so much emotional clarity around your parental trauma it wouldn't be showing up & manifesting in your present reality. This is a sign, there's still emotional nurturing & healing that needs to be done.

Many clients finally come out and admit that they just don't want to disrespect their parents or be ungrateful. I often have to remind them that, being grateful and respectful to your parents doesn't mean dismissing and disempowering your own emotions. Bypassing, understanding, ignoring & repression will keep you in self sabotaging, emotionally painful, unhealthy relationships, thoughts & behavioral patterns.

True healing is felt, not intellectualized.

Understanding is not healing.

It's the minds attempt to analyze a situation as a coping mechanism to deflect from emotional pain. You can understand and simultaneously honor your pain at the same time. When you unconsciously rush to understanding to find emotional comfort you bypass the process of healing & the necessary spectrum of emotion that must be felt to truly heal. Give yourself permission acknowledge how you feel, without attempting to protect your parents in the process.

Instead begin to nurture the inner child and adult child that has been silenced and unable to express the truth of their experiences. Again, this is not about blame. Acknowledging the various ways you've been silenced in how you reclaim your voice and your power without fear. Your job now, is to reparent yourself, acknowledge your truth and be the person you needed when you were younger.

self- expression is your birthright.

Spend the rest of your life reclaiming the voice that was silenced.

MAKE ROOM

If your spirit is giving you a bad vibe about a person, LISTEN. Remove yourself. Even if you don't have real concrete proof why it's time to remove yourself. Everything within your being is designed to keep you safe which also means your vessel is designed to pick up on subtle energies that don't serve you, deserve to be in your space or are potentially harmful to you.

When your spirit nudges you, that is your proof.

When your spirit nudges you, require no more proof.

When your spirit nudges you practice abiding by your discernment and intuition.

When your spirit nudges you, honor yourself and listen.

It's an invitation Clean up your circles, clean up your friendship groups, clean up your text threads and to clean up who you allow to have access to you, family included.

If a person doesn't feel good to your spirit, why allow them to have access to you?

You embody your power when you reclaim sovereignty over who has permission to have access to you & who doesn't.

This is a spiritual boundary, it's not personal.

This is an energetic boundary, it's not personal.

This is an intuitive boundary, it's not personal.

This is a soul boundary, it's not personal.

Some people won't evolve to their next phase of healing and growth because they continue to entertain people that energetically interrupt their frequency, purpose and evolution. They are attempting to heal, grow & evolve but their friends depression keeps seeping into their aura, causing them to remain energetically and spiritually stagnant. This is also karma for not listening to spiritual guidance.

There are people who want to hear you, see you & love your properly. There are people who deserve to share space with you. There are people who have such pure energy that will cause you to grow from just being around them. Go where your spirit is guiding you.

You don't have to continue entertaining relationships with people you don't like, don't care for or that aren't conducive to your healing. Removing yourself does not make you a bad person.

I don't work this hard

to be around people I don't like

UNCOMMUNICATED EXPECTATIONS

Uncommunicated Expectations are premeditated resentments. Typically, uncommunicated expectations stem from a person who just wants to be loved.

Often when a person has a love wound, meaning they weren't loved properly in their childhood or at some point in their lives, they us a subtle method of control to receive that love from others. A person with a love wound uses expectations as their way to control the environment of the relationship to ensure they receive the love they desire. A subtle attempt at force if you will. Even though on the surface uncommunicated expectations can seem harmless but those expectations can quickly become a huge issue when the person placing them doesn't get what they want or what they feel they deserve. This also becomes a huge issue for the person being blindsided and held accountable as if they did something wrong because they didn't meet the expectations they never agreed to.

This is not to say expectations are a bad thing even though as you heal, grow and evolve subtle methods of control like this won't be necessary because you will allow people the freedom to show up the best they can or remove yourself from the equation without expecting anything from them. So, it's not that expectations are bad it's that the people wielding the expectations as if it's their sword of honor are using them in unhealthy and wounded ways that either force another person into submission or completely does the opposite of what they desire and pushes the person they want love from, away. There is a healthy way to do everything and there is a healthy way to communicate expectations. The issue is many people are not communicating their expectations, they are expecting those they love to be mind readers and to just know what they need, how and when to show up for them. What also makes uncommunicated expectations unhealthy is, if the expectation hasn't been communicated that means the person hasn't had an opportunity to agree to those expectations or terms.

It's imperative that we normalize asking if a person has the capacity or desire to participate in our expectations before, we dare hold them accountable for something they never asked to be a part of or agreed to. Yes, you get to set the standard of how a person is allowed to show up in your life, and that person is also allowed to decide if they want to meet, participate or entertain those standards you've set.

Uncommunicated expectations also become an issue typically when the person setting the expectation doesn't receive what they want or believe they deserve. Unconsciously they become triggered because they couldn't control a person into loving them the way they desire, so they hold the person accountable, become sad, angry, frustrated, hurt, disappointed or even resentful. Simply because their needs weren't met and their ego feels pain from the loss of control.

Now the question is "Why didn't they just ask for what they needed?

Why not ask a person if they have the capacity or desire to meet your expectations?

Why have silent expectations and become resentful when they aren't met"? Typically, this type of behavior happens when a person's love wound is really being triggered. Sometimes when a child doesn't receive the proper love, care and nurturing at a young age, when they grow up, they may still search for love, deeply crave it and desire it. Because love was never readily available to them they may not know how to use their words and ask for it. Many people will openly say they refuse to ask for help or they hate asking for help so imagine how vulnerable a person has to be to ask for the love they need.

If a person was raised in environments where love was scarce, sometimes to survive those people had to put on hard shells, armor or build walls, or tough skin to protect themselves to not be hurt, causing them to grow into adult that deeply crave love but not fully know how allow themselves to receive it.

When I have a client who has a tough time receiving love, I give them an assignment to begin practicing asking for it. This assignment is not to help them rely on neediness, it's designed to help them take their healthy power back and learn how to use their words to ask for what they need instead of expecting or forcing someone to just know what they need by reading their minds. The truth is everyone wants to be celebrated, wanted, loved, seen, heard or acknowledged. When a version of us needs or wants to be nurtured in this way there is nothing wrong with asking friends

"I just got a promotion could you all please come over and celebrate me with me?"

"I'm having a tough time being a mom could you come over to hold space with me and reassure me?"

"I feel the most connected to you when you respond to my texts the same day, is that something you have to capacity to do?"

When a person practices, using their words they also practice vulnerability. By asking for what they need the person will no longer have to result to unrealistic expectations because by them using their words the other person has an opportunity to decide and make an informed decision if they'd like to participate or not. Not too long ago I was communicating with an acquaintance who one day told me, she didn't want to be my friend anymore or being in communication. The energy is her text message felt aggressive and upset. She explained that the reason she wanted to end communication is because I don't answer my phone when she calls, I take too long to text back and at that stage of her life she requires people who intuitively knows what she needs.

I was so caught off guard because I'd expressed to her previously that, I don't talk on the phone often at all and anyone who knows me knows I'm not a huge talker at all. I rarely answer my phone and it gives me anxiety and makes me overwhelmed when people text me often. In my line of work as an intuitive emotional guide I'm required to talk people through their emotional trauma daily, so when I'm not working, I spend most of my time in silence not speaking. This is how I personally allow my soul to recharge. I honor not using words especially if it's not necessary. Words can feel very heavy to me.

So, I explained to her, I always respond to her, it may not be within the allotted time she prefers however it's when I have the capacity to share energy. Unlike many people I don't give what I don't have within me to give, I deeply honor myself and if my soul is asking for silence and to put away my phone I comply. I told her, these feel like expectations I never agreed to and expectations I didn't even know she was holding me to. I told her how unfair it was to be met with her energy of being frustrated, angry and hurt but I'm just now being invited into the conversation that I wasn't even aware she was having with herself for months. I wanted to make sure she knew my intention wasn't to hurt her or upset her, so I asked were her feelings hurt, and she replied yes, but that was a long time ago, I'm over it now. This is was an indication for me that she had subtle uncommunicated expectations all along, even while knowing my capacity to use the phone or not be readily available, yet she was still hurt for a while without even bringing it to my attention before she was so overwhelmed with frustration that she was ready to cut all ties.

I instantly knew this person just wanted love, to be seen heard & acknowledged. HOWEVER, because the energy of the expectations, conversation and her frustration felt so aggressive my body felt the need to protect itself. Now her chances of receiving the love she actually wanted & the love I would have been genuinely happy to give in other ways that didn't involve talking on the phone was no longer accessible to her because my armor was reminding me to protect my peace from any energy attempting to disturb the peace that I must cultivate to continue my healing journey and be a conduit for others in my work.

The takeaway is she wasn't wrong at all for knowing how she wanted a person to show up in her life and she definitely wasn't wrong for cutting ties with me because communication is something that she personally desired. The aspect of this situation that could have been handled better, healthier or differently is actually asking me if I had the capacity to participate in her expectations the way she needed, asking specifically for the type of love she needed by using her words, this way we could have had a verbal conversation about needs and expectations of the friendship without me being blindsided or her having to experience unnecessary hurt that could have been avoided.

No one deserves to have their choice taken away. If you truly love someone or would like to build a deeper connection with someone, tell them what you expectations are, how you expect to be loved and treated and then ask them if they have the capacity, want or desire to show up with you in those ways. Everyone is allowed to decide how they have the capacity to show up in relationships and they are allowed to say no when they don't have the capacity or aren't' willing to meet your expectations.

The biggest lesson I've had to learn in my healing journey was to use my words & ask for what I needed without expecting others to know what my needs are. So many unnecessary arguments begin by holding a person accountable & expecting them to do something for you that you never even asked for. When you communicate your needs in a healthy way, the outcome is more likely to be healthy and less emotionally painful. It may be very uncomfortable to express this type of vulnerability, but this is how you invite someone you love to love you properly.

WHO DO YOU BECOME WHEN CONTROL ISN'T AN OPTION?

Who do you become when a deeply uncomfortable or painful situation has surfaced & you can't control, force or figure a way out of it?

Who do you become when your soul is saying "the version of you that uses control to make yourself feel safe can't come into this new phase of your life, surrender must be your new best friend"?

Many people Rely on control because it's their most dependent survival skill, especially if they had no control during their childhood, couldn't speak their truth, do what they liked, were abandoned or neglected by parents, not loved or supported properly or had unstable, unsafe. chaotic environments. The only way some people can feel safe is to control what they never had control over in their childhood & for most adults that looks like controlling everything, people, relationships, situations, success & expectations to outcomes.

So, who do you become when control isn't an option?

When you can't force your way into feeling safe?

Does fear take over?

Do you lose faith in your spirituality?

Do you panic, worry, stress, stress eat, find numerous ways to escape, emotionally project, place blame & make everyone else the problem, become triggered & cause chaos around you, lose sight of who you are?

If your soul told you right now surrender and submit to faith, let go of control & just trust that everything will work-out without you doing anything, do you have the capacity to trust that life is designed with perfect alignment, or do you just speak about "divine alignment" because it's sounds cute to say?

Releasing control also means to release the spirit of worry.

Donna Stoneham once said "Worrying is praying for things you don't want". Sometimes when a person is in survival, attempting to control their environments to feel safe, the second they realize control is no longer an option, they cling to worry, stress and overthinking. Let go or be dragged. If your soul is asking you to surrender and let go, do it or your worry and stress will drag you deeper into suffering. This is an opportunity to not just try to control your way into safety, this is an opportunity to dissect which version of you doesn't feel safe. How old is this version of you and when do you fist remember feeling an emotion similar to this? Do your best to begin taking a look at your childhood, you'll be amazed at how many answers live there.

When a person doesn't have the capacity to surrender their body, nervous system & spirit will always be in a state of resistance, out of flow & an inevitable debilitating stress is bound to ride their coat tails. When you practice daily letting go & trusting no matter what comes your way, you'll always have the capacity to evolve with grace.

RUSHING TO DEATH

When a person attempts to rush past an uncomfortable emotion or situation because they think happiness & comfortability will feel better, they rob themselves of their own life experiences and miss opportunities to fully experience the totality of LIFE.

Society has trained and programmed people to strive for happiness & peace so much that they've trained people to literally hate moments of their life.

People even say "I wish i could just skip this part of my life" because they only want to participate in the beautiful happy moments, but they completely dismiss, disregard & hate painful or uncomfortable moments that have just as much purpose, meaning as happiness and joy.

Society doesn't teach us how to be in harmony with the totality of life because true peace lives there.

I say all of the time, if my soul has been tasked with being a part of the human experience. I want my full experience. I want my Monies worth lol I want everything that comes with it. I want every experience & emotion that my soul has designed particularly for me! I don't want to run from my life or myself just because it's uncomfortable at times. I don't want to short change my experience by attempting to rush towards happiness that doesn't even last long. Happiness is FLEETING. It comes in waves & leaves quicker than it came.

When a person attempts to rush past moments of their life because they've deemed them as uncomfortable, before you know it, it'll be their last day to live and they'll have to sit with the fact that they robbed themselves of their own life by searching for happiness that came & went instead of being in harmony with what was present.

Even in the midst of uncomfortable moments you can still choose to embody joy, peace and harmony. You don't have to stress yourself out attempting to skip parts of your life, work harder to get to the next phase to achieve an energy you can embody right now in the midst of whatever emotion/situation is present.

Stop robbing yourself of your own life experiences, every single moment has purpose.

Remember Who The F*ck You Are.

Dear me,

I know you are scared,

But you can handle this.

Love, me

Keep healing love

Keep going and be prepare to go alone.

If that person is meant for you

They will evolve

Meet and match your frequency.

Live your life,

Love will never require you to be stagnant.

PROPER APOLOGIES

People don't just want apologies they want acknowledgment of how they feel and acknowledgment of what was done to them. They want people to acknowledge how their behavior effected or hurt them. They want undeniable self -accountability and acknowledgement of why someone treated them that way.

Apologies and intentions are not priority when someone just wants and deserves honest accountability, acknowledgement and ultimately to be seen, heard and felt.

I don't know about yall but I can't stand a "that wasn't my intention" ass person or an

"I apologize if that made you feel away" person.

Those are not real apologies and they damn sure don't have an energy of self- accountability and acknowledgment of the effects of behavior. Apologies don't mend relationships. Pure egoless, selfless, eager accountability does. When a person chooses to acknowledge the part they played, why they did what they did, what they felt to make them mistreat someone and to go even further to acknowledge how harmful their behavior was, that type of acknowledgment goes a lot further than an "I'm sorry".

I personally don't allow people to give me half assed apologies, I will literally stop someone in their tracks mid apology & tell them "That is not a real apology". I do this to interrupt the program that allows them to think they can rest on frivolous words in exchange for real and true accountability.

A real apology has vulnerability and self- awareness attached to it, but mostly the person apologizing should name their actions, identify clearly what they did, why and acknowledge that they understand how it affected you. People have been allowed for so long to maintain unhealthy relationships with people by brushing their unhealthy & unacceptable behaviors under the rug. They move on like nothing happened or apologize their way out of spiteful and toxic treatment by using cute language like

REMEMBER WHO THE F*CK YOU ARE

"that wasn't my intention" to the point they don't even know how to show up real, true or authentic when it's time truly take self- accountability for how they treat people.

True self accountability reflects real spiritual integrity. If you've treated someone badly acknowledge your behavior properly. If It's not pure, self-accountability and deep acknowledgment it's just manipulation wrapped in societally acceptable language. If you truly have "good intentions", the way you apologize should reflect that energy. There will be times when a person will have to learn to accept an apology that they will never receive and become their own avenue for closure. There may be parents, who refuse to honor your boundaries or admit their treatment towards you or someone who may have sexually abused you when younger etc. people who don't ever plan to acknowledge their treatment towards you. Accepting an apology, you may never be given goes for those who are not attempting to actively hold space in your life in healthy ways. However, If someone is actively attempting to hold space in your life, be a companion of any sort, accountability better come with their presence. It's nonnegotiable. Healthy boundaries for them are imperative because they need healthy guidelines and rules on how to show up in your space in a healthy way.

If someone is actively wanting to hold space in your life there's no such thing as accepting the apology I may never receive lol nah Fam. True love is creating space for people to practice owning and taking self-accountability. If someone actively wants to mend things with you, there is absolutely nothing wrong with you requiring them to do it the right way or don't do it at all. This is a firm boundary that says "this is how I desire to be treated & I won't allow anything less".

How a person "has the capacity" to take self -accountability matters because it shows how they have the capacity to love, be honest, nurturing, compassionate, understanding & display empathy. It's also very Important to mention that It's not always personal when a person cannot take accountability. Some people literally feel actual pain in their body when held accountable. The body attempts to protect itself from the pain of shame, guilt, unworthiness etc. & their ego defends them and teaches them defense mechanisms to protect them from truly seeing themselves so they don't have to feel that pain, that maybe connected to emotional trauma. We will speak about this more in depth in later chapters. But this is in no way an excuse, just an explanation of what is happening in the brain and body as a person attempts to or is asked to take accountability.

The proper way to apologize to someone is to fully acknowledge how they feel and how your behavior affected them. This is an opportunity to practice selflessness and true compassion.

When a person doesn't love themselves,

they battle themselves vicariously through others.

No more allowing people who are at war with themselves destroy your energy.

EVERYTHING SOUNDS DEEP TO A PERSON THAT DOESN'T READ

Do your own research.

Become passionate about doing your own research.

Your soul is your book, reclaim your guidance.

I don't care who said it. Even and especially if I said it.

A person should always have so much sovereignty their own minds that before they allow any information to enter their spirits they first do their own research and then they consult with their souls to decide and discern if the information being presented resonates with their spirit or not. Be so intentional about protecting the sacredness of the mind, body and spirit that you don't just feed it anything or allow anything or anyone to have access to you or your subconscious being.

Society today is full of information. The average person consumes 460% more information today than they did 10years ago. The brain isn't equipped to consume this much information daily. This is why so many people feel anxiety, depression, internal conflict, or why they distract themselves which pleasurable things like food, sex, tv, drugs or alcohol because they are constantly overwhelmed and overstimulated with information.

As we heal, grow and evolve on our journeys it's important that we stay mindful and aware of what information we consume, what is conducive to our healing and evolution and what is detrimental to our evolution. When on the journey of self-growth, the quest for knowledge becomes addictive at times, this is a form of ego. It can consume someone who is excited to learn new things or desperate to learn new things. Although everyone will be required to go down their own rabbit whole of information at some point, they must maintain self-awareness to know what information can't be trusted and then to cross reference the information they feel they can trust with the guidance of their soul.

There are so many people who have the gift for gab, they have mastered the art of memory and regurgitating information, but it doesn't always mean that they are speaking from a place of wisdom or from an energy that is pure enough to aid in your soul' evolution. Some people just be talking to hear themselves talk. Their teachings come from a place of ego not with the intention to active your soul level memory so you can remember who you are. Many people say don't pay attention to the messenger pay attention to the message, well around here we pay attention to both lol. It matters the energy you receive a message in. It matters the intention behind the message because how its delivered is how it will be received in your mind, body and soul. If you don't vet where you receive your information from, not only could you possibly receive a message your soul doesn't need or want, you could also receive anxiety attached to a message, causing your body to be tasked with attempting to get rid of the useless or harmful information that isn't conducive to your healing journey.

It's important to nurture such a healthy relationship with your soul, spirit and intuition that they become your wise council. Like I said at the start of this book, at some point reading books won't even be necessary or the egos ways to subconsciously feel wise because you'll have such a beautiful relationship with your soul that you recognize you are the book of wisdom, teachings and lessons. The more intentional you become in your healing journey the more all of your lessons evolve into wisdom. Nothing outside of us is teaching us anything new, it's either giving us misinformation or it's helping us remember what we already know. When we have a deep, true and pure relationship with ourselves we can download information, run it through our soul's data base, take what we need and leave what we don't. We'll naturally know "this feels true to me". When you intentionally heal, grow and evolve your lessons begin to write your own books of wisdom.

Everything Sounds Deep to a

Person That Doesn't Read

When you intentionally heal, grow and evolve

your lessons begin to write

your own books of wisdom.

THE BODY KEEPS THE SCORE

As an intuitive guide my clients come to me for advice, guidance and leadership. They ultimately want to know can they be fixed. The issue becomes that everything in society has taught many people that they need things and healers outside of themselves to be fixed, healed or better. I always start a session by journeying deep into my client's psyche, to understand how much of their memory they have access to and if they use any mind-altering substances like marijuana, alcohol, shrooms, edibles or drugs to escape their reality. I then proceed to ask them if they've been diagnosed with any mental illnesses or illnesses in the body, including aches and pains. I follow up with questions about their food intake and if they have a healthy relationship with food, their body and their weight. Initially this sounds a bit invasive but if a person is attempting to journey into healing on all levels these are questions that need answers.

Trauma can be loosely defined as when a person experiences any situation that produces so much emotional stress that becomes so overwhelming to the brain or body that it doesn't know how to properly process that energy or emotion that it effects the persons physical and emotional development. When this happens the symptoms of stress manifest physically in the body. The brain goes into fight or flight and does it's best to design methods to keep the human safe and alive. Sometimes the brain instructs the person to cry, become fearful, to emotionally detach, become angry or even extremely emotional as a way to help the person release emotional debris. The brain will also attempt to provide coping and defense mechanisms whether healthy or not to help keep the person alive. These can look like the brain forming mental illnesses, unbalanced eating habits, hoarding, addiction, unstable emotions, creating phobias or unhealthy and unbalanced personality traits.

When taking on a client the reason it's imperative to ask important questions is to get a feel of if their trauma has manifested in their present reality, in their behaviors, emotional patterns and physical bodies. This information will be proof that trauma still lives in their bodies, needs immediate attention, nurturing and clearing. A clear sign that notifies me when trauma is present is based on behavioral patterns or coping mechanisms like addiction, emotional detachments etc A clear sign to tell if trauma is present in the body is if a client complains of lack of memory, aches and pains in the body or mental illnesses. These are clear signs the body has stored emotional trauma and these are the long lasting effects of that trauma. Trauma changes the brain and the functionality of the brain and nervous system and can keep the person in a constant state of fight or flight.

The term the body keeps score simply means that the body remembers. It remembers every single moment of trauma you've experienced, every time you were embarrassed, emotionally manipulated, emotionally shut down, abused, neglected, abandoned, molested, deathly afraid, didn't feel protected, loved, nurtured, wanted, or taken care of. The body is such an intelligent machine that It works overtime just to keep you alive, so in certain emotionally stressful moments the brain may have shut down your memory so you could continue to live. Or maybe your overwhelming emotional stress manifested in your liver, kidney or as lupus, PTSD or bipolar disorder as an attempt to help you cope emotionally in stressful environments.

The reason this information is so necessary to know and understand is, just because you don't remember the full details of your childhood trauma, being molested, abandoned, or feeling unloved and unwanted when you were younger doesn't mean that it isn't directly affecting you today and playing a part in why you are promiscuous, angry, addicted to mind altering substances or feel a constant state of anxiety. Especially if you're someone who has been diagnosed with some sort of disease, illness, cancer or struggle to have children, these are clear signs trauma has manifested in your body.

It's not enough to just take medication without also healing the root cause of the sickness. The mind, body and emotional body are directly connected. This means each ailment has an emotional root. Those who suffer from asthma may also have unresolved trauma of deep grief that hasn't been healed or cleared from the body. Those who have cancers like ovarian cancers or tumor may have been molested in the past or experienced some sort of sexual trauma that is now stored in the womb. Those who have addictions to alcohol or issues with their liver may have an underlying emotion of anger that has manifested in toxic behaviors and toxicity in the body. Those who have chronic back pain may feel unsupported and those who suffer from heart issues may have roots of not feeling loved.

As we evolve in our healing journey, we are required to become conscious on all levels not just emotionally, but metaphysically, understanding anatomy, science, quantum physics, energy and brain functionality etc It all matters because everything is connected. When we adopt the perspective that the body keeps the score, we also give ourselves permission to heal deeper, to find the root causes of our emotional stress and discover how it is manifesting in our present lives and ultimately hindering us from living a free, liberated life without emotional or physical pain.

Earlier in this book I spoke about my four year process of not being in a relationship and not having sex. Throughout that entire four year period I had excruciating back pain that I always blamed on my size g cup breast. I was convinced that my large breasts were the only reason for my back pain. As a police officer I also had to wear a duty belt with a gun attached to it that was heavy including a bullet proof vest that was even heavier and certainly weighing on my back. On the surface these things made sense and it seemed as if these were the reasons for my back pain, until one day I decided to get a deep tissue massage to try to relive some of my pain. As I laid out on the table the first thing I felt was how relaxed I was in comparison to how relaxed I wasn't. It was clear that this moment felt like an escape from stress which was extremely relieving. As my massage began, I recognized sensation all throughout my body. I could feel sensation in my fingers, toes, elbows, neck and face. It was such an odd feeling for me because it felt so good and uncomfortable at the same time. Almost like it felt too good and this was a foreign feeling, especially since I hadn't been touched in four years. Once the massage therapist began to massage my back where pain was present, I noticed a sensation that felt like I was crying. I was so confused because, why the hell was I crying is all I could think of. As she continued to massage my back, the deeper she went into my tissue the deeper I began to cry and release emotion. At this point I was in full tears and snot was pouring out of my nose. Still confused but the cries were so deep and intense I had to give myself permission to allow them release from my body. Depending on where she massaged my back was dependent upon how much emotion I would release. I even began to have strong my visions of my dad, almost as if she knew which points in my back to touch for an emotional release and emotional memory to surface.

As she continued the massage, my cries became more powerful, I'd see more visions of my dad and would begin crying even more. Deep sadness, anger and grief felt so present as I cried uncontrollably.

When the massage ended, once I gathered myself emotionally, I apologized to her for crying and explained I had no idea where that came from. She replied by telling me how normal it was for clients to experience emotional releases and not to worry. This baffled me. It was normal? How? As soon as she left my home I went right into research mode and discovered how the body uses over 80% of its energy just to store trauma as a protective mechanism. This made It clear that I stored all of my trauma in my upper back. It was deeper than my breast size and my police uniform equipment. It was emotional stress weighing on my body and manifesting as physical pain as an indication there were still areas of emotional trauma from my past that needed my immediate attention.

I had gone four years without physical touch, not just sex but physical touch in general. Four years without connection of any kind especially deep meaningful hugs. The visions I had during my massage were indicators that my "father wound" was the wound that was stored in my back and if you remember the story I told early on in this book I spoke about when my dad took me to a park when I was four years old, I was on a swing while he spoke with his friends and at some point I fell out of the swing right onto my back knocking the air out of me. This was the first time I learned I didn't feel safe, but now after my massage I realized that the trauma from that fall was stored in my back, the trauma from not feeling safe and the trauma from not feeling protected in that moment were all lodged in my upper back and anytime my back would ach this was a signal that four year old candyss was attempting to get my attention and tell me she didn't feel safe, protected or loved properly.

Now because I was able to make this correlation, I didn't focus on a breast reduction or blame my uniform equipment because I understood there was a deeper -rooted issue. Now when my back pain occurred, I could go to the source, which was my four year old inner child and ask her "Are you ok? What are you feeling? Is there anything I can do? Do you need anything from me? How can I show up for you right now? How can I nurture you when you feel this way?"

I learned that when my body expresses pain those are opportunities for me to connect deeper with myself, acknowledge emotions that are still attached to memories and give myself permission to feel. Many times, physical pain is our bodies attempting to get our attention to guide on where we need to nurture ourselves more and sometimes these pains are the body begging for help to transmute the emotions that are building up. Soon after I became more mindful of physical touch. I recognized that I didn't allow people to hug me, and if I did it was a quick, short side hug during our greeting, but I never allowed anyone to actually hug me. I'd let go of our embrace quickly because hugs felt invasive, and I didn't realize any of this until after my massage. This massage highlighted how closed off I was. Even though I had just spent four years in isolation and solitude I didn't consider myself as closed off until I recognized how distant I was from people. When I became aware of my distance I suddenly was aware of all of my friends who gave great hugs, tight meaningful ten second hugs that made me feel seen, heard, loved and acknowledged. This stood out to me so much that I didn't want the hugs to end but I also didn't know how to ask for love in this phase of my healing journey just yet. I didn't know how to maintain a hug for longer that a couple of seconds without feeling awkward, but I was very clear these hugs felt like magic in my body, they felt good and warm and honestly like medicine.

The body expresses

what the mind suppresses.

CAN I GET A HUG?

The Hug I'd Never Given Myself. (written 1/27/2019)

For whatever reason today I've felt the need to connect. To be nurtured, seen & felt. & just sitting home tonight I really felt like i needed/wanted a hug. This, was strange to me because I have never felt the solution to what i was feeling was a hug. But in this moment i craved a loving embrace but because I was alone at the time i resorted to self - sabotaging thoughts of escaping, wanting to eat, or admiring the altered reality i was in during my mushroom ceremony. All of these realities I'm very aware are only coping mechanisms and distractions from looking within.

Honestly, I just felt open, void & empty. Not sad, nothing bad or painful going on in my life, not depressed. For some reason this is the emotion i woke up with this morning. I sat on my couch wishing i had someone to give me what i needed, then something just said "Candyss give YOURSELF a hug". The thought of doing this was extremely awkward. So awkward I almost didn't do it. I felt so weird about it as if there were hundreds of people watching a judging me for hugging myself. I hate to say it but I felt crazy smh. However, what I was feeling inside outweighed the fear of giving myself affection.

So, I did it, I wrapped my arms around my body and I hugged myself. Instantly all fear, shame, awkward and weirdness went out of the window and & the second both of my arms wrapped around my body i instantly began to cry. I closed my eyes & held myself as tightly as i could. & just broke down. The protection, safety, nurturing, love, affection & attention i was wanting so badly from an outside source, I had just given to myself. Then it dawned on me that i had never hugged myself. I had never made myself feel safe, seen, loved or nurtured. I had never hugged myself, rubbed my own shoulder & told Myself everything was going to be ok & that I'm doing a great job, until now. I had never given this gift to myself, only to others.

I felt like i had just met myself & mended a lifelong estranged friendship. As if i was living with a person I'd only talk to at times, see in the mirror, give food, apply makeup & clothing, watch cry & go through things, heal & grow. But still So detached from this person. I felt as if i hugged my inner child. The deeply innocent naive child that had no idea how to navigate the pressure of being a human. When i hugged Myself i felt like i merged with my twin, like I finally acknowledged & spoke to myself for the first time. I cried like a baby, saliva falling from my lips followed by deep hurtful moans. I felt so at home, so full of joy & yet so sad that I've never been my own friend before. The thought of feeling awkward or weird for giving my own self a hug in a moment that i needed it made me shake my head in disappointment. How could I have abandoned myself so deeply, been so detached from ME that I thought twice about hugging the body, temple, vessel and divine package that works to heal me and keep me alive every second of every day.?

As i continued to hug myself & cry i laid in my own arms. I laid on my own shoulder & caressed my back. Then words just started coming out. I remember saying,

"WOW you're so beautiful & so smart, you're doing such a great job here."

It felt like my soul had been waiting for me to LOVE MYSELF, accept myself & ACKNOWLEDGE MY OWN DAMN SELF!! I believe this is the first time I've ever shown myself "Self-Love" without it being about an external idea, practice, thing to do or a plan to not do anything. I've always viewed self-love as taking time for myself, rest, crying releasing emotion, massages to get rid of stored emotions, changing my thoughts, speaking nicely to myself etc and all of these things are definitely components of self-love, but how the hell did I not actually give myself the word " SELF LOVE" smh duh Candyss lol

This is the first time i had given myself exactly what i needed, A hug & embrace. I feel like I just met a completely new part of me. As I write this I continue to cry & each time I cry I put the phone down from writing & hug myself again. I've just told myself.

"Thank you for being here for me".

Have you ever hugged yourself tightly, took A deep breath & just relaxed into your own arms? Smh It's life changing to know that i can feel safe in my own arms. That i should feel safe in my own arms. That i deserve to feel safe in my own arms & that (I AM SAFE) in my own damn arms.

I AM safe with myself. I AM SAFE!!

It's the first time i truly felt that i wasn't alone. That I am my own friend, protector & soul mate. How far could i have possibly grown without a true deep connection to myself, afraid to hug myself or speak to myself in a nurturing voice out loud? I feel as if i just unlocked a deeper part of myself i haven't even been aware of. Like the source of me struggling to move into my next phase of growth is because not only was I not my own friend, I didn't love myself. This was the first time i felt like i wasn't battling & fighting myself. I understood why I had an alcohol addiction, I understood why I wanted to escape this reality so much, why my relationship with food is so unbalanced, I was using these external sources to give myself security, comfort, love & to self soothe, instead of turning inward. There was power in my newfound connection with self. Tonight, a bond was created that I'm overly excited & Eager to cultivate. I'm sooooo grateful the Universe gave me this life changing gift tonight. The gift was my first steps to learning how to truly love, like & cultivate a relationship with myself.

Every day I grow closer & closer to myself. My Life is Beautiful

<u>The Science Behind Hugs</u>

When we hug someone the brain releases chemicals called dopamine and oxytocin. Dopamine is known as the "Happy hormone". Dopamine is typically released during a kiss and is the same area of the brain that is activated by heroin and cocaine sending the feeling of euphoria or addictive behavior. Oxytocin is known as the "Cuddle Hormone" that is released when a person is touched or kissed. Although these two hormones are released when a hug is formed, I don't mean a 1 second awkward greeting type of hug. Studies show that to get the maximum benefit, a hug should last for 20 seconds. An intentional hug, not only helps us release dopamine and oxytocin but the help

1. Reduce Stress

2. Boost Heart Health

3. Protects against illness

4. Makes you happier

5. Reduce fear

6. Reduce pain

7. Easier to express a variety of emotions

"We need 4 hugs a day for survival. We need 8 hugs a day for maintenance. We need 12 hugs a day for growth."

—Virginia Satir, family therapist

American psychologist Harry Harlow Conducted a study called "Contact Comfort" Where his study showed that infants need physical touch, embrace from their mothers are just as equally important as food and without physical touch the infant has a higher probability of dying.

<u>Physical touch is a requirement for human beings.</u>

Maslows Heirchy of needs research shows that for a person who survive, their psychological needs of intimacy, belonging and love have to be met.

So, what happens when you hug yourself?

You begin the process of creating a fundamental relationship with yourself, almost like a mother holding her baby for the first time initiating that necessary bond. The second you hug yourself you rewire your brain to begin a trusting relationship with yourself, you being to feel safe within your own arms, to know that you are taken care of. You take your power back from solely depending on an outside source to give you comforting by reminding and teaching your brain that you are already comforted. The exact same hormones that are released in the brain while hugging another person are even released when you hug yourself. All it takes is 20 seconds for a hug to do it's magic.

Anytime you recall an emotional pain or trauma without the intention to heal and nurture it,

you re-traumatize yourself and your nervous system.

PRAY INTO THE BODY

The body is the subconscious mind, the portal to heaven and the living manifestation of God.

So often we pray to and for things outside out us, forgetting that prayer is nourishment to the soul not just language to beg and ask for things. Prayer is our superpower. It allows us to create realities within us and outside of us with intention. When we pray into our bodies, we create an environment that is nurtured and nourished with our own divine magic. Praying into our bodies is how we send love notes to our internal world, our heart, liver, kidneys and all organs. Internal prayer softens the fascial connective tissue that runs through our bodies like an electrical system. Internal prayer reminds the body that it has purpose, that it is loved, safe and honored.

Healing requires us to have a deep relationship with our bodies. Many yogis teach the philosophy of detaching from the body, but I believe there are moments to detach from many things and moments to deeply honor things. The body is our vehicle that allows us to carry out our soul's divine mission, to fulfill our souls purpose and journey within our human experience. It's not necessary to identify as a human but acknowledging the body and the miracle that it is, can serve as a daily reminder to practice gratitude for our opportunity to experience life. Internal prayer is how we practice self-love on the deepest levels and how we connect with the aspects of our being we forget about daily. My first time praying into my body I cried deeply because I was now aware of all of the parts of my being that I was painfully unaware of, neglected and disempowered. I heard body parts cry out for acknowledgment, yearn to be seen, touched, apologized to and honored.

When I began to pray into my body, I was able to see my own self neglect and abandonment. I then was able to see that any fear I ever had of being abandoned was solely me projecting because of the many ways I'd already abandoned myself, daily. My internal prayer practice healed my relationship with self and helped me form a healthy dialogue that allows me to pour into the areas of my being that need to be seen, heard, loved, acknowledged, nurtured and nourished.

My Internal Prayer

(use this if you need or create your own)

Thank you.

I see me, I acknowledge me and I am grateful for me.

Is there any part of me that wishes to be acknowledged?

Breath, thank you. Thank you for choosing to breathe life into me even when I am deeply confused about how to show up in this life.

Ankles, feet, knees and legs. Thank you. Every single day you make sure I keep going. Not only do you take me from place to place you remind me to intentionally only take one step at a time. You send me small reminders to take my time and give myself permission not to rush.

Heart, Thank you. Even when I was the reason for your pain you never gave up on me. The fact that you continue to show up for me even when I'm unconscious of your continual beating, you remind me that I am worthy, and I do have deep purpose.

Forearms and hands. Thank you. Many times, I disregard how much work you put in for me daily. I don't acknowledge the pain that you feel when I refuse to let things go. I apologize for how my lack of awareness and my choices to hold on to things that no longer serves me affects you. Thank you for still choosing to intentionally show up for me.

My Tongue, Thank you. You give me the opportunity to enjoy and explore sensation. You add value to my life experience and thank you for that.

Womb. Thank you and I'm so sorry. I've put you through a lot, I've allowed people to have access to you that were undeserving. I apologize for the times I used for sex as an exchange for love. You never deserved that. Thank you for loving me through my pain and for still loving as I make our relationship right.

Soul. I admire you so much. You are the epitome of perfection and everything I do is to make you proud and to honor you. I respect you. I respect how far you've traveled, how many lifetimes you've chosen to experience to continue your journey of evolution. Thank you for your guidance even when I didn't have the ears to listen nor the maturity to follow your lead. Thank you for not giving up on me.

Only you know what your internal prayer should sound and feel like. Only you know the words that you need to hear. Right now, put this book down and go inward. Honor yourself right now and pray into your body.

When we start to honor the wisdom of the body,

We open the channels that lead us to Source.

IF YOU'RE NOT EATING RIGHT, YOU'RE NOT THINKING RIGHT

So much emotional pain, tension or stress can be cured with a healthy diet and a healthy digestive system. When emotional pain is present or a person feels lost in life with no ambition, no connection to themselves and no passion for life, we must first dissect what this person is eating, drinking and consuming energetically. Food isn't just for enjoyment or feeling satiated, its information to the body, cells and DNA. The food a person eats sends information to their body. Foods can be categorized as living foods of dead foods. High vibrational foods or low vibrational foods. The food a person eats is either sending healing and rejuvenation to the body or depletion and decay. The average person can find out what types of food they should be eating based on their blood type. This will tell them if they should be eating meat, a plant- based diet and what foods they specifically need for the best functionality of the body.

When speaking in terms of emotional healing, we must be so mindful and conscious of the food we eat because our food has a direct impact on our emotional well-being, our thoughts, how we perceive situations, how we receive and give love, our mental health as well as our energy, aura and energetic field. Our food directly impacts the frequency we emit from our bodies ultimately determining the types of people, love, relationships, situations and opportunities we attract. When I speak to my clients and they tell me they're sad, depressed, always anxious, confused about life and have no drive I instantly know there's a possibility that their food plays a part in their low vibrational energy. The gut is considered the bodies first brain. It is the link between a person's emotional body health, mood, physical health and how they think. The average person can hold up to 8-25 pounds of poop in their colon, also causing a disruption in a person's emotional health, mood, body health and how they think. When a person isn't eating the foods that best benefit their bodies their internal systems that are directly correlated with emotions, thought and brain functions become effected. Many people complain of sadness or anxiety and what they may be experiencing are symptoms of the chaos that's happening in their internal world. If the body is struggling to process and digest food or poop then it seems fair that a person's emotional health would reflect the dysfunction that is happening within them.

Animal Based Foods

I'd like to start by saying, I by no means am attempting to convince anyone to be vegan, However I do believe that a choice can only be a conscious choice if all facts are revealed and you still choose that option for yourself. If there's information that hasn't been presented and that you are not aware of sometimes a choice can be based on ignorance and a lack of information. This is typically what happens with people who consume animal-based products and meats. We've all grown up in a society that doesn't tell us anything about where our food comes from, we just know its steak, chicken, beef, milk or eggs. Society has never really shown us visuals of where our foods come from because they know if that happens many other things will be exposed that expose the unhealthy, immoral and unethical methods they go about supplying these animals-based products.

Specifically, but not limited to animals like cows, pigs, chickens many companies mass produce these animals. They are artificially inseminated, pumped with chemicals and hormones to make them grow bigger and faster. They are hoarded in unsanitary places and most if not, all have some sort of wound, disease or cancer physically visible on their bodies. These animals go without care, nurturing or nourishment. Many have pockets of pus and blood oozing from their bodies. Instead of caring for these animals, the slaughter houses typically just cut the wound off of the animals, which leaves a huge problem. The physical wound may have been cut off of the flesh, but the cancer still lives in the animal's body. Even all milk has a regulated percentage of pus that is allowed to be in the milk and approved by the FDA.

The Animals Emotional Wellbeing

In our society we also aren't taught to care for the emotional wellbeing of animals but for any person who is intentional about their healing journey at some point will have to acknowledge that spirituality also plays a huge part of the healing journey which requires compassion for all living things, as all living beings are a reflection of God. However, our society just teaches us to only care for animals we can possess, specifically dogs or cats. No other animals are typically held to the standard of house pets but there is a deep sense of possession an ownership over all animals which also dismisses and disregards the animal's personal freedom, spiritual intelligence and brain function intelligence.

Studies show that cows and pigs are just as intelligent as dogs. It has been proven that most animals have the capacity to display emotion, the same types of emotions as humans. They can feel sadness, anxiety, depression, fear, despair, pain, abandonment, anger, confusion and much more. Cows have been documented crying, literally shedding tears when they feel certain emotions. Pigs are so intelligent they have the ability to play catch just as a dog would. The emotional awareness of an animal that you typically eat is important because you should be mindful that when you consume animals you aren't just consuming their flesh, but you are also consuming their emotional wellbeing.

This poses the question well, what is the animals well-being and emotional state before being slaughtered and packaged as food? Because the slaughterhouses are so immorally run, animals have no personal living room. They are on top of on another day in and day out, stuck in the same positions and living in their own urine and fecal matter. The conditions cause animals to develop psychosis, become volatile, anxious and to kill and harm other animals near them. The animals begin to feel sadness, depression, anxiety and fear. Many of the workers in these facilities are cruel to the animals. They beat them, kick them, stomp them to death, hit them with poles amongst many other heinous things. Other animals see this treatment, they hear the animals near them being beaten and they feel fear just as humans do.

Typically, when it's time for an animal such as a cow to be slaughtered the cows cry out in despair and feel full fledge fear causing their bodies to tense up. As the cow is being killed all of the fear, anxiety, depression and confusion the cow feels becomes so overwhelming that the cow begins to release hormones into its body causing the muscles and tissue to tense up and constrict. This is typically what people call tender. They say things like "my steak was tender" not realizing their steak wasn't tender, it was fear, anxiety and depression. This is where the issue comes into play because A person is not just eating a steak, chicken, eggs or drinking milk they are eating cancer, disease, fear, anxiety, despair, anger, pus and mental illness, yet the average person can't understand why they are riddled with depression and anxiety. For many people their depression, sadness and anxiety isn't even theirs, it's the animals they eat on a daily basis. For more understanding on the topic of how animals are treated in these situations you can refer to a documentary called "Earthlings". It is very graphic, it is very true, and it is emotionally difficult to watch, however it will provide much awareness and may even prompt you to make healthier choices.

When a person consumes animals not only does the body and the digestive system have to figure out how to digest and process this foreign animal or being it also is forced to figure out how to digest and process that animal's emotions as well. The body isn't equipped with coding that is capable of digesting, processing or transmuting another animal's emotional state causing many peoples emotional dysfunction to stem from foreign entities in their bodies. They are taking medication for anxiety and depression but they're still consuming it in their food on a daily bases. This is how easy it is to genuinely want to thrive on your emotional healing journey but takes huge steps back and interfere with your progress because of lack of knowledge.

This is partially why prayer over food exists. Indigenous people who ate animals were clear that they were sacred beings that had emotions, governments, systems and souls. They'd kill the animal and immediately afterward they have a moment of gratitude for the animal. The indigenous people would thank the animal for being a source of food and pray that the animal would be nourishment to their bodies. This prayer was an attempt to transmute the emotional and cellular information within the animal so that information would be healthy information downloaded into the cells and DNA of the consumer. Another difference in these times were how the animals were raised, respected and treated. They lived in their native natural habitats that were conducive to healthy emotional regulation and they also weren't pumped with artificial chemicals and growth hormones. So, the prayer indigenous people did over their food truly had to the power to transmute energy.

Dr. Masaru Emoto & The Hidden Messages of Water

In the 1990's Japanese Researcher Dr. Masaur Emoto would label petri dishes of water with positive or negative words or emotions. Some dishes he'd label "Love" and other dishes he'd label "Hate". Emoto proved that when water was labeled with positive intentions and then frozen, they'd reflect sacred geometry. The labels with negativity were unsymmetrical and blurry. This proves that thoughts and emotions can change the molecular structure of water. This proves that water holds memory. This is important because our bodies are 60-70% water. This is just a little more clarity on why the intelligent indigenous people understood they had to pray over their food so whatever emotions were within the animals would be transmuted before the human consumed it.

While we are speaking about water, it's very important you also pray over your water and set intentions for your water. Acknowledge the source of that water and what it may have had to endure to make its way to you. Water holds memory. This is why Indian cultures do not drink water as soon as they fetch it from a well. They allow water to sit for a certain amount of time before consuming it because they're clear that water holds memory. For those of us in the USA our water is sources through machinery, tanks, drills and large manufacturing companies which means before our water arrives to us in stores is has to endure much instability and chaos. It is very important that we are mindful of this, or just like animals we could also be consuming the energy of the water. Prayer, intention and charging our water are beautiful practices to change it molecular structure before consuming it.

Living Foods?

If you never give yourself permission to unlearn the things you've be taught and things you deem as normal, you'll never be able to create new paradigms for yourself or explore what else can work for you that is conducive to your healing journey and not sabotaging it.

Living foods should always be 80% of a person eating regimen that is on their emotional healing journey. Not to shame anyone about eating meat, but to remind those that if you want to heal then you must send the messages to your body and use the foods that reflect healing, life, vitality and rejuvenation. Fresh fruits are a beautiful way to create a healthy environment in the body. All things have their own vibration, frequency and energetic resonance. Plants have their own sound and energetic frequency. People have their own energetic frequencies. The earth has its own energetic frequency and so does our food. Obviously dead foods like animal products have a low vibrational frequency while fruits and vegetables have a high vibrational frequency meaning that these foods are more in alignment with what the body, mind and soul need to live, function and thrive properly.

When you give yourself permission to explore clean foods like fruits and veggies, make fresh fruit and veggie juices daily, you'll get the see the benefits of adding high value frequencies into your body. Fruits have so many enzymes that are perfect for clearing emotional debris, brain fog and unnecessary emotional distress. I'ts important to become mindful of what foods make you feel the best vs. which foods make you feel lethargic. What foods make you feel weightless vs. what foods make you feel heavy. What foods give your energy vs. which food gives you the "Itis". Many people love to laugh about having the "itits" during holidays like thanksgiving.

This means the food was good and they ate so much they got sleepy. But what they don't know is the body doesn't agree with that sentiment at all. What's happening is the body has become so overwhelmed with attempting to process food, break down the food, process the emotions attached to the food that it needs extra energy to do so much work, so the body forces the person to pass out and become temporarily unconscious so it can utilize more energy to process the food. The issue is people think they just took a nap, went to sleep or got some rest. Their lack of awareness is so dangerous that they don't understand their body was so overwhelmed it forced them to go unconscious just because it needed more energy to function. This is how subtleties of our regular "normal" day life becomes a disservice to our healing journeys, the lack of self-awareness directly impacts our emotional, physical, mental and spiritual health. Healing requires us to be mindful, aware and conscious on all levels, even the levels that require us to unlearn and relearn. With more awareness we can make healthier decisions from a place of wisdom and no longer a place of ignorance.

Let's change the way we eat,

Let's change the way we live,

Let's change the way we treat eachother

Tupac Shakur

Warriors in Training

It's ok if you're exhausted.

It's ok if trying to be the best version of yourself is taking everything you must give.

True warriors that embody the power of the universe don't just show up to mindlessly fight, they feel the grief that comes with having to fight their opponent.

As most of us evolve the grief we truly feel is the outcome of battling ourselves. We feel grief from battling the parts of ourselves that self-sabotage, feel unworthy, are not ready to do what it takes to evolve or the parts of ourselves that is doing all of the necessary things to evolve but are exhausted by the lifelong process of healing. & all are ok.

Maybe today is the day your warrior spirit doesn't show up to fight these versions of yourself but to bow to those versions of yourself that are deeply struggling. Maybe today is the day your warrior spirit says

"I see you, i know what you're experiencing is hard, I'm here & i hold space for you as you experience the natural growing pains of evolving".

You build spiritual stamina in the moments your soul feels heavy but you keep moving forward one moment at a time, one minute at a time. Fuck a day at a time let's just give ourselves grace for right now. Stay here. Stay in your now. Stay in your present. Show up for yourself right now.

THE FUNKY AURA

"**A** plane can't land until the coast is clear. Some of your blessings and the things you are attempting to manifest are stuck in the air because your internal world, spiritual and emotional body is not clear. There's too much mess on the landing strip.

The healthier and the more-clear the mind, body, soul and nervous system are the easier it becomes to manifest what you want in this reality. When you are clear on all channels not only can you manifest what you desire but you'll also have the capacity to receive it and maintain it without sabotaging it.

Our aura is the natural energy we exude from our body. It reflects how we feel about ourselves, our lives, relationships, parents, work and even how food makes us feel. Our aura is what a person sees when they look at us. For example, I know when a person says I'm glowing they believe they are speaking about my skin but I know they're seeing my aura because it's a reflection of how great I feel at that time in my life. This is when people say" There's something different about you but I can't put my finger on it, did you change your hair?" These are clear signs that your aura is very powerful. The more in harmony you are with life, the happier or at peace you are with all things in life the more your aura reflects that. This is why people know how you feel about yourself before you even open your mouth. Everyone can see auras but most just aren't aware that is what they are seeing. When you actively move through emotional pain, trauma, limiting beliefs, fears and anger your aura begins to shine brighter. The more a person holds on to those same limitations the more they dim their own auric light.

A person's energetic field has many different layers. The physical auric body, Etheric or Astral body, Emotional body, Mental body, Spirit body and Universal awareness body. It is a reflection of the persons frequency, emotional health, physical health, spiritual health, psychological health and energetic health. The energetic field can also stem from the heart, many people have such a weak energetic field because they've suffered so many heart breaks by the hands of themselves and others and have yet to do the healing work to clear the energetic pain/stress of the heart. The energetic field extends to at minimum a foot beyond our physical bodies. It's like our personal data bank that sends messages out into the universe and other people. It sends messages to other people, communicates and depending on how healthy our energetic field is, it decides what you have the capacity to allow into your energetic field or what you have to repel and turn away.

Good things come to those who feel at home in their bodies.

This is where the issue with manifesting and attracting comes into play. The energetic field will only allow in what you have the capacity to receive, better yet, what you've done the work to receive. Many people swear up and down they want to experience blissful love, but they still hold grudges against their ex-partners, they're still angry about how they were treated in their past relationships and their hearts have never fully mended from those emotional pains. These unhealed experiences weaken & dim the aura and these experiences are also encoded into the energetic field. What happens is you meet a person, you smile, you look nice, have great conversation, yet that person never shows interest or calls you back. This is because your words are saying you want love, but the messages that are encoded in your energetic field are saying you are deeply afraid of love and you sabotage any resemblance of love once you receive it. The unresolved emotional traumas from your past that are encoded in your energetic field are now sending danger signs and red flags to potential partners. Have you ever been in contact with someone who looks the part yet you say "I have a bad feeling about that person?" This is because our energetic field is also an extension of our intuition and everyone has it, so essentially everyone's body is doing it's best to decipher if the person in front of them is a safe place. Remember the bodies only job is to keep us alive, so it works overtime to read auras and dissect energetic fields to keep it's person safe. When you have so many unresolved emotional, spiritual, psychological and mental wounds other people's energetic fields repel yours. They send signals to that person to run, have no interest, don't return phone calls because something feels off. That person may have not called you back because unconsciously they picked up on your daddy issues, abandonment fears, and sexual trauma in your energetic field. This isn't a sign that you're damaged and incapable of being loved, this is just an indication that there are areas within your being that still need nurturing so you can finally receive it.

When a person has unresolved aspects of their lives it directly impacts their ability to receive the opportunities, blessings, love, money and life they desire and want. The blessings they wish to receive have no place or space to land because the person is too clogged with hatred, unhealthy toxic foods, unresolved emotional trauma, grudges, resentments, fears, working hard as a trauma response, feeling overwhelmed, unworthy, undeserving and insecure. If a person feels all of these things plus more where does a blessing have space to land within that person. The follow up question is, how can a blessing land in an environment that is not conducive to its growth? So now all of that person's blessings are just held hostage outside of their energetic field, waiting for them to heal, grow, evolve and make room for the things they want so deeply. You must make room for the blessings you want. You must prepare yourself for what you desire and you must heal for what you attempt to manifest. Create an environment within your being that is so healthy, that anything that lands within your energetic field flourishes as if your aura has become the sun. When you feel good, empowered, at peace and in harmony with the totality of your being, that energy exudes from your heart into your aura into your energetic field. Begin doing whatever it takes to decode and re-code your energetic field, so it reflects the version of you that is healing, growing and evolving intentionally.

May your aura be

Warm, soft and peaceful

You May Be The Problem

" If you list all of your ex's in a row you can make a flow chart of your own mental illness".

This quote is so intrusively beautiful because it forces a person to instantly take self-accountability for not one but all of the relationships they've allowed themselves to be a part of. This quote holds a mirror to those who find solace in placing blame after their failed relationships and even become addicted to seeking validation from those they vent to. When a person chooses to make a career out of complaining about their ex, they do themselves a disservice by not giving themselves an opportunity to take accountability for their repetitive relationship choices that ultimately lead to their relationships ending in unhealthy ways and bringing out the worse in them.

When a person continues to enter, attract or entertain relationships that are unhealthy relationships this may be the universe nudging them to begin reflecting and taking accountability for the energy they're emitting into the universe.

"Bash My Ex" Syndrome

Often when a person ends a relationship they tend to go on a "bash their ex" spree. They find comfort in blaming the other person for their bad behavior or mistreatment while failing to acknowledge they were a willing participant. When relationships end some people are in so much pain, the feel so emotionally raw & triggered, instead of seeking a healthy solution like therapy or identifying to the source of the problem which is themselves, they rest on blaming the other person to distract themselves from doing their own healing work. Crafting mental narratives and stories about all of the things their ex did wrong gives them an opportunity to have a self-inflicted pity party, another opportunity to seek love through their victim mentality that offers an opportunity to run from acknowledging their own wounds, traumas and voids that lead them to that relationship.

When a person displays the "bash their ex" syndrome, it doesn't' mean they are a bad person, it could be a sign of emotional immaturity, low emotional intelligence but mostly just an attempt to feel better. Sometimes at the end of relationships so much emotional residue surfaces, so much emotional pain, anger and unsaid words begin to rear their heads. When these emotions become so uncomfortable the brain finds ways to help the human find comfort to keep the human safe. Remember the bodies only job is to keep A person alive. So, the brain looks for opportunities, conversations and anyone who will listen so the person can finally vent and release some of that emotional pent-up energy.

Most times people bash their exs and become addicted to telling unhealthy stories because they aren't emotionally or spiritually mature enough to know how to nurture their emotions in a healthy way, so the only way they can get rid of this emotional energy temporally is to vent. Some people even take on the vengeful ex approach, they may want others to dislike their ex just as much as they do, not because they are a bad people but on an unconscious level, they just don't want to be in pain, alone. They don't want to experience those chaotic, turbulent and explosive energies alone so they recruit friends, family or anyone who will listen and tell their ex bashing stories, so they'll have someone who is mad, angry or hurt, with them. It's an unconscious tactic to not have to deal with their breakup alone and feel painful emotions alone.

Unhealthy relationships are a huge part of the healing journey. Most will find that unhealthy relationships were the conduit and catalyst to their spiritual awakening. We must not stop at only acknowledging unhealthy relationships, you must create a flow chart of your ex's, their behaviors, similarities, as well as your own so you can identify what wounds led you to them to ultimately be nurtured. When an emotionally painful relationship ends, you take your power back by focusing on the real topic at hand, which is your lessons and what you were meant to take away from that situation.

<u>What Wound Allowed You to Look Past Red Flags</u>

Typically, when a relationship ends both partners are very clear on what they believe the other person's shortcomings are. They become great at dissecting what the other person should work on, and heal but when it comes to themselves, they are oblivious to the fact that their own woundedness is what landed them in this unhealthy relationship to begin with.

During my sessions with my clients, I always give them opportunities to vent about their past relationships if they need to. Sometimes just being able to speak their truth is an avenue to healing but I'd do them a disservice if I didn't also ask

"Why are you so clear on what the other person's traumas are but unclear of the trauma that allowed you to enter such an unhealthy relationship to begin with?

What wounds do you have that convinced you to look past red flags?

Why didn't you love yourself enough to leave, sooner?

Why did you allow yourself to be a part of a relationship that was so unhealthy?

What part of you felt so undeserving that you allowed yourself to accept crumbs masked as love?

I always give my clients an opportunity to rewrite the narratives they've been replaying in their minds because it invites them to take their power back by acknowledging that things were not just done to them, they played a part in those moments. People are able to take their power back when they choose accountability.

<u>Gifts Wrapped in Pain</u>

When I was younger, I dated someone with narcissistic behaviors and when that relationship ended, I screamed from the rooftop how narcissistic that person was. I told people how they treated me, things they said, how controlling they were, how jealous, manipulative and how much of a cheater they were. However, what I didn't do was tell the parts that I did. I never admitted, I stayed in that relationship for a little over a year and willfully participated in the madness. I never admitted to the many times I forgave that person, because I didn't love myself. How many times I forgave that person for cheating because I was deeply insecure about my body. And I damn sure never acknowledged that I only stayed in that relationship after being cheated on to make the girl they cheated on me with believe we were happy and in love. Ultimately, I stayed because I didn't love myself enough to believe that I deserved better. It wasn't until maybe a year after finally leaving this relationship that I realized that person caused so much emotional pain that it was the perfect conduit to my emotional healing journey. I was in so much pain I had to seek ways to help myself feel better. I learned about real spirituality, the law of attraction, energy, frequencies and meditation. As I continued to heal, grow and evolve I recognized my ex gave me a huge gift, Pain.

Once I gave myself permission to unwrap the immense pain, I realized that the gift of growth and soul level evolution was inside of that pain. I realized that I may have never come to that exact phase of my healing journey had my ex not caused so much pain. Suddenly anger and resentment began to subside and all I could feel was gratitude and exactment. I was grateful for my ex because I could see that their soul was in divine alignment with my soul and caused just enough emotional discomfort for me to being my soul ascension. I was excited because I had just unlocked a new version of my being. My entire life was about to begin with this newfound spiritual and emotional healing information I was learning. I became passionate about healing and vowed to never bash my ex's again. I honored them as soul beings, and as divine teachers. I no longer chose to see them as humans, that was baby consciousness. When I recognized their souls were answering to my souls call for deeper evolution I could only thank my ex's and acknowledge them as the angels they were. Now don't get me wrong, I ain't call them and tell them thank you lol although there would not have been anything wrong with that, but I chose to internally send a message to their soul and acknowledged the part they played in my healing journey. I thanked them for being a divine teacher and for my gift wrapped in pain.

Blame Robs You of Opportunities to Heal

When a person chooses to rest of placing blame & pointing fingers, they rob themselves of their opportunity to heal, grow and evolve. They rob themselves of their own divine lessons that are in the midst of their pain. They rob themselves of seeing their ex-partners as a conduit to help them heal deeper wounds. Remember,

you don't blame a clown for being a clown, you ask yourself why do you keep going to the circus?

Healing can only happen when we intentionally choose self-accountability and become passionate about seeing more of ourselves and exploring the depths of our own psyche, emotional wounds and unhealed traumas. Obviously, there are many instances where the person you've dated was wrong, did abused or manipulate you. You deserve to feel your full spectrum of emotions and simultaneously remember all roads will always lead you, back to you. Even if they were wrong & deeply hurt you, you can't help what a person has done to you, but your healing is still your responsibility. You must love yourself enough to Keep healing & never stop taking your power back.

Soul Level Healing Is the Cake, Love is the Icing

After so many painful relationships I recognized that these relationships were not failures. They were all deeply successful because I gave myself permission to receive my lessons that were attached to the pain. I gave myself permission to let go of the anger I had towards the human and chose to adhere to the divine message that relationships are not about bringing me happiness, joy, peace, love, kids & family. Many times, it's quite the opposite. Relationships are only here to help us heal, grow & evolve. They are designed for souls to connect and give one another the exact medicine needed for soul evolution. Sometimes that's love, peace and joy. Other times it's a soul that holds a mirror to your face that is so clear it triggers, every childhood trauma of not being loved, seen, heard, acknowledged, wanted, abandoned, neglected and abused.

Sometimes relationships are only meant to show you what emotional wounds you have that still need your attention and nurturing. The lovey dovey stuff is just icing on the cake. If someone gifts you with pain, please love yourself enough to unwrap it because your lessons are waiting for you inside.

Healing also means
taking accountability for the role
you play in your own suffering.

FORGIVE YOURSELF FOR NEEDING HARD LESSONS

Y ou can show yourself compassion and still hold yourself
accountable.

As you heal, grow and evolve never forget that you can choose
how you'd like to receive your lessons.

You can choose to receive your lessons from a place of
love or from a place of pain.

You deserve grace

Wherever You Go, There You Are.

I just need a fresh start.

Once I lose 30 pounds I'll be confident.

Once I get this new job I'll make more money and I'll be able to enjoy my life.

Once I start traveling I'll feel happiness and freedom.

Once I get married, I'll always feel loved.

When I have my baby I'll never have to feel alone again.

I'm moving to Hawaii to start over, I just need a new environment.

March 1, 2020 My favorite cousin Jarret, was killed and I was devastated. I truly didn't know how my body would still living. The pain that I felt was so paralyzing the thought of what had happened to him made me feel as if I was going to vomit but as each week went by grief became less volatile and easier to navigate and feel. June on 2020 I began renovating my cargo van into a camper van. I'd decided I was going to explore VanLife with my German Shepherd Cleo. I had been wanting to experience this for a long time and that Christmas my momma purchased me the van as a gift. I decided summertime was the time to set out, explore some national parks and have a good time on the road. I was no stranger to solo travel at all, I'd done my fair share of traveling while recovering from my alcohol addiction. I'd spent a lot of time camping in the mountains and exploring nature to aid in my healing process, but this was different I was now traveling with my baby girl as my first vanlife video went viral.

I was so excited to share my experience, so I created a youtube channel and grew my following to over 40k subscribers on YouTube and tiktok within a matter of months. I was having the time of my life going from national park to national park. I explored all of Utah, New Mexico, Denver, Arizona, calli, Oregon and more. Cleo and I were on the road like best friends, taking photos, lots of videos and exploring true freedom until one day I recognized I'm recording a lot of videos but I must get back to dedicating my mornings to my spiritual routine, which was mediation, tea, followed by an hour of intentional listening. This is when I sit in silence or only allow silence for the first hour of my morning. There's no music, no activity just me giving myself permission to listen to whatever dialogue is taking place within my being. This way I'm not ignoring any voices, thoughts or intuitive messages that are attempting to get my attention by being distracted by constantly moving and doing things.

In my moments of intentional listening I realized, I wasn't as happy as I thought. I didn't feel as free as I thought. I was deeply sad. I was traveling from state to state in what felt like an adventure BUT my by silent moments helped me see that I was using travel, constant movement and creating travel content as a way to escape my pain. Once I recognized that I was attempting to escape, the flood gates opened. I now had miles and miles of open road to cry on as I drove from state to state. I now had vast mountain tops I could cry at the top of as Cleo and I did our daily hikes. I was all over the place until I chose to go arches national park and just sit still. I stayed there for maybe 2 weeks and set up camp.

Arches national park is a black out sky which means its one of the darkest skies in the USA and you can see every star visible to the human eye. There are unlimited shooting stars, the milky way is visible with the naked eyes and just the sight of them while laying on my back made me feel as if I was levitating. I would heat up my vegan chili, sit in my lawn chair and just wait for the sun to set every night. Once the sun set, I'd make smores for myself, give Cleo her nightly treats and then I'd climb to the roof of my van, lay on my back and watch the stars until id fall asleep. These moments felt like pure freedom because I wasn't running, moving or doing I was just being. After a few months, being on the road became exhausting so I began to make my way back home. My plan was to travel through California to see my friend Jamele, stay with him a few days to recoup and then travel back home.

My first night in cali was at the golden gate bridge. I was amazed. It was huge and I was in awe of how small it made me feel. Cleo and I stayed in our campervan overnight watching the lights of the cars drive across the bridge was such a romantic experience, yet I remember being so exhausted I passed out as soon as the sun set. The next morning before hitting the road I chose to take photos near the golden gate bridge. I turned the camera to selfie mode and when I saw myself, I just burst out in tears. I was having an emotional melt down. When I saw myself, I saw the months of grief I had been running from, the sadness I'd avoided, my spiritual practices I'd ignored and the selfcare I'd disregarded. Here I was at the golden gate bridge and I couldn't even see it, not just because my eyes were full of tears. I couldn't see the golden gate bridge because emotionally I wasn't there, emotionally I was still stuck in march 1st the moment I was told my cousin was killed. I was a prisoner to the grief I tried to travel my way out of and not only had grief come to reclaim its time with me, it had shown up on my face so drastically I didn't even look like myself. My complexion was darker than it had ever been, my face had broken out with acne and rashes and my under-eye circles were so dark I looked sick and malnourished. I cried so hard at the golden gate bridge and the only words I could hear in my head were

"Where ever you go, there you are".

This was a huge aha moment for me, now I had an opportunity to experience the wisdom of this quote for myself. In that moment I was able to own how I had neglected myself, run towards fresh starts, new beginnings and new ideas of freedom to erase the reality of pain that was waiting for me.

This day was so monumental for me because it was the last day I gave myself permission to consciously or unconsciously escape from anything.

Wherever you go there you are simply means, you take you with you wherever you go. You become the mountain, the relationship, the new city to live in, the new career or the new travel destination, they all begin to reflect you, and your internal world. No matter how beautiful a new travel destination, how perfect a new job, how refreshing a new city is to live in, how healthy a new relationship is you will always drag the unhealed parts of yourself with you into your new experiences. The fresh start is only a fresh start at the beginning until the excitement wears off and the emotional debris begins to resurface. No matter how beautiful an environment is the unhealed residue of the past will always bleed on your present moment.

This is why it's imperative to heal where you are, to stop what you're doing and give yourself permission to feel. So often people are waiting for new opportunities to make them feel good, better or healed, but these new opportunities are just distractions from the unhealed parts of our being that lye dormant in our bodies. This is why a person can get into a beautiful healthy new relationship that feels like the answer to their prayers and months later all of their trauma starts to rush to the surface, and they realize they actually don't even know how to receive healthy love. I personally know so many friends who have moved out of the USA into other countries and their experience started out so beautiful then a few months later the exact emotional pains they were experiencing in the US they were now feeling in the other country.

So many of my clients tell me they just need a change of environment because the environment they are in is unhealthy and not conducive to their healing journey and my advice to them is stop forcing people, places and things to be the medicine to your wounds. Become your own medicine, embody your power and heal where you are. When you do this, when you evolve where you are, you no longer give your power away to outside sources to do your work for you and heal you. When you intentionally heal without running or hiding from yourself you own the truth that you are powerful and only you have the capacity and ability to heal you. You now remind your being that you are capable of cultivating joy, happiness, peace and harmony within you without searching for these things outside of yourself. This is true power. When you learn to heal where you are, you can go anyplace, enter any relationship and explore any new opportunity and it just be that an adventure and opportunity to explore, not a desperate measure to find the love, joy and healing that is already within you.

Love yourself enough to make room for your blessings.

Prepare yourself for what you desire and

heal for what you attempt to manifest.

Create an environment within your being that is so healthy,

that anything that lands within your energetic field flourishes

as if your aura has become the sun.

FORGIVENESS IS BABY CONSCIOUSNESS

When I journeyed into the amazon jungles of Peru to explore plant medicine ayahuasca my goal was to forgive my dad. When the shamans facilitating the ceremonies asked my intention for taking this medicine, I explained how I was ready to move forward, release resentment, anger and grudges. I was ready to forgive. The shaman patiently listened and when I finished explaining my intention he responded.

"As you heal, grow and evolve you won't need forgiveness because only compassion will be present."

This was the first time someone had use the word "compassion" in regard to how I show it. This instantly prompted a question inside of me "Do I know how to show compassion even when I feel resentment? Do I know how to have compassion? Is compassion something I should have, show, give or is compassion who I am or who I should be? Does compassion exude from my being? How do I acquire compassion and how do I know if when I give it, it's authentic? These questions instantly showed me that when I become emotionally triggered, I lack compassion. I can use logic and understand but my emotions override my ability to simultaneously exude compassion. At that time, I realized that I didn't know how to emotionally love someone, not just show compassion but genuinely feel compassionate towards them and be angry at the same time.

Years later what the shaman said to me, stayed with me. It helped me dive deeper into my perspective around forgiveness. I began to see forgiveness as a very egoistical concept. To think that I'm powerful enough to forgive someone. That a person owes me an explanation and I'm so powerful I can grant them forgiveness. I realized ego thinks this way. Many people begin to use forgiveness as their chess piece, their way to maintain control, power or emotional leverage that signifies only that person has the power to free another with their forgiveness. Even as a person apologizes, they ask "Will you forgive me?" Placing that person's ego in an unconscious position of power to say yes or no. Our society typically uses forgiveness as a gift to someone else when truthfully, it's a gift ourselves. Forgiveness is baby consciousness. When we allow the essence of forgiveness to evolve into compassion true healing has surfaced.

When there's no need to let a person off the hook, or make them feel bad for how they showed up because your only intention to nurture your internal world so beautifully that only compassion, patience, love and understanding have permission to live in your heart. This does not mean that you have to condone certain behaviors or even allow those who've wronged you an opportunity to stay apart of your life. Compassion can still be present as you simultaneously tell someone to "Get the hell on". When we being to adopt the perspective that many truths can exist at the same time, we don't have to relegate ourselves to one emotion, one thought process, one perspective and one way of understanding or handling situations.

I had to learn how to practice compassion, daily. I began praying for a softer heart daily and I'd also apologize to my heart for all of the heaviness, the emotions, resentments, hurts and pains that I was CHOOSING to willingly hold onto because I didn't want to let go, and I wasn't ready to forgive. I had to apologize to my heart because now just like others who had broken my heart, I was just like them harming my heart when I all I had to do was simply let go and allow love in. I realized I wasn't as nice and loving as I wanted to think I was. Honestly, I was very forgiving to those I didn't care about because they didn't matter enough to me to hold on to anything they did or said, but those who I'd formed relationships with forgiveness was always in my heart but the pain and resentment of how they treated me followed so it was never true forgiveness if I still remembered and replayed in my mind how they made me feel.

I learned that practicing compassion helped me detach from moments ego attempted to take control. I gave myself permission to not focus on how I felt but to also have compassion and understanding for the fact that everyone is trying to figure out their personal levels of being human. I began to practice giving people the grace that I would want someone to give me, even if that was from a very far distance. They could have access to my compassion just no access to me unless my spirit felt safe enough to warrant that level of re-entry.

Compassion doesn't mean you must forget; it isn't a pass for what someone did to you and it isn't saying that you aren't allowed to feel how you feel but holding on to that deep rooted toxic energy of not wanting to let go only harms YOU. It only festers in your body, it only causes you disease and cancer. It only manifests in your relationships, your inability to manifest the life you desire and your ability to actually attract the healthy type of love you deserve.

Let go or be dragged.

If you continue to hold on to the thoughts, feelings, emotions, grudges and resentments that don't serve you and aren't' conducive to your healing journey only YOU will be affected. Love yourself enough to practice letting that shit go and giving yourself permission to invite compassion back into your heart.

Soul Level Communication

As you Heal, Grow & Evolve
Forgiveness Won't Be Necessary,
Only Compassion Will Be Present

As Spiritual beings as we meet new people and potential romantic partners, we must learn to utilize the language of the soul instead of only resting on a language that was never ours to begin with.

When it comes to vetting future partners and the reason so many relationships and friendships fail is because people are using languages that are not native to their soul, which causes them to misinterpret signals, red flags & clear messages the other person is sending. In my past I was a person who used isolation as a defense mechanism I mastered telling people only what I wanted them to know, I mastered making a person feel close to me even with little information about me.

This was how I coped with not feeling safe around people & how I coped with the fear of potentially being hurt. In high school I learned how to adapt to the needs of people, perform to receive love and be whoever I needed to be to be wanted. It wasn't until I began my healing journey that I recognized the many masks I was wearing. It dawned on me that no one truly knew me because I didn't even know myself outside of those masks. This is why we must utilize multiple methods to get to know another person that doesn't just rely on words or questions a person can consciously or unconsciously lie about.

So, like my momma always says "you can make your mouth say anything". At some point we must graduate to the practice of utilizing our soul's native language to decipher who deserves to hold space in our lives & who doesn't.

Many men & women have a list of questions that they ask a person to get a feel for who they are & there is absolutely nothing wrong with this, but to a certain degree you will have to rely on them having integrity & trust their words to be true until they show you otherwise.

When your first conversation is a conversation between souls without the use of words, your soul can tell you instantly "they lying" lol and boom, your soul just saved you from having sex with someone that didn't deserve you and a year of pain & unnecessary heartbreak. The soul doesn't need a year to feel into if a person is meant to play a role in your journey or not. When you rest on WORDS to get to know a person you must also be mindful of your ears.

Do your ears hear what the person is actually saying or do your ear hear what your wounds need to hear to feel loved, seen, wanted, acknowledged or chosen? This matters because your wounds allow you to hear what you want you hear & this can be a unhealthy situation. When you listen from your wounds you begin to look past clear red flags. When we take our time to see past infatuation, when we practice learning someone with intentionality and begin asking that person's soul, why are you here, what did you come to teach me & how will you teach me these lessons, you give your soul permission to play apart in your journey instead of just going from relationship to relationship based on words that never held value. When you hear the intentions of that person's soul then you get to choose and decide if what was revealed to you resonates with your spirit. Words and language can be beautiful and definitely serve a purpose when they are coupled with the true language of our soul.

The doors to

Other dimensions are open

Compassion Fatigue

Compassion fatigue is when you give of yourself but don't give to yourself.

When you pour from a cup that's empty.

When you give what you don't have and when you spend so much time caring for others you simultaneously neglect, abandon and disregard your own self-care and personal needs.

This is the epitome of self -sabotage. Although most people will mask the sabotage with saying they just have a good and caring heart, but doesn't your heart need nurturing too? Don't you need emotionally safe spaces to be vulnerable, be taken care of, held space for, heard and nurtured?

Many people become addicted to helping others as an unconscious way to escape their own emotional pain. They hide behind how well they show up for people, care for them and attempt to love or help them back to health. Because helping others to some degree requires a level of compassion, the spirit becomes exhausted when a person is giving all of their love and care to outside sources without creating space to love and care for themselves. As a result of the lack of proper self-care the love & compassion that person gives to others becomes emotionally, physically and psychologically draining. The act of caring so deeply for others slowly becomes an unconscious method for self-sabotage, escapism and leads to deep soul-dishonor.

Usually, the term compassion fatigue is reserved for caregivers who care for others as their paid job. It acknowledges that the field of caregiving be it a nurse, doula, therapist or intuitive guide haven't been successfully taught how to not take their work home. How not to become consumed with all of their clients energy and allow their clients emotional pain to also weigh them down. Although this is all true, what about the people who show compassion simply because it's a trauma response to how they were raised. So many children were raised to take care of their siblings.

They learned how to be responsible at a young age, cook, clean get their siblings ready for school and ultimately missed out on their own childhood to care for others. Many children even had to emotionally take care of their own parents. These behaviors don't just build a responsible adult, these behaviors also become trauma responses and teach children how to care for others and be responsible for others before they ever care for themselves. This causes the child to grow up as an adult depleting themselves to show up for others with no knowledge of how to show up, care for, nurture and have compassion for themselves.

Typically, when a person has cared for others for so long and has disregarded their own self care for so long, by the time compassion fatigue sets in they are so emotionally exhausted they don't even know where to being to start loving themselves. They feel deep guilt when they take time for themselves or when they set healthy boundaries that allow them to only love and care for themselves and release the responsibility to care for others. They prioritize the needs of others over their own needs and tend to have a very tough time giving to themselves what they give to others. They put so much effort into fixing others so they can avoid fixing themselves. They care for others, so they don't have to feel the emotional weight that comes with caring for themselves.

Essentially people use compassion for others as an unconscious method of escapism because they either don't know how to have compassion for themselves, they may not believe they are worthy of compassion, or they are afraid of the many emotional traumas that will be exposed once they practice self-care compassion. When a person goes for so long giving what they don't have the capacity to give, when they continue to pour from an empty cup they deplete themselves and disregard their soul so much that their "compassion" now becomes an invitation to feel the pain that comes with self-neglect and abandonment.

My advice, stop what you're doing a remind yourself you can only meet a person as deeply as you've met yourself. Which means that it's impossible for you to fix, have compassion for anyone or help anyone else through their moments of need if you don't even have the ability to do the same for yourself. This a moment where spiritual integrity and self-reflection comes into play because if you're helping people, showing up for them, and ultimately giving them the energy, love, support and compassion that you don't even have to give to yourself, your energy of self-neglect and dishonor energetically bleeds onto them. They receive your help and compassion as well as your fatigue and depletion. Energetically they consume whatever energy you care for them in which isn't fair or safe.

Parents tend to do this a lot with their children, showing up playing the part of a parent, exhausted from compassion fatigue but will continue wearing that mask instead of cultivating healthy methods to get them the help they need so they can begin to take care of and nurture themselves, because their children feel that self-neglect, fatigue and emotional exhaustion.

You can only love someone or care for someone the way you love and care for yourself. You are deserving and worthy of reclaiming your compassionate power and saving it only for you. You are allowed to only give people the love, care, compassion and nurturing that you have when it's in abundance. As mother Ayanla Vanzant always says "What is in your cup is for you, what runneth of is for everyone else.". You must learn how to care for yourself, too. If you don't know how to care for yourself, then the care you give to others isn't care at all, it's a trauma response to avoid your own selfcare needs and emotional pains. Love yourself enough to begin setting healthy boundaries that allow you to only focus on you. The world will not crash and burn because you choose to develop healthy self-care routines and rituals. When you learn to embody your own compassion, there won't be a need for fatigue to set it, because all versions of your being will be nurtured, watered and flourishing in a healthy manner.

Experiencing love will always be stressful

when you only know how to love people

you think you have to fix

WHY PARENT'S STRUGGLE WITH ACCOUNTABILITY

So many adult children are still plagued by the trauma caused by their parents. Most adult children ages 18-60+ still wish parents would acknowledge or take accountability for the pain or the wounds they caused. These adult children to a certain degree hold themselves hostage in their own self-inflicted prison of pain refusing to heal their wounds and trauma without first receiving acknowledgment or an apology from their parents. Each time the adult child hopes for this type of closure but doesn't receive it, and refuses to do their own healing work they re-traumatize themselves and experience the emotional pain & memories all over again.

The truth is not all parents will have the capacity to take accountability in this lifetime & for many, it isn't because they don't want to. It's because they don't know how to without also having to feel emotional pain of shame, guilt & embarrassment for the pain they caused. This is not an excuse for their behavior towards you, this is just an explanation of what is happening scientifically within the brain and body when we attempt to hold a person accountable. Many adult children who've experiences trauma from their parents who won't take accountability may be very triggered by this chapter and that is ok. The emotions that arise are an indication that more healing is to be done around this topic, but even more so if a person is triggered by this chapter it's proof that you're still triggered by your parents are still deeply hurt they won't acknowledge, see and hear you the way you need. And that is ok.

This sentiment goes for anyone, not just parents. When we hold any person accountable, force them to see themselves, quickly, without an opportunity to prepare themselves emotionally. So quick that the brain feels attacked, the nervous system goes into shock & the body responds by going into fight or flight by attempting to protect & defend itself. This is why when you attempt to hold a person accountable sometimes their first reaction is to defend themselves(fight) shut down communication (flight) or become angry or aggressive (fight). These are all signs that they've become emotionally overwhelmed & the brain has stepped in to keep them safe or alive. Many times, parents have spent such a long time avoiding taking accountability that their brains have created STRONG defense mechanisms to help them avoid the emotional pain that is attached to accountability.

To gain a little more clarity, maybe begin to reflect on how you or the average person responds to moments they are being required to take accountability before they have the capacity. The average person deflects, gaslights, defends, plays victim, becomes emotional, shuts down emotionally, becomes angry or aggressive. There is a reason accountability isn't too high on many people's priority list. Some of those people have narcissistic mental illness traits, but for most people their body is in fight or flight and others may simply just not know how to take accountability and own such harmful, egregious, abusive and neglectful behaviors. When you hold a parent accountable and you expect them to acknowledge how they neglected you emotionally, abandoned you, chose drugs over you, didn't listen when you said you were sexually touched, hurt you, abused you & caused emotional damage or even get help for your mental illness, imagine the amount of shame, guilt, embarrassment, pain, trauma they'd have to feel right then & there in that moment. Imagine how the powerful emotions will rush through their body energetically, the average person runs from accountability for simple things, and the average person could never own up to causing so much trauma so imagine what a parent has to feel owning they're the cause of this type of trauma. The body literally feels physical pain when it becomes emotionally overwhelmed.

Lack of accountability isn't always because a person doesn't love you and it doesn't always mean they are a bad person. This unhealthy behavior of not having the ability to take accountability reflects them not you. This unhealthy and harmful behavior reflects an individual who is still amid their trauma and can't meet you as deeply as you're requiring. They may have a very young, underdeveloped soul that has only incarnated into this life only

REMEMBER WHO THE F*CK YOU ARE

a few times and is still learning deep soul lessons and accumulating deep soul level karmic debt. This is where we have to begin to separate the human, the parent and the soul. It's understandable to be hurt on a human level, but on a soul level the person who refuses to take accountability does so, so you can heal your emotional traumas and wounds by tapping into your own soul level power. The souls who cause the most pain, harm and trauma are your angels sent to send you to the depths of yourself so you can activate your healing, activate your power and evolve as a soul.

Even when it feels personal it's not personal, it's spiritual business.

Even when it seems personal it's still in alignment.

The pain is still an angel guiding you back home to yourself so you can embody your innate power, and learn how to reparent, nurture and love yourself without needing an outside source to do it for you.

This is not an excuse for anyone to treat you badly and not rectify their behavior. This also doesn't mean that people or parents are allowed to make you feel horribly and you must take it or even stay apart of their lives. You are allowed to set healthy boundaries and decided if continuing this relationship is best for your healing and growth without feeling any guilt behind your decision. You are allowed to feel into if your relationship with your parents or anyone is a healthy or toxic space for you and pivot accordingly. I want to make sure that people, you the reader understands that many truths can exist at the same time.

That your parent may be the root cause of some of your emotional trauma,

Now that you're an adult you can't help what's happened to you, but your healing is your responsibility,

You deserve acknowledgement, apologies and accountability from you parent,

They may not have the capacity to give you that type of closure and acknowledgment and this lack of accountability doesn't mean that they don't love you.

If you're someone who has a parent of someone in their life that is continuing to display unhealthy and emotionally harmful behavior, this is an invitation to begin setting healthy boundaries so you can embark on your healing journey without continual reminders of your pain and trauma. You still deserve to be heard, your experience deserves to be acknowledged & your feelings are true and valid. Again, some of your parents not acknowledging that isn't a sign that they don't love you, it's a sign that they too are plagued with their own trauma & bypassing, avoidance & emotional detachment is their brains unhealthy defense mechanism. It's very easy to say "They should still know how to take accountability for their child's sake" in a perfect world this would be true, but when we are speaking about the brain in survival mode, it will do anything to avoid emotional pain and many parent's and people have not evolved to have enough mental and emotional maturity to heal this part of themselves.

"As you heal & evolve in your journey forgiveness won't be necessary only compassion will be present". You're allowed to own the truth of how you feel, ask for the apologies you deserve & accept the apologies you may never receive for the benefit of your own healing & soul progression. No matter what you do always love yourself enough to give yourself permission to leave the door of your heart open, so when the trauma and wounds begin to ache less, you'll always be able to return to love.

Everybody is Grown Until It's Time to
Communicate, Tell the Truth, Apologize or
Take Accountability.

2/27/23

After writing about parents, or people in general and their inability to take accountability the same night a lot of emotion surfaced for me. I refer to myself as an intuitive guide, because what I share is solely from a place of wisdom or intuition, especially when I write. Anytime I write anything, it feels like a sixth sense, like a nudge or voice. I never plan what I'm going to write, I don't make outlines or rough drafts like we were taught in school I just write from my soul and when I feel it or I'm given a topic from my spirit I stop everything I'm doing to write that thought out and follow wherever it leads me. So much of my writing is for me and my own healing and much of it is my intuition guiding me to write for others to help them through what they are currently experiencing or to validate what they're feeling or currently attempting to heal through. This is why when I share my writing so many people ask me "how did you know I needed this right now? Or you're always right on time when I need to hear a message". It's as if a huge part of me is deeply connected to the collective (quantum entanglement) and feels what they need in certain moments. I realized I was guided to speak about parents to prepare myself for the resurfacing of my own grief I'd experienced as a result of my own parental trauma.

Last night i cried so hard because i missed my dad which was something I've only said twice in my life. Last night and when I experienced my first mushroom ceremony. I felt so much sorrow, gratitude, grief and regret all at the same time. Regret of not being there to form a relationship with him as much as I could have while he was dying, not allowing myself to move past the anger and resentment to get to know him more and form a relationship with him. He wanted to be a part of my life but I didn't have the tools to allow that to happen. He would call me and leave messages on my voicemail and I was so angry I wouldn't allow myself to respond or call him back. My defense mechanism of detachment was still so strong I didn't know how to form a relationship with him and still allow the truth of how I felt to be present.

Last night i was watching a show called "the Outer Banks" on Netflix. It's about a group of teenagers who go on dangerous life changes adventures to search for historically hidden treasure. I love this show because it allows my inner child to explore, come face to face with danger, admire friends that deeply love each other but what i didn't realize is how much my inner child also related to the characters who didn't have fathers that were present in their lives the way they should have been or in the healthiest way, just like me. I thought I was just watching a tv show that my inner child liked but towards the end of the movie I found out this was not the case.

At the end of the show they found the gold during a treasure hunt, & finally the not so good dads showed up for their kids by sacrificing their lives for them. The dads in the show had been absent fathers, engaged in many things other than maintaining the relationship with their children so the aspect of them dying to save their kids lives was a huge closure to the show for the teenagers and then me. Seeing the dads give their life for their kids made me cry so deeply because my dad also sacrificed his life for me as well, on a soul level I know that he chose the role of an alcoholic & non present dad so my soul could evolve from that pain of absence & fulfill my souls purpose. My dad died from liver cancer in 2016 because of his alcohol addiction which is also why he couldn't be apart of my life & what also paved the way for my own alcohol addiction

(I'll b 5 years sober in March)

I couldn't help but cry & say my dad would have loved to find treasure too. This is when I knew my inner child was also present experiencing these emotions with me as well as my young adult self that was conflicted with grief and regret. My dad was a huge kid & he loved surfing, skateboarding , & playing the guitar. He thought he was Bob Marley lol. Even in his 50's before he died he was still surfing at the beach in Texas and still at skate parks trying to ride his skateboard. My dad even broke his hip and his arm trying to skateboard before he died, then healed then went right back out and broke his other arm and leg again lol. He was such a kid he could careless about no broke arms or legs lol and he'd even say "as soon as I heal I'm going back out there again because they just built this new skate park I want to try out". I continued to cry heavily because I could now see the life my dad wanted but sacrificed in so many ways and for so many reasons, me being one of them. I'm sure there's many things my dads soul wanted to experience outside of alcoholism. I felt much guilt because for years i chose to be angry at him instead of acknowledging how his soul sacrificed his life on earth & his opportunity to be a dad just so my soul could have the fuel it needed to evolve through the pain. Now that pain I felt from his absence is wisdom i use to help so many others & on top of that I get paid to share. This is the epitome of divine alignment. My life couldn't be what it is today with the decisions my dad made. This is proof that souls choose one another before entering human form. We choose our parents, what pains our parents will cause so we can acquire specific lessons for the evolution of our soul. Unwavering love has to be present on a soul level for a soul to agree to hurt you so much, for you own good. Isn't this exactly what people say God does. God gives us hard lessons, takes us through the most difficult moments so we can evolve. I see absolutely no difference here. On a human level the pain was difficult and still is at times, but on a soul level on a God level, I understand and I'm grateful that my dad played a part in who I am today. This understanding soothed my deep gratitude and regret.

I've done so much healing around my dad for years and this is a reminder that the journey to healing is a lifelong process. Our main job as humans is to remember who we are, why came here and allow every single circumstance, pain, emotion or trauma guide us back home to ourselves. In this process not matter how much you heal, grow or evolve Grief, sadness, regret and many other emotions will surface randomly, and that is ok befriend them. They'll leave when the lesson is received.

KARMA IS NOT YOUR PERSONAL ASSASSIN

Written 12-16-16

Last night I had a very disturbing yet insightful dream. Regarding karma. In my dream I was A part of an Aboriginal tribe & my people were at war with Giant humans almost like Nephilim. The etymology of Nephilim can also mean giants in some translations, they're mentioned across the history and in the Bible, Hebrew Bible and the book of "Enoch". They're known as mysterious giant people or fallen angels. We were fighting with spheres, and I recognized I was myself but I was also an aboriginal teenage young adult boy.

I was partially fearful of fighting and simultaneously fearless, almost as if I knew to survive and be a part of my tribe this was something I had to do. It was the norm but a first time, war for me. Obviously, the only way to win a war is to fight & sadly kill. I was being chased throughout the whole damn war by one giant a** man thing. His only focus was me. I was terrified & I tried throwing my sphere at him to stab him so many times, it didn't work. I remember being too afraid to hide, too afraid to allow my fear to take over me, but it was clear that I wasn't a fighter and I didn't enjoy having to protect myself in this way. (kind of like in my real life and physical reality). The giant continued to chase me, as an attempt to stop him I attempted to stab him again with my sphere and it worked, I got him.

Once I stabbed him, he immediately went down and collapsed on the ground. I ran over to him with mixed emotions, relief that I no longer had to run or be afraid and then fear set in again, now instead of being afraid of him killing me, I was now afraid that I'd killed him. Even though I knew it was him or me and I knew I'd have to kill him so he wouldn't harm me, I still didn't truly want to be a killer. I didn't want him to die. I went over to him as he was dying, and he spoke very clearly a few words to me that shook me. His last words right before he died were.

"We will meet again, you will feel me again"

& Instantly more fear rushed over me and I couldn't help but to think "OH SH*T ! What the f*ck does that mean? lol For the remainder of my dream I lived in fear that he was going to haunt me or come back alive & get me.

When the 2nd part of my dream started I was in a car with 3 other people. (yall know dreams be all over the place lol) I was no longer an aboriginal person fighting with spheres, I was a regular person in my car with friends. The paranoia and fear of the man I killed still haunted me but, in this moment, I was free of thinking of him and what I'd done. I was just living my life in the car with what appeared to be faceless friends of mine. Although just a second the thought crossed my mind of who are these friends, why don't they have faces, can I trust them and the most random question that surfaced was, are they me? All of a sudden, I could see and feel a presence around the car. The presence was trying to get in the car to hurt us, but I knew it was after me.

As I sat in the back seat, I witnessed this presence kill the three people in the car with me. The presence shot them then turned and shot me as well. I was terrified before he pulled the trigger. But mostly I was confused. Once the presence shot me, I could feel the pain, feel the blood pouring from my body until it felt as if I died. Suddenly the same man I had killed during war appeared in my backseat & said

"I Told you that you'd meet me again"

I instantly burst into tears, I was so confused and afraid. He then held a mirror to my face & I could see all of the things I had done or said to people to cause joy, love, harm, hurt or pain written all over my face in black ink, the good & bad. As I looked into the mirror and saw all of my past actions written all over my face I felt an extreme wave of guilty consumed me and I began to cry even harder. I couldn't help but to also still be in shock that I killed this man, yet he is here. How? I cried and explained to him "I didn't want to kill you, it wasn't my INTENTION to kill you, I was afraid for my life I had to do something because I thought you were trying to kill me. I was only attempting to protect myself, you were chasing me, I was afraid, I never intended for you to die.

The Man Replied,

just because you can JUSTIFY your reason does not mean you are right & it doesn't mean you are wrong, However, what you put into the Universe you WILL get back. There is no right or wrong, it just is and you must experience the alternate side of each action. Your Intention does not change the act itself. Your death is your payment and lesson.

"YOU MUST LEARN"

THE LESSON LEARNED

I've learned that when dreams like this come to us, they are divine downloads, messages sent from GOD to guide us. I also know that dreams aren't just dreams they are reality in other dimensions, so if it happened in a dream then I really happened in another dimension, universe or timeline. This dream was a reminder to become more intentional, conscious and aware of what type of energy I put into the universe. To be mindful of how I treat people, speak to them and treat them. To protect my words and maintain spiritual integrity with my actions. To always remember that universal law must teach us, must make us aware and we must learn. Like James Baldwin said "If I love you I must make you conscious of the things you don't' see".

This lesson also taught me that good intentions don't eradicate lessons, karma or karmic debt. Having the ability to justify our actions also doesn't eradicate lessons, karma or karmic debt. Just like the angel in my dream said "there is no right or wrong". This matters because people use karma as their personal assassin. They even say "Karma is. A B*tch or karma will get them". They think karma is their personal assassin waiting to harm those that have harmed them and it's far from the truth. Karma is pure love and pure guidance. How can a person learn if they don't experience the same energy or emotion that they caused another to experience? In my dream the angel had to kill me so I could be aware of how it felt. This is why the angel allowed me to see my face in the mirror with all of my actions written all over it. I had to see the many ways "d affected others with good intention, bad intentions, misguidance, lack of loved and pure love. I had to learn that all energy I put out is what I will receive in return, not as a punishment but just to expand awareness, mindfulness and intentionality.

Many people have assigned a low vibrational energy to karma and its truly the epitome of God's guidance. It's an opportunity to learn, heal, grow and evolve continually. So often a person has treated another badly, a now someone is treating that person badly. Instant Karma. Often those people learn deep lessons and even come back to make amends because they now understand in hindsight what they couldn't previously. Then there are those people who refuse to learn their karmic lesson, abide by them and evolve that create more karmic debt for themselves, causing them to experience lifetimes of hard, painful, and emotionally heavy lessons.

Recently an acquaintance who could have potentially grown into a friend (I spoke about this in the uncommunicated expectations chapter) expressed she didn't want to be my friend anymore because I wasn't as available as she'd like. She highlighted that it took me too long to respond to text, sometimes I didn't answer the phone and these aren't the types of friends she wanted in her life. I explained to her that I was always there for her when she needed me, just not for frivolous conversation but I showed up, offered things, time, advice and even money when it was needed. I explained other that it takes a lot out of me to be super accessible to others and I truly nurture my alone time, my silence and my lack of communication.

I nurture my energy and don't give away what I don't have. I also mentioned that she had expectations for me to show up for her in a way that I didn't have the capacity, but that doesn't discount that I did show up for her very beautifully when I could and did have the capacity. She refused to acknowledge that truth, However I deeply understood her perspective because my ways of communicating bothers many people. Not all are used to and care to understand why I operate this way. She chose to end all communication with me and we amicably parted ways.

Recently as I wrote this book I received a message from her, it was an apology letter. She stated that she had given so much of her time and had poured into another person all that she could and later felt betrayed that the person she'd helped didn't acknowledge her help but instead insisted that she gave more of herself, more time and more energy that she didn't have to give. She acknowledged how horrible this made her feel and instantly thought about how she had treated me and expected more of me than I could give while simultaneously disregarding all that I'd actually given in my own way. She apologized and explained that she now knows what that must have felt like for me because it was also done to her.

This was the epitome of karma and such a beautiful expression of karma reflecting how its intentionally designed for our greater good, not our detriment. When she chose to end communication with me and disregard the many ways I had shown up for her I never said "Karma is a b*tch). I never needed another force to get pay back for me and that's what people are desiring. They want karma to make someone feel how that person made them feel, they want payback which highlights that person has more work to do in the evolving journey. Karma wasn't there to reprimand her it was there to show her, herself. To remind her of the energy she was putting out and to show her a healthier way. To make her conscious of the things she didn't see and give her a lesson on how to move forward in a healthier way in relationships with others. The beautiful part about her karma was that she instantly acknowledged it, she saw herself and gave herself permission to own that her karma was teaching her a lesson. Then she obeyed her spirit when it nudged her to reach out to me, take accountability, apologize and own her part. This is spiritual integrity. The reason so many people have so much unpaid karmic debt is because they refuse to see themselves in their karma. They write their karma off as bad things randomly happening to them and don't acknowledge that these bad things are happening because of lifetimes of not owning, taking accountability, making amends and implementing the lessons karma is attempting to teach them.

To a large degree she was justified in acknowledging she required and wanted more from her friendships, karma wasn't there to tell her she did anything wrong it was just present to allow her to feel what her behavior felt like. Karma is one of our greatest teachers and when we give ourselves permission to see all things in life wanting to help us by giving us lessons it makes our journey of evolving a lot easier. Our healing becomes a lot easier when we stop running from ourselves, running from accountability and running from lessons that are only reflections of our own energy, spiritual integrity and how we treat others.

The same is for our good energy that we put into the world, karma isn't biased that energy doesn't just acknowledge pain, mistreatment or lessons that need to be learned. This is why in my dream I was also allowed to see the great things I'd had done written on my face. We get o experience those energies of karma as well. Sometimes people have run from their karmic lessons for so long that they can't feel the love that karma is also sending them, they feel so much of the pain because of taking accountability for those parts of themselves.

Karma is not your personal assassin. It won't get people back to make you feel better. Karma will show up to guide those people with whatever grace or force is necessary to give them the lessons they need to heal, grow and evolve. Karma is God expressing the deepest and most pure love.

You will be presented with the same lessons

In different variations, people, relationships and situations

Over and over again until you master it.

Karmic debt isn't just about the acts of other people.

It's also about your acts against yourself.

Many are living out their karmic debt,

by repeating the same self-sabotaging

life cycles repeatedly.

They don't have to wait for karma to appear because

It's in the food they eat, relationships they entertain,

jobs they choose

And emotional trauma they refuse to heal.

Acknowledge your lessons, implement your wisdom

Or your personal karmic will force you to, repeat.

Evolve or Repeat

TIME IS AN ILLUSION

As young children and young adults, family and society plague us all with questions like,

What do you want to be when you get older?

What college will you go to?

Do you want kids?

Will you get married?

How much money do you want to make?

They tell us very young to start planning these things now or if we don't, we'll end up flipping burgers at McDonalds. From youth, time and the lack of time is continually implied. So, most people spend their youth daydreaming about what their life will be like once they're finally older. I remember I would always say "I'm going to go to college and study law to become a lawyer. I wanted to be married by the time I was 24 and I wanted four boys as children. I even had a backup plan just in case my timeline didn't work out, If I wasn't married, engaged or had no children. My backup plan was if I'm not married by the time I'm 28 then I'll adopt kids. I had my life's timeline mapped out and in high school this was my goal to someday achieve. Until my senior year in high school I experienced the deepest and most painful trauma of my life that derailed my goals, plans and ambition to do or become anything.

I graduated high school with the bare minimum of everything. I had just enough credits to graduate, A GPA that was just good enough to get into community college and just enough energy to wake up everyday to keep trying. I was so depressed that I didn't even know I missed deadlines to apply for colleges. Even though I took a college and careers course in high school I was too depressed to actually pay attention in class. I was so depressed and out of my mind I had no idea while I slept in class everyone around me was applying for college, receiving grants, loans and receiving their acceptance letters. Just attempting to listen to my instructor give us detail after detail was so painful and overwhelming all I could do was put my head down on the desk and sleep. I was so out of it that I didn't realize everyone around me had started their college experience as I attempted to sleep my depression away.

After high school graduation, the next day I started my journey into community college. My timeline had shifted, and I didn't even know if I had the capacity to be a lawyer at this point and now my goal was to make it to Sam Houston University to Study law after two years of community college. Those first few months I was plagued by time and comparison. It felt as if everyone I had gone to school with was ahead of me. I felt as if I was behind because I had to go to community college. This changed the trajectory of my life and made me feels small, ashamed, embarrassed, less than and like a failure. I felt as if I wasn't where I wanted to be or should be in life.

My momma was always super supportive. She always told me, I didn't have to work or go to school that I could take as much time as I needed to feel better, got to therapy and heal my depression. We'd create routines for me to feel better about my day. Write out meal plans so I could eat healthy. She helped me do so many things to ease my depression but the trauma I'd experienced in high school on top of my new college dilemma, he artificial societal timeline was already ingrained in my psyche.

Eventually attempting to go to college was to much for me so I went away to the military in hopes it would help me escape my depression and the timeline, and to some degree it did. I was no longer on the same timeline as others. I now had immersed myself in a complexly different world that didn't require me to compare myself to others. A couple of years went by, then everyone began to graduate college and I felt that embarrassment come back so, I decided to go back to college and this time I told myself, I'm going to finish when its meant for me to finish as a way to give myself grace for not meeting the timeline.

At some point during college a friend told me I should apply to be a police officer. I did and then I got the job. Graduated the academy at the top of my class and no longer needed college to pursue my career. My job as a police officer saved me from the college timeline. The opportunity to become a police officer showed me that not all timelines are real for everyone. Everyone doesn't need college to have a good paying career and that truth opened my eyes in many ways. I was now able to see how many other people were trapped in the prison of societal timelines. I was now able to see how many other people felt like they weren't where they wanted to be and so many people who felt like they weren't where they "Should Be".

Many were plagued by the idea that they were supposed to be further along, with a much better career, a family, married, with more money, more established in life and more financially stable. For the first time I was able to see that it wasn't just me feeling the pressure of holding myself accountable to this invisible societal timeline. Honestly, I said to myself "If my momma ain't holding me to an invisible timeline of when I should do or accomplish certain things then why am I stressing or trippin?" My mommas unwavering support held space for me to come to my own conclusion that time did not exist and not only did her support allow me to let go of the timeline, it also allowed me to ask questions that needed answers like,

who the hell came up with this timeline mess?

Who said we had to have children, be married, make a lot of money, have prestigious careers, buy a house, buy a car and do all of these things by a certain age?

Who made these rules?

Are they even still alive?

Why am I following rules created by someone that I've never even met?

What if these rules were designed to keep me in obedience to societal structures?

What if we don't share the same morals, ethics, goals and values?

Why would I follow rules created by someone who may have created these rules in a time where they actually mattered?

It may have been a time in history where college education was imperative for financial stability, or a time where being married, having kids and a family by a certain age added value to society.

I had to really just sit with the truth that, it's a new dawn and a new day and I was no longer participating in artificial timelines that did not benefit me. The societal timeline felt like a trap, a cage, a prison and such an unauthentic way to live my life. It felt as if this timeline took my power away, my ability to choose, took away my freedom and ultimately caused stress and created a spirit of comparison all the while I wasn't even sure who I was trying to impress.

There was even a time when I got home from the military all of my friends were graduating college living in their own apartments and I thought maybe I need my own apartment too. I was still living at home with my mom which wasn't a bad thing at all to me. My momma and I were best friends so I didn't have a pressing reason to move out, other than seeing my peers my age do it.

I remember my momma saying "Apartments are a trap baby, trust me if your friends could stay at home and save their money, they all would. Nobody wants to pay a whole bunch of bills". So, instead of moving out I chose to build an efficiency apartment behind our house this way I still had my own space and my own apartment. I had a beautiful loft apartment, water, electrical, high ceilings, water, kitchen and bathroom. I chose to release the timeline and do things my way. I chose to intentionally create my own paradigm, my own rules and do my own thing. Then suddenly I started seeing all of my peers on twitter talk about how they wished they could still stay at home to save money and not have to pay so many bills. This was another aha moment, reminding me to follow my own path. No one else's path is my path, no one else's timeline is my timeline and I'm allowed to do what is best for me even if it conflicts and is so very different from my peers, people my age, people on social media or society.

I was no longer following the status quo and shaming myself because my journey was different and didn't look like everyone else's. I began to find that notion empowering because I was doing what was best for me. Even as a police officer making great money, I didn't want a house, I didn't want a mortgage I didn't want to pay random unnecessary bills just to be able to tell people I had a house. I just wanted my own personal space and I had it. I realized what was important to others wasn't important to me and that was ok. It wasn't important to me be married or have kids. When I was around 25-29 all of my friends or peers were working on their second or third child I was still feeling into, do I even want kids? I came the conclusion that I didn't want kids at all, I enjoyed my freedom, my cats and my dog. I began owning my truth more and more.

One day while on police duty we were called to a briefing about our retirement. I remember asking at what age will I be able to retire with my benefits? I was told I would only be able to retire at 67years old and if I retired before then I would lose benefits. I instantly said "Who came up with this? Who designed this method because it doesn't work for me." At this time, I was about 23 or 24 years old and I couldn't imagine working for the rest of my life. I remember I got so upset I left the entire department retirement meeting. I had to leave that meeting because it was clear I was only around others that still believed in the societal timeline. They followed the rules of society and by this time in my 20's I was a rebel with a cause, and they could never pay me enough to work until I was 67 out of obligation. I always said, "God didn't put me here to just work, my life has so much more purpose that working at a job". But I was also very clear that this was jackpot to generations that were raised to follow societal norms and work. I was also clear I'd have to find a way to do what was best for me. When I went to my car before I drove off, I put my face in my hands and I just cried. I felt defeated by this invisible system of societal norms that was attempting to force me into submission and attempting to force me into living a life I never agreed to.

I felt as if I was suffocating and being controlled by paradigms and entities I couldn't even call and curse out or ask questions. I was pissed, but underneath that I felt helpless because I didn't know how to live a life on my own terms, I didn't know how to live the life I desired, I just knew that

I deeply wanted to. I sat in my driver's seat while warm tears began to run down my face and land on my bullet proof vest. I knew I was going against the grain. I was stepping into my truth in a society that was designed to make people forget who they are and CONFORM. As I cried, I just began to pray and ask God for a way out, for something different, better, more freeing, and more fulfilling. I asked to live a life that best resonated with my spirit, that was on my own terms and that didn't resort to me shrinking under societal norms. I wasn't fully clear what I wanted my life to look like, I just knew I wasn't working until I was 67 years old, I wasn't wasting my life away at a job because I knew my soul was meant for much more. I drove away that day, angry, sad, defeated but encouraged.

I kept saying "They got me f*cked up" lol.

I drove home listening to one of my rebellious anthems "Meant to Live" By Switchfoot. I was determined to find ways, even small ways to take my power back. I began looking for opportunities in my regular life to have fun, explore go on adventures and travel. I questioned everything, I didn't care who said it, I was determined to only live my own truth. When I first chose to travel out of the country alone, everyone said "women shouldn't travel alone, especially out of the country", and my response was who said that? Who made that rule?

So many people are prisoners to the societal timelines and rules that are placed on them and the truth is time doesn't exist. You can be 60 years old and choose to go to school to study math just for fun. You can be 40 years old a choose to try having a baby. You can choose not to marry, you can choose to not own a home a spend your savings traveling the world backpacking and thriving living in your tent. You can choose that you prefer to live an emotionally healthy life and give up the job that stresses you and be ok with taking a large pay cut for the sake of being at peace and happy. You can choose to marry and divorce three times and still be open to finding love without carrying societies judgment. And guess what, you can do all of these things, make you own rules and live on your own terms and this will still be considered successful.

Your life choices are successful because they are successful to you, because you followed your heart, your intuition and did what make your soul smile. You are the only person that matters. There's a movie titled "They live" that depicts beings that are similar to robots, conforming to societal norms, they wear the same clothes, buy the same houses and cars, they speak the same, the way up at 9am and come home at 5pm. They keep the same routine and only live their lives on the weekends. This movie shows how society has programmed us to obey the norm. When we give ourselves permission to create our own lifetime line we choose to obey our souls and not invisible dictators that have decided for us how we should live.

You are powerful enough to choose your own path, without the guilt of your parents constantly questioning you about when you're going to get married, have kids or get your life together. They are following societal norms as well so they may not have the capacity to understand you making and living by your own rules.

At age 31 I finally decided to quit my job and become an entrepreneur. I told my mom I couldn't bare going to work another day, it was literally killing me. Initially my momma was nervous, and her protective mom brain kicked in, understandably so. I was about to quite a career job paying great money to become an entrepreneur making unstable money. I was honestly ok If I didn't make any money at all, I just needed the freedom to choose. I needed to have the freedom to wake up and choose to work or go to the park and read.

During my emotional healing journey as a police officer I was processing a lot of emotions and traumas. Some days I needed to cry the entire day but I had to put my tears on hold so I could go to work. To some this is normal, work now, make money provide for yourself cry later, but this wasn't how I wanted to live my life. I needed the freedom to decided, the freedom to say I need take the day off just to cry today without there being a punishment or a supervisor threatening to write me up because I didn't have a doctor excuse. My momma saw that I was redefining what normal was for myself. I was the first entrepreneur of our family so this was uncharted territory. No one had gone against this societal norm. The day after telling my momma I had to do this for me she was with it, she saw that I was in my power, that I was more than capable of living on my own terms and she was so supportive of my transition. She helped me budget my money, create a daily routine and maintain my responsibilities during my transition.

I had out grown the environment of waking up to a 9 to 5. It was now time for me to fully step into entrepreneurship. After that retirement conversation I utilized the next few years by visualizing the life I wanted for myself, writing about it, romanticizing it and owning that it would one day be my future. I also didn't just live in the future, I created the reality I wanted to live right then and there. I began traveling, exploring and honoring my present moments. I lived in the present how I wished to live in the future. I told God I wanted healing to become my career and now years later I was able to retire at 31 years old and truly create my own rule book and delete the idea of time.

The invisible societal timeline only exists if you give it power. It's your birthright to live your life on your own terms, within your own time and in a way that best resonates with your sprit. Take your power back however and whenever you need to. No more allowing an invisible timeline guilt, shame or embarrass you into conforming. When you do your due diligence and make you emotional and spiritual healing a priority the life that is meant for you will be waiting for you.

All of the rules are fake.

Do you.

You Are Allowed to Change Your Mind

As A person heals, grows and evolves what resonated with their spirit last year may not resonate with their spirit today. The things they could participate in five months ago may be subtle ways of dishonoring their soul today. What methods, relationships, ideas, careers, beliefs, goals, desires, drugs, drinks, business models, communication skills and behaviors worked previously may not work now. At some point every person enters a liminal phase that is an opportunity for them to allow change to occur, for them to allow themselves to pivot, adapt to their growth or change their minds. So often people are so resistant to change that they will allow things that are no longer working to continue. They'll force their old business models, relationships, jobs, thoughts and behaviors into submission.

Cognitive Dissonance

Cognitive dissonance can be described as a mental conflict that occurs when a person's core beliefs are challenged or contradicted by new information. Even when that person is the one challenging their own core beliefs. This conflict activates areas of the brain involved in personal identity and emotional response to threats, meaning the brain goes into fight or flight. The person begins to feel threatened on a deeply personal and emotional level causing them to shut down, shut out and disregard any rational evidence that contradicts what they previously thought to be true. It becomes so important for them to protect their core belief that they begin to rationalize, ignore and even deny anything that doesn't agree with their core belief.

This proves that it is not easy for a person to change their minds, not only is it difficult it is also physically painful because stress on the brain manifests as physical pain in the body. A person may have to fight themselves internally just to allow change to occur. They may have to convince their bodies that they are safe enough to allow new information in and remind their brains that no threat is present. Essentially for a person to change their minds and introduce new beliefs they must convince the old version of themselves that is holding onto old core beliefs that they are safe enough to let it go. This is the epitome of internal conflict. They are in internal conflict with themselves and unaware that this is what is making their decision making so cloudy and difficult. They fear adapting to their new phase of being and they fear change because it requires them to enter new uncharted territory. This can feel uncomfortable because it's unfamiliar or because they fear appearing as a hypocrite.

<u>The Hypocrite</u>

Let's face it, as we heal grow and evolve at some point we will contradict ourselves. We will contradict our past beliefs, thought processes, what we thought was right, wrong, what we defended and even what we shouted to the mountain tops. Personally, once I realized how often I began contradicting myself along my healing journey I just learned to shut the hell up lol. This is where giving ourselves permission to unlearn and relearn comes into play and really taking pride in being a student of life. So often people don't allow themselves to change their minds because They fear what it looks like on the outside to show up a specific way one day and the next day show up as a completely different person. This is why many people struggle with setting boundaries, it requires them to change their minds about how they allow people to show up in their lives, what they accepted yesterday may be completely different than what they accept today and that is ok. However, many people fear how they'll appear to others when they begin to embody this new version of themselves.

Another example is religious beliefs. Many times, people grow up practicing a certain religion, preaching and teaching that religion and suddenly one day they are presented with new or different information that changes their ideology, perception, perspectives and beliefs. These people tend to feel deep shame, embarrassment or fear around changing their minds because of the fear of appearing as a hypocrite. On a deeper level this is where cognitive dissonance kicks in. I learned at a very young age you do not argue religion, no one will ever win because you are arguing core beliefs that the brain physically will not allow you to contradict. But the truth is, self-contradiction is a beautiful sign of growth. It shows that a person is giving themselves permission to remain open mided to receiving new information without being closed off and closed minded. This is the epitome of evolution.

Personally, as I began my healing journey years ago, I recognized I was learning so much information daily that I was a walking contradiction. Not because I was a bad person, gullible or believed anything I read but because I learned what it felt like to decipher what actually resonated with my spirit as true and not just go along with information that was fed to me as true. I was now able to feel into what felt true to me. Once I realized how often I began contradicting myself along my healing journey I just learned to shut the hell up about what I thought I knew lol. Students don't speak they learn, they observe, and they receive. I learned that it's not necessary to hold myself hostage to anything, no core belief, no ideologies, no perspectives, no opinions. I learned to say "I don't have an opinion on that" this gave me an opportunity to not attach to judgment, just to allow myself to observe.

When I began to no longer attach to beliefs, I no longer had to change my mind about anything because I was free to explore all things. My freedom began to feel like an adventure learning about new ideologies, I read a lot of philosophy, conspiracy theories and quantum physics. If I hadn't chosen to release myself of my religious beliefs, I would have still thought that science was disrespectful to God. Now that I was free of mental constraints because I gave myself permission to change my mind, now as I studied science I realized, science is God. Now I could explore any religion I wanted, and it didn't mean I believed in that religion but I was open to learning from them all taking what I needed and leaving what I didn't. This was true freedom for me in all aspects of life especially business and relationships. In relationships I learned to say, that doesn't feel good to me anymore, I know I allowed you to speak to me this way yesterday but that doesn't work for me anymore. Even in business I learned that changing my mind was also a reflection of my relationship with my intuition and spirit.

Intuitional Guidance

A huge reason people don't allow themselves to change their minds is because they don't have a strong relationship with their intuition or their spirit. They are in such internal conflict with themselves that they don't hear the internal voice that is telling them "It's time". This is true for some but for others they hear that internal voice and intentionally ignore and disregard it and act like they're confused calling everybody and they momma to ask for advice talking about "I just don't know what to do" lol and the truth is, yes they do. Their intuition is loud and clear that It's time to make changes, change their minds about what they allow, how they show up in the world, or change their minds about their business strategies but they fear the change and the outcome that is attached to change. Many fear what they will lose, how they will look to others and ultimately how they will be affected.

The Beyonce of Van Life

In 2020 when I began to travel the USA in my van with my German Shepherd Cleo I was so excited. My Instagram, TikTok and YouTube platforms were growing so quickly. I personally grew my platform by speaking about things that mattered to me like emotional healing, but I was clear I also had to mix in things about my van because ultimately people were following me to enjoy my Van Life experience with me and most of those people stayed because they valued the emotional healing topics that I'd speak about. But I instantly recognized a conflict. I realized that Van Life could quickly become a box that shrunk my potential. People in the vanlife community grew their platforms solely by speaking about van life. They'd make videos about things like "This is how I cook in my van or This is how I shower in my van or This is how I use the restroom in my van or This is how much I spent on my van build or This is what a day in the life looks like in my van". No shade to anyone in the vanlife community that speak about those things to spread awareness for future Van Lifers, but I was tired of talking about that sh*t lol. No one could pay me to talk about another water pump or solar panel. Because words matter to me, silence matters to me I don't speak unless it's a conversation I actually desire to be a part of and I don't speak on topics unless I actually have a desire to share something with meaning.

In my videos of speaking about my van I felt my body becoming more and more drained. I knew my spirit was asking me to change my mind and to pivot. Business strategist love a good "niche" and Van Life was my unintentional niche. When a person has a niche, they are told to not stray from that niche, meaning if I make videos about van life and I speak about emotional healing, don't start randomly making videos talking about my love for pancakes. A niche means to honor and speak about what people came to hear you speak about. Van Life was never how I wanted to market myself, it just kind of happened and I went with it and enjoyed it initially only because I was able to sneak in meaningful messages. But I felt a deep calling to stop driving my van to rest, which meant not having vanlife content and I felt the need to only speak about emotional healing. My expansion from my Van Life videos going viral helped me begin my online 1 on 1 emotional healing intuitive guidance session with hundreds of clients. I was clear that if I changed what I spoke about many other changes would follow but one day I just went for it. I couldn't ignore my intuition anymore regardless of what I would lose or how this change would affect me.

I began getting hundreds on questions daily "are you still traveling in your van, she's a hypocrite that's not even her van, she's not a real van lifer that van is probably parked in her drive way, where's Cleo?, did you give away Cleo because you're in a relationship, I'm unfollowing". Every single day these were the messages I was getting followed by 200-300 followers unfollowing me on all platforms every single day. My amount of emotional healing clients got fewer and fewer and so did the sales on my skincare business, but I knew it was the right thing for me to do. I had to change my mind regardless of how it affected me, I was being asked to evolve and expand and I only had the energy to speak about things that I was passionate about like emotional healing.

Even though many changes occurred that were emotionally uncomfortable from me listening to my intuition I learned a valuable lesson. If it no longer resonates with my spirit, I'm off of it immediately. There's no attempt to talk myself out of it, weigh the pros and cons or attempts to understand how the change will affect me, I'm just allowing myself to adapt to the flow. When new information is presented, when we see what we are doing is not working, when we feel our spirit guiding us to do something different change is inevitable.

The answers you may be looking for, the healing you desire, the success you seek, the love you deserve and the guidance you need may be on the other side of changing your mind when you're being called to. Give yourself permission to move in alignment with your intuitive guidance.

Changing your mind

when presented with new information is a sign of

soul level intelligence.

Happy is the man that is nothing

and knows nothing.

NORMALIZE SITTING YO A** DOWN

When a person can't find a deep sense of meaning they distract themselves with pleasure.

Distractions don't feel like distractions until they're done distracting you. When a person consciously or unconsciously distracts themselves it's a reflection of their internal fear of sitting with themselves and or their thoughts for long or intentional periods of time. When the body rests at night it's in repair mode while our spirits dance & astral project into other realms & dimensions. The physical vessel requires rest and stillness to repair & to sustain its life in this reality.

Healing is found in stillness. A huge distraction for many is social media because they haven't learned the proper way to use it and again, when a person can't find deep meaning they distract themselves with pleasure and Instagram is full of opportunities for dopamine hits. Sitting in silence, being still or putting the phone away for long periods of time can be a hard concept to grasp because the average person is afraid and doesn't know how to stop doing. So, they continue to enter relationships, create, travel & build businesses even when their soul is begging them to rest, they do this to subconsciously distract themselves from being with themselves. They are afraid of the thoughts and emotions that will surface when they finally get still.

Many will even make excuses like "I have kids, I don't have time to rest". But you make time to get your nails done. You make time to eat the food you desire. You make time to watch your favorite shows. The bottom line is people make time for what they want to make time for and what a person chooses to make time for is a reflection of their priorities.

The average person doesn't know how to rest. Resting, meditating, sitting in silence for a couple hours, taking a nap, not doing anything even if there's work to be done. Resting is a personal boundary that everyone is allowed to set to honor their souls. Giving yourself permission to not do anything, to embody your stillness in spite of the guilt or that programmed nagging voice that tells you "You should be doing more". Releasing yourself of distractions is how you honor yourself.

The advice you need is in your silence. The next move you should make, the next goal you should set, the next caption you should write is in your ability to detach from the world outside of you & align with the world inside you. Like our mommas use to say, sit down somewhere! Allow your soul, God & your intuition guide you properly. REST, you know your soul is begging for it.

Constantly staying busy is a trauma response,

Slowing down is medicine.

THE REAL GENERATIONAL CURSE
(How your family shame & secrets ruin your child's life)

T he real generational curses are the untold secrets, the shame around mental health and the hidden trauma that effects the family for generations. Families do their kids, their lineage and future generations a disservice when they hide vital information and hold on to family secrets that continue cycles of trauma, abuse, mental illness and lives of despair.

Many families, especially black families or families of specific cultures were raised to not to talk about many things within the family and don't tell family business. Huge life changing events are swept under the rug and everyone goes on like nothing has happened but trauma is brewing in the core of the family and the individuals that were directly affected. Not only is the trauma what took place in the family, there is a second layer of trauma of not being able to speak about it, tell anyone and having to hide and keep the secrets of very traumatic events.

So many children and adult children have no idea who their parents are. They have no idea why their parents don't show love or affection. They have no Idea what their parent's upbringing was like, what trauma their parents experienced or what traumatic events changed the course of their lives. Many of my clients who suffer from parental trauma don't know or suspect that their parent's may have mental illness but the generation their parents grew up in silenced them so much the parents were never able to get proper mental diagnosis or have been so programmed to remain silent that they still won't say anything or give any detail to their children that could provide a lot of clarity on why their relationship is so turbulent and painful.

So many adults are in pain hurting because they can't figure out why their parents don't love them or why their parent's behavior feels as if they don't love them. Not knowing their parents deeply love them but they were never given love as a child, their parent never nurtured them or supported them so the example of how to love properly was never shown and they truly just don't know how to show or give affection to their child.

When I was younger, I deeply resented my dad for not being present in my life. I felt as If he chose alcohol over me which wasn't true at all, but as a child with limited brain functioning that's how I interpreted his absence. This daddy wound later evolved into a wound I call "Why no me syndrome". It's the wound that never allowed me to feel chosen and not only did I never feel chosen I attracted a reality within relationships of men who never chose me, who always chose an ex-girlfriend over me. My life began to match my perception, my dad chose alcohol over me and then every man I loved seemed choose another woman over me. As I continued to evolve in my healing journey I realized, I knew absolutely nothing about my dad.

My mom one day randomly told me that there were times he suffered from deep depression. This shocked me, firstly because I'm in my 20's and I'm just now learning this valuable information that proves what he was going through had absolutely nothing to do with me, secondly if I was privy to this information there's a possibility, I would have had more compassion for him instead of downloading his absence as him not choosing me. Lastly what stood out to me the most is, if he experienced deep depression, why?

What had happened in his life that was so traumatic that he'd need to use alcohol to escape his reality and that would ultimately keep him away from his child. In that moment I realized had I known more of my dad's life story, his experiences, his wounds his traumas and even mental illnesses if any were present, I'd have a clearer idea who he was as a person and ultimately I'd be aware that whatever trauma he experienced also lives in my cells and DNA as well. When my first deep depression was triggered at 17 I wouldn't have been in shock and confused about what I was feeling or what was going on with me I wouldn't have known that my dad also experienced this feeling. I would have also been a little more mindful of some of our parallel patterns that would later evolve into my own alcohol addiction.

So many children are raped or molested by their own family members because no one speaks about the cousin, uncle or aunt that has been molesting the youth of the family. To make matters worse no one even acknowledges that the cousin, uncle and aunts were touched themselves and what they're doing to the youth of the family is what was done to them.

Most families refuse to acknowledge the mental illness that plagues their family. It's kept secret. Imagine if children grew up knowing depression, which is just emotional trauma passed down generationally ran in their family. They could have natural remedies, therapy etc lined up before signs ever appeared. When important information of any kind is hidden the elders in the family allow their younger family members to maneuver through the confusion, abuse, parental trauma & fear of mental illness alone. Thinking they're crazy, not worthy of being loved, their abuse was their fault and ultimately causing them to fear getting help.

Addiction is so common in families it should be a pre-requisite for the child to know about it and understand it. When I was 3 years old my mom went to rehab for drug addiction and every single day after she got out of rehab, I was with her. She took me to every single AA or CA meeting she went to. My mom raised me to be aware that addiction ran in our family. She explained why & how people suffered from it. My dad and many family members have either suffered from it or died from it. She taught me early & never kept her life story from me. That openness she shared gave me an awareness at a young age & it's how I was able to identify I had a problem as an adult. Thank you, momma.

Family silence causes family trauma to continue. This lack of honesty and lack of intention to heal causes generations to have to figure things out after the trauma has already happened. When the adults of the family heal, they also heal their lineage.

GROW WHERE YOU ARE

You're exactly where you're supposed to be, so GROW where you are.

Stop waiting for a new job, new opportunity, next vacation, next relationship & Heal where you are, cry where you are, explore where you are, love & Elevate where you are.

There is no such thing as being out of alignment with yourself, actually the more out of alignment you feel the more you should pause & find a space of gratitude because there are so many elements protecting & guiding you. So even when you feel out of alignment, you're very much still in alignment.

When the relationship fails, when you feel as if you've lost yourself again, when you feel unhappy or like you don't know what you're doing or not sure what you even want to do with your life, you are in the midst of creating your power and purpose.

It's imperative that you remember each step of your journey is meaningful, each relationship, heartbreak, loss, every bit of confusion is a gift to you, for you to unravel & tell your soul thank you!

When my life gets extremely difficult the first thing I do is cry lol & then I Thank God, the universe, & my spirit guides for allowing my uncomfortable moment to be my teacher & my lesson. I thank them for the gift to see things from a healthy perspective & then I listen to what the moment is attempting to teach me instead of being resistant.

I continue to choose to grow Where I Am, in the midst of the pain, in the depth of the confusion, in the thick of the heartbreak, in the middle of the unraveling. Even if where I am isn't ideally where I'd like to be.

You deserve to heal and step into your power now, No longer waiting until you feel better, saying things like "I'll follow my dream once I lose weight or once I get over this life hurdle". Remind yourself that the perfect time to take your power back is always right now, the only thing that is real is the present moment. Grow where you are and

Remember Who The F*ck You Are.

May you rest in peace

May you laugh in love

May you cry in safety

YOU ARE DOING SO MUCH BETTER THAN YOU THINK YOU ARE

Healing doesn't always feel too good, especially not as good as Instagram makes it seem.

It's not always peaceful, sensual, liberating and fun. Most of the time your healing journey may feel as if your bones are aching, like you're standing in fire while you're simultaneously drowning in your own tears. Sometimes the healing process feels as if we are re-traumatizing ourselves just to heal our trauma and to some degree this is true. Even when a person has a surgery and the wound heals perfectly, years later that wound may still ache or itch. This isn't a sign that something is wrong, this is a sign that the wound is still healing.

<u>Give Yourself Credit</u>

Honor how far you've come. Write in your journal the many obstacles you've overcome so you don't forget and applaud yourself for your endurance to keep going and traveling on your journey even if may seem as if you haven't even received any benefits yet. Most people feel down, defeated and discouraged on their journey because they've forgotten where they come from. They've forgotten the versions of themselves that worked hard to be where they are now. Acknowledge your faith and honor your intentionality. Applaud the spiritual stamina that it takes to continue showing up for yourself daily. There's so much honor in choosing to get up every day to keep trying, even when every bone in your body is ready to give up and give in. Hug yourself for being your own support system. You may not have the support you want, need or desire but the fact that you choose to remember that your soul is equipped with every single tool you need to continue your healing journey is bad ass.

<u>Honor Yourself</u>

Immediately when healing becomes hard, Move. Move your body, don't allow that energy to of defeat a change to become stored in the body.

Sing, dance, stretch, go ride go carts, take a soap making class, listen to a comedy show, invite friends over that make you feel joyful, find a way to make you inner child smile like swinging on a nearby park swing. Celebrate yourself just because. Celebrate yourself because the work you're doing can be difficult. Celebrate yourself just as a reminder not to become stuck on consumed with your healing journey. Celebrate yourself to reminder yourself that you can heal and simultaneously live your life and thrive in a beautiful way.

You are the divine manifestation of God.

There is nothing that you can't do,

There is nothing you can't heal through

There is nothing you can't overcome.

Give yourself grace love, you are meeting new parts of yourself while also reconciling with parts of your past. You're doing just fine and no matter what is happening you're still exactly where you are supposed to be.

Honor the liminal space between

No longer and not yet

LET THEM SUFFER IN PEACE

Sometimes the greatest expression of LOVE is allowing someone you love to suffer without attempting to step in & "Fix It" for them or "Heal" them. Sometimes the epitome of love is allowing them to suffer in peace. Giving them permission to be exactly where they are. Holding space for them to grow painfully in this level of their healing and spiritual evolution.

You do people a disservice when you attempt to end their pain prematurely disregarding the fact that their pain is their teacher, not you.

When you help people prematurely you become a thief & rob them of the lessons they could only find in the midst of their pain. When you step in to relieve a person from their pain you could also be interrupting their karma, their necessary lessons created by the soul for their own benefit.

When you force someone to grow or evolve before their soul is ready you aid in helping them do more damage to themselves in the long run. Difficulty, pain & hard lessons are a part of most if not all people's souls journey, these difficult moments are exactly what their souls need to become strong enough to endure the process of evolution.

If you force them to grow at your pace & help them avoid their painful struggles you also help weaken the muscles they'll need to evolve & fulfill their soul's mission. True healing requires spiritual stamina, which means people must learn how to evolve through hardship to earn their methods to obtaining their peace as the heal, grow and evolve.

Growing up learning I couldn't help everyone I loved forced me to learn Healthy detachment. Now When I see people in the midst of their soul pain, I'm happy for them, I send them love & guidance if they ask but I detach & allow them to fully experience their process of evolving without my interruption.

Everything won't get figured out in this lifetime and some people will require lifetimes to evolve, grow & heal & that is ok. Some people will stay stuck in their addictions, trauma or toxic behaviors & won't fully grasp their lessons until their next lifetime. We all deserve to experience the totality of our journeys without interruption. If you help a struggling butterfly out of its cocoon before it's ready, it dies because it wasn't able to build enough strength to adapt to its environment for its own growth.

Helping people is about having deep discernment & a deep connection to your own intuition to know when it's necessary to help someone or when you're impeding on another person's journey.

Acknowledge if there is a savior complex present within you as you practice allowing people to be exactly where they are. This is love too.

I cannot heal you

But I can commit to

supporting you and holding space for you

As you learn how to heal yourself

YOUR LOVE IS TOXIC?

Society, Disney and romantic movies have programmed us to believe all relationships should, be positive, healthy, healing and make us feel deeply in love. Not all relationships are supposed to be positive, happy & healing. Some relationships are supposed to be so toxic, confusing & hurtful that they bring the person to their knees because through this pain is where the quest for growth, self-reflection & healthy change occur.

When someone hurts you so bad that you seek healthier ways to feel better & you notice the only way out of the pain is to awaken to the high frequency life of healing, growing and evolving you've never been aware of. This is where you realize, you can choose love that teaches you lesson without so much pain. This is where you realize yourself worth and where your spirituality strengthens.

Society has created a world that romanticizes positive, happy, healthy relationships which causes people to demonize the unhealthy toxic relationships. When we demonize something or someone for being the cause of all of your pain or problems, we simultaneously tend to miss the lessons, gems and messages that are in the midst of that pain. Even though these hurtful relationships are not ideal, God still lives there as well.

You're not meant to spend the rest of your life with every person you love.

Try meeting a person & instead of having sex with them or romanticizing your future together sit across from them in silence or meditation & speak to their spirit. Close your eyes and connect on a soul level by asking,

What did you come to here teach me?

Ask their spirit, why are you here?

Why did our paths cross?

Instead of assuming this person came to be your husband/wife.

Some people (souls) only come into our lives to drop off a message & sometimes the deeper the pain the better the lesson. As you heal, grow and evolve at some point hard lessons in love won't be necessary because you'll learn that you can begin to choose your lesson from a place of joy and peace and no longer hurt and pain.

In the meantime, its ok to practice gratitude for our worst relationships, they were the vehicle to get us to the next level of ourselves. Imagine shifting your perspective & acknowledging your romantic partners as being placed in your life only to be your teacher, beings that were sent to activate your soul's memory to heal karmic contracts. This helps you release the unhealthy societal programming of attachment, expectations and unnecessary resentment.

Relationships are tools, guides & teachers. Respect & honor them & their true purpose. LOVE is the bonus.

LOVE IS NOT POSSESSION

You can't possess people; you can only experience them.

Love is not possession & whenever we try to possess people, hold on to them & keep them past our souls divine timing with them, it's out of fear. Fear of losing them & fear of the reality that when they are no longer here our voids would be exposed. The voids they'd helped us temporarily fill.

Fear & love cannot co-exist.

When a person embodies fear of their relationship ending, or fear of their partner cheating, love no longer lives there, obsession does. No matter how short, long, toxic or unhealthy my past relationships they were all successful because I chose to receive the lesson & leave the pain/resentment. The only time a relationship is a failure is when you choose to be surface by blaming the other person, holding grudges and resentment towards them instead of also seeing the lessons and God's messages in the pain.

We all have our own individual soul journeys to fulfill & people are divinely placed in our lives as vehicles to help us get to our next phase of growth, & after they serve that purpose, sometimes they must leave. Once they fulfill their soul's purpose they must continue on their personal path & that is ok. People are not ours to keep, our dogs, our partners, our friends & our children. People leaving, finding another relationship or even transitioning/passing away isn't a bad thing, it's a sign their soul was given another mission that didn't include you. My husband who is a meditation teacher says, "We don't even get to keep our bodies, at some point we even have to give up our bodies". Nothing is ours to keep. Everything In life is teaching us how to nurture healthy detachment and freedom.

Your forfeit your gift of a lesson when you focus on the whys, what ifs & how things happened. Take the lesson leave the pain or you can bring the pain too but when you adopt a healthier perspective like this it medicates the wound of that pain a lot more. It's selfish of us to want people we love to stay for the sake of our own happiness.

We should want them to do whatever it takes to fulfill their individual soul's purpose even if that means we can't be a part of it. If you truly love someone, you'll love them while they are with you & you'll have understanding when it's times to part ways. Before we are humans, we are reflections of God and soul's beings having a human experience. We all must complete our own souls mission and Identify our souls purpose & understand that everyone can't come with you along your journey, let them go with love & continue on your path. Love is an experience to help you grow.

Even when the physical person is gone you can still hold on to the love, but the person is not yours to keep. Practice seeing those you love as soul beings and begin practicing the art of non- attachment and letting go. Be connected to everything, attached to nothing.

WHEN YOU FALL IN LOVE THE END IS PAINFUL

When you fall in love the end is painful.

When you grow in love there is no end,

you continue to grow in love whether together or apart.

To be in love, not with a person but to be in the midst of love at all times even if your partner isn't present, love still lives within you, around you and beside you.

True love is yet another path that brings you closer to you, closer to fulfilling your souls purpose.

Love is not a place to fall in (fall in love) or an experience meant to lose yourself in, those are (karmic entanglements/teachers). Even in your journey through love, you're still on an individual path that just so happened to cross paths with another beautiful soul. Your job isn't even to figure out, expect, plan or predict how long your paths will intermingle. Your only job is to enjoy the experience in your present moment.

When intentional growth is your priority personally & for your relationship it doesn't matter what happens, who chooses to come or go, who must transition out of your life, you are still on your path to intentional grow with complete surrender to whatever God needs to happen, whatever emotions are needed to surface inside you, painful or happy.

Intentional growth means to be committed to your journey at all times no matter what love is formed or lost. The Love you've cultivated with your own soul, spirit & God remains fully intact & you remain fully dedicated to continuing your path with intentionality, even if you have to walk alone with tears in your eyes.

In Every relationship both individuals should have a WHY? Why are your apart of this union? My why for my partnership with my husband is to intentionally work towards fulfilling my soul's purpose, to allow myself to experience the highest frequency of love I believe there is & to give the highest frequency of love I'm capable of to myself and my partner. My why is bigger than the human form of Candyss. My why is my reminder that even in the midst of my greatest love story all roads still lead me back to me.

Don't commit to me

Commit to evolving

I'll meet you there.

I LOVE HARD

I become concerned when I hear a person say "I love hard" or I give my all when I love, because in a healthy reality it doesn't, and it shouldn't even take all of that to love someone.

When a person say's I love hard what that person is truly saying is,

"I give so much of myself to others that I have nothing left over for myself."

"I give so much (love) to others that I'm depleted in the process."

"I give so much love to others in hopes that they'll love me the way my voids crave"

This is not love. This is a person using love to get what they want in return, for someone to love them back the same. A person loves hard in attempt to use love to subconsciously fill their voids & nurture their own wounds. It's another form of codependency & control. Always showing up, doing & being there for others & giving your all to others to the point you have nothing to give yourself. To the point you've neglected yourself.

This is not love, it's self-sabotage masked as "I love hard" or My love is intense".

This is unhealthy & most times after a person like this "loves you" at some point they start to resent you & feel that you don't reciprocate their "Hard Love". They begin to think you don't love them as strongly as they love you, you don't show up for them, make them feel safe, cared for, you don't do for them on the level they do for you.

But what they're really saying subconsciously is

"Why don't you deplete yourself for me the way I deplete myself for you?

Why don't you focus on loving me so "Hard" that you forget to love yourself like I did?

Why don't you put yourself to the side & go out of your way for me the way I do for you?

This type of "love" is a subconscious bargaining chip used when a person is so fearful of loving themselves that they choose to love others intensely to avoid & escape themselves. Bragging about their exaggerated quality of love, gives them a false sense validation. It's doesn't take giving all of yourself to love someone. Listening, cultivating safe spaces to be heard & seen authentically are intentional & effective ways to show love. Love doesn't always require being something & doing something for someone. That same love you're "Attempting" to give away at your own risk, practice giving that to yourself. You deserve weightless love that doesn't require you to do anything hard and doesn't require you to deplete yourself in the process.

Stop replacing your healing with,

Relationships.

You deserve weightless love

that doesn't require you to do anything hard

and doesn't require you to

deplete yourself in the process

CAN YOU BE UPSET WITHOUT REMOVING LOVE?

D o you know how to be upset without removing love?

In relationships it's ok to allow ourselves to be upset but it's emotionally healthy to still practice maintaining compassion & not removing love from our spouses, family or children.

A form of Emotional Abuse is when a person is upset with you, they intentionally remove their love, become cold, give silent treatment, don't care for you or take care of you & intentionally make you feel guilt, shame, embarrassed & bad.

Psychology studies show that when a person is ignored by someone who attention means a lot to them, the reaction in the brain is similar to physical pain. When a person is angry without a healthy balance of compassion, they attempt to use this form of emotional abuse to make a person feel, how they feel or worse.

When you truly love someone both truths can exist at the same time.

Anger doesn't have to be void of love or compassion.

You can let someone know how deeply upset you are with them & be very clear & firm on why, while still maintaining compassionate love in you approach. You can convey why you're upset without making them think you will leave them and without beating them up emotionally when they already feel horrible, or continually throwing their mistake in their face to shame them. People who do this lack healthy conflict resolution skills & on a deeper level are suffering from deep rooted emotional pain & want others to feel that pain with them.

A healthier way of not removing love while upset looks like, being open & communicating about why you're upset, but still being able to say I love you before you leave the house or before you get off the phone. Still making sure your spouse's well-being is ok, that they're safe. As you work together to find a solution.

Withdrawing love, because you're angry can causes deep trauma and trigger a person's past wounds of abandonment, unworthiness, feeling like a burden and their wounds of neglect. This then can also trigger lack of self-worth & lack of confidence in a person, especially if this is something they experienced in childhood. When you truly love someone, if you truly love yourself no matter how angry you are, you still lead with love & compassion. You always do your best to leave people better than you found them.

This is what healthy balanced love looks like. Still honoring how you feel while still holding space for love to remain present. When moments become emotionally difficult for you to maneuver just take a moment to breath and begin to remind yourself "Love lives here".

Love lives here.

EMOTIONAL IDENTIFICATION

When you're healing, what you feel doesn't always have to be identified.

As humans our bodies are processing energies, experiences, memories & shocks to our nervous system that we aren't even conscious of moment to moment. Sometimes when you wake up & you just don't feel your best, you may feel down or even just heavy emotionally, but you don't know why. Sometimes this emotional heaviness isn't because you're sad about anything that's happening now, this may actually be a sign that your body is processing energies, memories, emotions & thoughts from traumas & situations that happened days, months, years & even lifetimes ago.

Sometimes my clients will say they don't feel like they are healing, but they don't think about the fact that you are always healing, whether you physically/emotionally feel better or not. Healing doesn't mean you feel good, joyous and happy, it just means. Progression in your life journey is taking place and that can look and feel many ways.

Your body is always repairing & helping you process emotions, energies & feelings. When an emotion surfaces the body is already at work attempting help you process & release it, but you must be still long enough to acknowledge it & allow that wave of emotion to pass.

During thanksgiving my husband & I randomly experienced moments where we woke up & felt a little heavy energetically. Nothing was "wrong " & we never attempted to identify what we felt or why this wave of heaviness was present, we just honored how each other felt & catered to one another. He took me on an intuitive walk & helped me play through my inner child at a playground & I massaged his feet & read a book to him.

Being conscious that what you feel is just A passing wave that doesn't always need to be identified, dissected & figured out gives you freedom to feel however you feel without being attached to why & how to fix it. You can just be, until it passes.

Trust & allow your soul to renew itself without your help. You entire being was designed to heal as a human, trust yourself. Even when you are consciously clueless trust that you subconsciously know exactly what you are doing.

Find your cape.

Praying Like A Beggar

I prayed for this, why am I afraid of this?

Sometimes we ask for things we want, but don't fully believe we are worthy, just yet.

Sometimes when we pray for things we romanticize how it will look, feel, change our lives & make us happy, but we don't acknowledge that pain, un-comfortability, confusion, new behavioral emotional requirements that will come with what we asked for.

Somehow in our romanticism of what we desire, we completely disregard that with new levels of receiving come new requirements of growing & new requirements of shedding people, behaviors, emotions & thoughts that can't come with you in your season of receivership & that can be deeply scary.

It's important to remind ourselves that just because we receive what we pray for doesn't mean the work is done, we still must continue our process of evolving, healing & growing to maintain our spiritual stamina & keep what we've been blessed with. Anything that grows or expands has the capacity to feel uncomfortable or even painful no matter how beautiful the expansion is. When the fear sets in it can become very easy to talk your way out of our new healthy relationship, career opportunity, creative ideas etc. this is called self-sabotage. These are moments where it's imperative to check in with yourself to dissect which version of you is afraid of elevating & ask why? Which version of you doesn't believe you deserve love, a career or new opportunities. Which part of your being doesn't feel worthy and where does this belief stem from, where is it rooted? Ultimately this is what it comes down to.

"I am afraid of receiving what I asked for because deep inside there's a part of me that doesn't feel worthy."

"Nurture that part of yourself. Cultivate a relationship with that aspect of your being that is so fearful of living the life you desire, asked for and worked for. It's ok to feel growing pains as you intentionally heal, grow & evolve.

STOP SHRINKING

Stop shrinking yourself to fit into spaces you are meant to outgrow.
Take up space,be outlandish with your confidence

Stop "humbling" yourself to feel accepted, to not step on toes or to be perceived in a "good" way.

Stop hiding your greatness, your power & your light.

Release the fear that keeps you from and sabotages you out of embodying the essence of your being.

As a woman it's taken me 33 years to feel at home in my body, to allow myself to take up space, to show up big and bold. I now know that when I gained 60 pounds seven years ago it was my bodies subconscious way of expanding to be seen & acknowledged, because I so desperately wanted to show up big in the world & show my light, but my fear hindered me & manifested in me showing up big in the world as 60pound weight gain.

Everything in society tells us to minimize ourselves to make others accept us. Society tells us that a "humble" person is attractive, & nah. We are not doing that anymore. Take up space, promote your business unapologetically, be loud, hype yourself up, show out because you feel good & embody the depths of your beautiful essence. No more hiding, humbling yourself or being modest. Imagine GOD giving you the brightest light & you turn around dim it out of fear of how it'll make others feel.

Give yourself permission to embody your greatness and step into your power. Embrace your gifts, sensuality, talents, intelligence etc. It's time love.

Real healing requires

touching pieces of yourself that terrify you

THE LOVE BIBLE

When a person isn't raised in a loving environment as a child, as they become an adult they're forced to look for outside role models to teach them what love is supposed to look & feel like.

If a person wasn't nurtured as a child, supported, allowed to cry, wasn't held as they cried, didn't feel safe, protected, if their emotions weren't acknowledged, if they didn't feel seen, heard or they weren't told I love you. When that child evolves into an adult they begin chasing an idea of love, what they think love should look and feel like. The lack of love they received as children forces them to look to outside sources for an idea of what love is. They begin to learn about love from unrealistic sources like music, tv, movies and society.

If a person wasn't raised with love, they have no blueprint on what love truly looks or feels like, leaving them to guess & take other people's advice for how it's "supposed to be". Not only does this cause confusion in their adult relationships & friendships it also causes confusion in how they show up to love themselves. It manifests as a lack of boundaries, saying yes when they really want to say no, living & thriving in survival mode, craving love but having no idea what it looks like and how to actual accept it when it arrives. When a person isn't raised with love, their entire perception of what love can be distorted. However, there is hope. Even though they may not know what love looks or feels like they now have a blank canvas to create their own idea of what love looks/feels like to them. They get to create their own love blueprint, love manual or love bible. There is no one rule book on what love is or isn't. Love is whatever resonates with your spirit. As you create your own manual you have the freedom to add too, take away, & change your mind. As you grow & evolve what looked like love to you as a teenager doesn't feel like love as an adult. You get to decide what behaviors, tones of voice, types of words or gestures look and feel like love to you. When you're eating healthy compared to only fried chicken, based on how that makes your body feel you get to decide which one of those

~ 297 ~

eating habits feels like self-love to you. As you continue to heal, grow and evolve you can always return to your love bible to update the information.

Even those who were raised in loving environments still had opportunities to explore their own versions of love growing up. We've all at some point experienced love that we want more of and love that was never love to begin with. Everyone in life is given an opportunity to learn their own concept of love as they heal, grow and evolve. It becomes an adventure to explore love and the different' types of love.

You may not have experienced love growing up, but you still have the power to decide what love looks & feels like to you & adjust as you grow, heal & evolve.

KARMIC SEX

Don't have sex with that person if you aren't Prepared to absorb their emotional, spiritual & karmic residue.

As you embark on your spiritual journey the meaning "Sexual Freedom" and "Sexual Liberation" changes, now spiritual integrity becomes priority and the term spiritual integrity isn't used to be or sound righteous, it's used as a reminder that as you heal, grow and evolve sex is no longer just sex, it becomes prayer.

There is a deeper consciousness & awareness that comes with exchanging sexual energy. Women must be mindful of what types of spirits they allow into their womb of creation, the portal that brings all souls into this realm & men must be conscious of giving away his seed which is his life force & each time he gives his seed away without sacred intention and lacks the ability to control his lustful desires & ejaculates he loses his life force, ages himself & dies a little each time.

Most People use sex as an emotional escape. When they don't want to deal with the depths of themselves, they choose to get lost in another, ignoring the karmic consequences that come with allowing sexual partners into their reality that have no business there. Sexual energy exchanges are so strong you start to absorb your partners characteristics, depression, you absorb their emotions, you even start to look like them. How many times have you seen someone who's dating and thought to yourself, they actually look alike. This is no coincidence; it is how strong energy is. Imagine what happens when you exchange sex with a partner that is emotionally unhealthy, in the midst of their trauma & spiritually lacks integrity. What do you think happens to you, your sprit, aura, & soul?

Society has convinced people to practice "Sexual Freedom" because there's a deep societal knowing that as long as you're spiritually connected & enmeshed to another, you'll never fully be able to inhibit & embody the fullness of yourself, your power & your own soul because your energies will be constantly in conflict trying to cleanse themselves from your partners toxic and karmic residue.

When having sex acknowledge you're inviting that person into your spirit. So many are allowing others to leave stains on their souls & what's worse is they have zero idea how to cleanse their vessel of that energy.

Spiritual Integrity is taking pride in who you allow into you home body. Honoring your soul with connections that raise your serve a purpose in your soul's evolution, not help you forget who you are.

Don't have sex with that person if

you aren't prepared to absorb and transmute their emotional, spiritual & karmic residue.

As you heal, grow and evolve sex is no longer just sex,

it becomes prayer.

When You Don't Know Who You Are

When you don't know who you are, you invite other people to tell you.

When you don't know who you are, you the door open for other people to create their own narratives & describe your character in your own book.

When you don't have a clear idea of who you are, you become susceptible to others opinions, perspectives & their personal views of you and heir false perceptions of you can quickly become your reality.

It's imperative that you know your own soul because when you leave room for doubt narcissistic people will begin calling you the narcissist & actually have you believing it. The selfish will call you selfish & the those who deeply don't love or like themselves will unconsciously project all of their self-hatred on to you & make you out to be the villain & the problem, while the entire time they are the devils in disguise.

When you aren't clear on who you are their opinions can ruin you, hurt, scar & even traumatize you. Make you feel worthless, like a bad person, unattractive, unlovable & so much more. This is why the journey to healing ourselves is a non-negotiable and an urgency. Not just in relationships but in society as well. Everything around us does it's best to make us forget or dislike who we are, our jobs as humans having a spiritual experience is to remember who the f*ck we are and to shut off all of the noise, opinions & perceptions of others & return back home to our truest selves.

When you know who you are it becomes very easy to stand in your power, set healthy boundaries, & only allow what you deserve. When you are clear on the type of beautiful being you are no one has the power to make you believe otherwise.

But this first comes with full self-reflection & acknowledgement of not just your greatness but the spaces that can also use some work, love & nurturing. Intentionally seeking your own blind spots & loving on them, & no one will ever be able to use, you against you. Ever again.

You either know yo self or you ho yo self.

Your call.

Trigger Fingers

Your feelings are always valid, but your assessment of the situation may be inaccurate.

When a person becomes triggered their emotions are always valid, however this doesn't mean that they are seeing things from the healthiest perspective and it doesn't mean they are right in a situation. It just means they are allowed to feel how they feel. Most times when people are "triggered" they are reminded of hurtful memories from their past & unconsciously see the current situation as a reflection of that. Being triggered is like entering a time machine, the second your wound is tampered with you begin to see the world from your place of pain, unhealed emotions & no longer from a place of clarity & sound mind. You even revert to the age you first experienced those unhealed pains.

Many people have disagreements and think that they are speaking to another adult, but subconsciously the person you are speaking to could have reverted back to their 12 year old self and this I why it is so difficult to come to a mature resolution. This is how triggers formed from trauma manifest in our adult lives.

When you choose to practice self-awareness these emotional episodes can be managed & will less likely end in damaged relationships. Triggers aren't about blame they're opportunities to learn more of ourselves & to feel into why these emotions have surfaced & dissect where they stem from. How you feel is valid, but your perspective & Perception maybe distorted & coming from unhealed spaces within yourself. Self-accountability doesn't always feel good. Healing & growth doesn't always feel good, but triggers are opportunities take accountability & simply self-reflect so you can heal deeper, honor yourself, honor your soul & empower your journey of healing.

When you refuse to acknowledge the source of your triggers and rest on placing blame on the person who triggered you, you subconsciously reinforce the idea that you are powerless & anything outside of your is power-full. You reinforce the toxic idea that you need others to make you feel better, happy & at peace & you also reinforce the idea that other people have the Power to make you feel angry, agitated and unwanted emotions. No matter what another person does or say any emotion that you feel in your body was your choice to feel & hold onto.

I do my best to refrain from saying "you made me feel" because if we journey deep into self-accountability we know, no one can make us feel anything. We choose how we feel, how we respond and how we react. No one has that much power over us, even when we unconsciously give our power away. No matter what a person does we are responsible for the emotions we choose to acknowledge and hold onto.

When we adopt this perspective, it gives us the freedom of choice to remember a person may have behaviors that trigger me, but all emotions come from inside me, they aren't given to me which mean I have to take accountability for the emotions I chose to feel, acknowledge and hold on to.

When A healing opportunity presents itself to you, take pride in doing your own work without projecting it onto others, making it their responsibility to heal things that only you have the power to heal. When you choose to intentionally grow & heal you empower every cell in your body. You motivate every space within your being to be better & show up as the highest version of yourself.

Show up for yourself, especially in the moments you feel like blaming another person for how you chose to feel. The moments a person plays apart in triggering us are opportunities for us to return back home to the depth of ourselves.

Those who trigger us

to feel negative emotions are messengers.

They hold messengers for the unhealed

parts of our being.

FULL OF LOVE, LOW ON TRUST

Imagine not being able to express the one thing you feel most. The one thing you're full of, love. Because you "Think" you're supposed to trust people.

Trust is a subconscious need to control & stems from a deep void. It's a defense mechanism used so you don't have to deal with the truth that you subconsciously already know, that you aren't & will never be able to control anything, anyone & no Situation. Spiritually on a deeper level the need to trust & control stems from the fact that the Ego feels it had no control over its birth into this reality. No control over the choice in parents you received. No control over the way you were raised, how people perceive you, how people choose to love you, want you, need you, see & acknowledge you.

The need to trust comes from the fact that you're living in a world that you have no idea what is really going on. A God you can't see, but you can feel. Which calls you to have "Faith" & choose (trust) You never know when something bad can happen. You can't control the weather. Most people can't even control their own emotions. What around you in life do you actually trust fully and whole heartedly?

As spiritual beings we subconsciously know we must surrender to life & all that comes with it. However, most people are so fearful of trust they use relationships as their last attempt to gain control of the unknown. They attempt to use their partners and children & make them behave in ways that solidifies that they have control over their own realities.

"I Trust you" typically means, I trust you not to hurt me, lie to me, do me wrong, I trust you to not do anything that brings me emotions I'm not prepared to handle. I trust you to hold the status quo that we agreed to. Don't change anything, don't lie, cheat or do what's best for you if it'll affect me because then my life will become unstable and reflect the unknown. Trust has been used by us as a weapon to subconsciously make ourselves feel safe. But everything in life is based in the unknown & asks us to continually surrender to what comes.

To truly trust anything or anyone requires deep surrender & detachment from the deep fear of being hurt. It requires the demolishing of expectations & the acceptance of what is & what will be. I now believe that the inability to trust others, let your guards down, embody the freedom that is LOVE, is a clear reflection of the deep confusion a person feels around being human, your deep confusion around living in a realm called "Earth" where nothing makes sense. We are literally spinning in in space that has over 2 trillion galaxies and thousands of planetary systems. The people are confusing, the rules are dumb & the situations can be extremely heart breaking. On top of that we experience random miracles that remind us there is a higher power & can't be by coincidence. We receive confirmation in the exact moments we need it & we randomly see beautiful moments in this life that makes us grateful for life.

On a subconscious level, many "Humans" deeply wonder Wtf is this? How am I here? Why Am I here? Etc as beautiful as life can be, just the idea of how miraculous life is can make you feel powerless & even confused. My personal opinion is that humans attempt to subconsciously feel safe or attempt to regain power in a world that is so confusing by protecting themselves in relationships. Romantic or platonic. I believe the ego put up walls not just out of fear of being hurt but as an innate coping & defense mechanism that comes with not fully understanding life in general. Unconsciously believing the only way to feel grounded or safe in this world is to protect themselves against the beings we must come in contact with daily. It's not that you don't trust them, it's that you don't fully trust anything because you don't fully understand anything.

What's beautiful is when you cultivate a relationship with your soul & a deeper relationship with source, God, The universe, whatever name resonates with your spirit. Protective walls are no longer necessary because trust is now who you are. Fear is no longer needed because trust is now a part of your being, knowing that everything is working for you & not against you whether you understand life or not. This type of trust makes it easier to thrive in relationships because you trust that no matter how any situation unfolds it is always designed & in alignment with your best interest. I believe this is a huge purpose of life, learning to trust, live, let go & just be without attempting to always protect ourselves. What do you believe the purpose of life is?

Stop Breaking Your Own Heart.

Cry, yell, scream or explode if you must.

Thug it out and then step into your power.

FORGIVENESS DOESN'T MEAN RE-ENTRY

As we heal, grow and evolve in our own personal healing and spiritual journeys it is important that we always leave the door of our hearts open as a reminder to always return to love. In life there may be many times when someone mistreats you, doesn't honor your value or takes your love for granted. In these situations, especially when our emotions are involved, we feel hurt of offended we must always take time to decide how we choose to show up in that relationship or with that person moving forward. When a person apologizes and you honor their apology with compassion, understanding or forgiveness, you must also decide how you'd like to move forward. You must take into consideration what is emotionally safe for you and ultimately what is a healthy decision for your personal peace.

Forgiveness does not mean Re-entry.

It doesn't permit a second chance &

It doesn't mean a relationship with the person you're forgiving must look the same, go back to normal or even continue.

When a person has treated you in a way that presents red flags, make you question their character, morality or spiritual and makes you feel uncomfortable or hurt, you are allowed to readjust how that person has permission to show up in your life, it they have permission at all. Loving someone doesn't constitute a right to have a relationship with you. Being in relationship with you of any kind is a privilege and you choosing to reassess a person's privileges doesn't mean you're a bad person, it means you honor and love yourself so much that you are mindful of who you allow into you space based on their intentions, actions and ultimately how their energy effects your energy.

You can deeply love someone & still say "I forgive you , I love you and I deserve better" or "I forgive you and allowing you to still hold space in my life isn't healthy for me".

This isn't to say when a person makes a mistake they should be reprimanded, it's to say become clear on what mistakes are understandable and grant further access and what mistakes show you who a person truly is and requires their access to be denied or revoked. Many people learn the same tough lessons because their loving heart outweighs their logic & the truth is sometimes the people you love most, want to experience life with, co-parent with, be married to, be best friends with are not healthy relationships for you until those people learn that your forgiveness to their apologies aren't permission for second chances to display the same unhealthy behaviors. Sometimes you will have to learn to love people from & distance & forgive them without dishonoring yourself & allowing them back in to potentially make the same mistakes.

Personally, I've always been done my best to forgive or at least understand a person's behavior because on a soul level I understand people's behavior is a direct reflection of their inner world & I have compassion as people work out their personal levels of being human. However, they get a full access pass to practice healing their emotional dysfunction far away from me, from a good healthy distance lol my forgiveness and understanding doesn't always warrant re-entry. Once A person shows me who they are and what karmic debt, they are actively working through based on how they've emotionally projected and treated me I deeply, whole heartedly believe them, I adjust & I implement boundaries to love people from a distance. I can still love a person beautifully from a distance, by acknowledging.

"All of the love I have for them still exists within me and in my heart, they just lose access to it".

Case by case you get to build your intuitive muscle & practice discernment on who should be allowed to hold space in your life, set boundaries on what that looks like & listen to the guidance of your spirit when it's says "Aht Aht" or to welcome someone back in with a soft heart.

The only way to have pure access to your intuition & hear your spirit is if you heal emotionally & spiritually so you can decipher whether your intuitive discernment hears from a place of pure love or trauma based on wounds & voids.

Forgiveness doesn't mean re-entry.

It means,

All of the love I have for them

still exists within me and in my heart,

they just lose access to it.

SPIRITUAL STAMINA

Sometimes being able to pull through dark, uninspired, depressing, unhealthy & painful moments is dependent on how much work a person puts in to heal during their happy, positive, peaceful & inspired moments.

So often when people are happy, inspired & full of peace they forget about doing the work to heal. They stop going to therapy, they stop learning themselves, they stop self-reflecting, holding themselves accountable and doing their emotional healing and spiritual practices. They subconsciously carry the mindset of

"if pain isn't present, if my situation is no longer bad I'm not going to focus on it"

and they allow themselves to get distracted with fun, tv, relationships, food, drinking, smoking or anything that aids in them feeling good or better. However, when the fun runs out, pain resurfaces, they realize they never created a real blueprint to pull themselves out of their own self-inflicted hell.

The peaceful, happy, joyful and inspiring times are the best and easiest times to practice spiritual, emotional & psychological stamina. This is the time to focus & write the book, to practice meditation, to dig deeper into your emotions, to dissect your thought processes, to start cultivating a healthy relationship with your body and your higher power. The moments you feel great are not a time for distractions, but time for cultivating, creating, becoming & embodying the best version of yourself, so when the pain resurfaces it doesn't dismantle your entire being.

When the fleeting wave of happiness dissipates, the motivation has run out, the negative self-talk starts to come back, the confidence isn't there, you're emotionally eating, can't think of what your next steps in life are. You quickly realize that it's beyond difficult to pull yourself out of a rut when you haven't spent any of your time practicing spiritual, emotional &

psychological stamina. When you're intentionally dedicated to healing as a lifestyle and a passion, when dark moments come, you'll still be able to thrive in them. Thrive in your depression, pain & uncomfortable moments.

One day you may feel really low, but you'll also be empowered enough to say

"I've developed this part of myself and I have the tools to pull myself out this rut, I don't have to stay here".

Do your work now so when tough times come, you can evolve in those spaces with grace and confidence. Deep down you know exactly what you're capable of. There's even moments where you get a glimpse of all the potential you have. You can get there. You just have to be willing to sacrifice habits, things and situations that are standing in the way of your healing, your growth and you evolution.

When you make an intentional decision to heal

Everything in the universe agrees with you

And works towards helping you complete your mission.

As long as you are trying to do better,

Better is going to come.

EVERYONE IS MY TEACHER

Your relationship with another person reflects the relationship you have with yourself.

Relationships are perfect opportunities for people to dissect themselves on a deeper level, to feel sensations of what emotions come up during uncomfortable moments. To pay close attention to how the body responds to those uncomfortable moments & get curious about why?

So often people think healing only happens when they are single, alone and in solitude, this is true to a certain extent. Solitude is one of our greatest and deepest teachers because it provides enough silence to hear the guidance of the soul. However, even deeper healing occurs when in relationship with another, because other people are just reflections of us (they are you) they have the power to point out our blind spots, to trigger our emotions, to hold a mirror up to our faces and make us see ourselves in ways that are not possible in our oneness. Even when someone doesn't love you the way you'd prefer they are still loving you by ushering you to love yourself.

People don't just enter our lives so we can be in love and give them titles "friend, husband, wife, mother, child" they are our guides. We learn our greatest lessons by having relationships with other people. One of the most value lessons I've learned on my journey was to not get caught up in

"The Relationship" instead get curious and ask, what is this soul asking me to see within myself? When in relationship of any kind practice being present enough to see how that person is guiding you back home to yourself & teaching you about yourself no matter how painful or angry their methods make you feel. There maybe things that you need to pay closer attention to within your being, emotions that may arise that may need a little more nurturing or behaviors that may need to be rectified. Even if a person gifts you with immense pain this is actually one of the most beautiful gifts because through pain, many lessons can be extrapolated through that experience with that one person.

I honor that My husband and I see one another as guides, teachers & gurus. As much healing & spiritual work we've done alone before our souls re-connected in this lifetime, we are always excited to learn from one another, to see things within ourselves we didn't see before & still feel free and loved enough to heal and grow right in front of one another. Even when it's uncomfortable. No arguing or disagreements just open hearts eager to be students to one another's wisdom. When we give ourselves permission to remain a student of life, we open ourselves up to receive guidance, lessons and teachings from any person, place or situation. The wisdom isn't in just in the books, it's in the teachers you walk past daily.

How Does This Make You Feel?

S ometimes the healthiest way to maintain a relationship is to simply
ask "How does this make you feel?"

   Put yourself in their shoes, to explore their perspectives and thought
processes without attempting to decipher who's right or wrong, but to help
yourself find a deeper level of compassion, connection, patience &
understanding for what they may be experiencing or feeling.

   George Bernard Shaw's famous quote says, "The simple biggest
problem with communication is the illusion that it has taken place."

   Sometimes it's easy to forget how things you do, say or partake in effect
the people closest to you. Especially in romantic relationships. It's easy to
get caught in selfishness and completely disregard how even simple things,
can make your partner feel unintentionally. It's imperative to check in with
your partner and ask questions about how certain things may make them
feel. Take the initiative to inquire, to dig deeper into their emotional
psyche. Sometimes just asking feels like checking in on them, it feels like
support, nurturing, provision and care. Sometimes just asking about how
certain things make them feel is all the medicine that's needed to sooth
whatever feelings are surfacing for them.

   No, you absolutely don't have to be a mind reader and its ok to
acknowledge your partner may feel some emotions rising but they may not
have the words to express them just yet and sometimes you inquiring opens
the door for open healthy conversation to take place. This also doesn't mean
that whatever they feel is "right, makes sense or is logical". Many times
when a person is still processing how they feel, they may not express
themselves the best or most articulate because they are still getting a grasp
on how they actually feel, but how they feel is still valid and they deserve to
be heard or nurtured even in those spaces.

   When you begin to ask yourself "I wonder how this makes him/her
feel? I'm curious how this affects him/her? You start opening doors to put

yourself in your spouse's shoes to understand their experience in your life. What you may feel to be "ok" may be causing the complete opposite types of emotions in your spouse. Get comfortable asking "how does this make you feel?" It's important to take time to check in with your partner and the health of your relationship. Dissecting if there's anything you two can do better or differently to enhance your love, communication, understanding & intimacy. This can truly help put out any romantic fires before they even begin.

Healthy communication is a practice.

Remind one another to take off your armor.

Let down your walls and disarm your heart.

Start the conversation with the mantra

"Love lives here"

And when you begin to feel uncomfortable

Breathe, Then remind yourself to

return back to love

A Reminder to Let Go

S urrender is GOD
The unknown is GOD
Trust & flow is GOD
Letting go & allowing is GOD

Allowing yourself to befriend your fear is a deep connection with your soul. The practice of staying in flow & surrendering when you feel resistance or fear or the need to control is truly a practice. A daily & even moment to moment practice for those who need to have control over people, situations, goals & outcomes. Those that feel unnecessary pressure that is mostly self-inflicted. You will have to stay mindful that the only path to the things you desire is learning how to surrender at the depths of your soul.

Your attempt to always control is a sign you feel powerless deep down & that you have zero trust for life, yourself, your soul, your process of evolving and a higher power or GOD of your own understanding. Where there is surrender there is peace. Where there is trust there is harmony, not just with the beautiful aspects of life but you'll find harmony in being at peace with anything that comes your way because you'll see that all is happening exactly how it should & there is no need to control or fix what is already perfect. If you want to experience peace. Let go of the need to control. Practice the art of Surrender when resistance surfaces. Let go or be dragged. Remember who the f*ck you are.

Movement is Medicine.

When you move your body

Stretch and work towards strength

You remind your body

it is safe to open up

THE SUN & ALL HER FLOWERS

I smell life when i breath in the air of the forest trees. I see God when the sun gloriously shines her light to brag about her creation.

Her light helps me see into the pain & struggles they endured to grow. Many trees are distorted, crooked, hunched over, broken, with lumps, scars, vines & even sumps that could grow no longer it's clear many trees had to adapt to stay alive in environments that never nurtured them the way they deserved. Some trees grow straight up into the heavens, they seem like their journey was the easiest but truthfully, we'll never know the depths of their branches. For all we know their branches touch heaven but their roots are rooted in hell. Some branches experience so much trauma they had to split personalities and grow in different ways to survive.

Every year the trees & plants teach us how to shed, release & let go of what no longer serves us. They intentionally die to be an example of how to surrender to life & death gracefully. They show us how to slow down take our time, evolve naturally with flow. They also show us how things can dangerously erupt when we choose to force.

With all of the innate trauma the trees & the flowers have to experience in their lifetime. They never stop returning home to themselves. They never stop growing & they always choose to love so deeply that they never stop providing a home for others.

The sun raised them well.

The sun loves them well.

The sun nurtures them well.

YOU ARE ALLOWED TO EXPLORE ANGER

If anger is present, you're allowed to honor it and feel it to the depths of your being without rushing past it because "society says it's the right thing to do".

As I journeyed into anger in a healthy way I realized I didn't give myself permission to be angry. I was deeply afraid of my rage that I now see as a beautiful visitor I deserve to explore myself with time to time. When I allowed myself to befriend my fiery rage, I found parts of myself I'd abandoned covered in ashes.

Years ago, I would not say anything, hold all of my emotions in and later explode in anger. I'd just go off and explode uncontrollably. As I journeyed into my healing and spirituality journey learning how to control my emotions and my anger was one of the first things I worked on. I read A book called "Anger, the wisdom of cooling the flames" By Thich Nhat Hanh that helped me learn more about my anger. I hated giving my power away to anger and having to apologize for my reaction later on.

So, I perfected responding and not reacting. I perfected controlling my emotions, remaining calm and levelheaded. Even as a police officer of seven years amid crazy, chaotic and unsafe situations I would always get asked "how are you so f*ckin calm"? I taught myself how to become so calm in the midst of turbulent situations and even crisis's that some people have admitted that my demeanor scares or intimidates them. I become extremely observant, my voice never elevates and I maintain beautiful composure and control over my emotions, however one thing I never truly allowed myself to feel again was, anger. I got so good at staying calm and keeping my composure that I bypassed how I actually felt.

Now when anger surfaces, I realize that I cannot move on or transmute this energy until I admit that anger is present. A necessary mention is those who also suffer or suffered from alcohol addiction like myself at some point in their lives may also suffer from un-nurtured & unprocessed anger.

Alcohol directly affects, irritates and agitates the liver, this is why when many people drink they become angry, hostile or aggressive. Now that I'm sober all of those years of anger were stored in my liver and still needed a place to go to be transmuted. So, when situations arise that trigger the energy of anger, I also must stay mindful that my liver is purging emotional residue.

As I invited myself to befriend anger, I realized that I had been a thief in my own healing journey. I had robbed myself of my natural expression of emotion because I thought forgiving and rushing past anger made me a "good person". I muzzled myself & learned extremely unbalanced coping skills. Although it was necessary for me to learn control and composure years ago, now I also had to learn that anger is allowed just like any other emotion, anger serves a beautiful purpose & healing cannot occur until the truth of all emotions are fully expressed, felt & acknowledged. As Caroline Myss would say "Liars don't heal". Ignoring the truth of our feelings, convincing ourselves things don't bother us anymore, and believing our own lies robs us of the opportunity to heal wounds & sometimes that means allowing passionate anger to be present without focusing on how it looks or its outcome. I had to apologize to myself for silencing myself and for years of dishonoring my own self-expression. Now I deeply honor anger, explosive energy and rage. I embody it as my teacher and a messenger that comes to help me release energies that no longer serve me. I've created my own explosive energy practices that allow me to honor these emotions without them being directed at a person or spiritually irresponsibly projected on to a person. I personally enjoy going out into nature, journaling about what emotions is present and what I feel and then yelling and screaming to the top of my lungs to allow that explosive energy to release from my body. Another beautiful practice is punching, hitting and slamming pillows to release explosive energy. I instruct many of my clients to go to smash rooms that allow them to beat objects like TVs, wood, glass, walls and other things to help them release their emotions.

When you allow all emotions to be present without rushing past them you honor yourself.

If anger is present, you're allowed to honor it

& feel it to the depths of your being

without rushing past it because

"society says it's the right thing to do".

When I allowed myself to befriend my fiery rage,

I found parts of myself I'd abandoned covered in ashes.

The Spectrum of Emotion

While working with clients, as they share deep personal life experiences and traumas, I'm always guided to ask them "How does that make you feel".

This is how I gauge if that person even has the capacity to feel emotion, acknowledge emotion, be vulnerable or if they have the capacity to identify how they feel. Typically, the average person doesn't know how to identify what they feel so the attempt to explain it in a story form.

An example would be

Me: How did it make you feel that your mom was abusive to you.

Them: She was always mean to me, I just never thought she loved me.

Me: So, how did it make you feel that you never felt loved?

Them: I understand her mom never showed her love so how could she show it to me? It's hurtful by I'm used to it by now

Me: What are three emotions that describe how it felt to never feel loved by your mom?

Them: Angry, Sad, Hurt

When a person has experienced deep soul penetrating pain, but they only have the capacity to describe that pain with words like "Angry, Sad, Hurt" I know they have a very limited emotional vocabulary, a very limited understanding of emotions and may not fully in be in touch with what they actually feel and what emotions are present.

In our society this is very normal because growing up we typically only learn three emotions "happy, sad, angry". This paradigm isn't always helpful because our emotions are much more intricate. Most times multiple emotions exist at once and each emotion has a root emotion. An example is when a person says they're angry, underneath anger could be let down, underneath let down could be, betrayed, underneath betrayed could be hurt, underneath hurt could be, unworthy, underneath unworthy could be, unloved or un-loveable.

Being able to identify the root emotion matters because it doesn't give a person permission to rest on "I'm angry". It allows them to explore the root causes of their emotions which for the most part will always lead back to what I call the "The Love Wound". When a person wasn't loved properly the way they needed to be loved as a child or the innate wound of just wanting to be loved, seen, heard, acknowledged, wanted, chosen, safe and protected. In my client example, she could only identify with the emotions of "Angry, Sad, Hurt" we now know that underneath those emotions are possibly 10+ other emotions that are lying dormant and that have gone unacknowledged and unexpressed. This can be emotionally dangerous because what if a person only feels as if they are angry? They may spend the rest of their lives only identifying with anger, now their demeanor reflects an angry person, they show up in their present relationships as angry and ultimately attract more situations that allow them to express that anger. But what happens if that same person is now aware that underneath their anger is pain, fear of abandonment, unworthiness, neglect, not feeling good enough, or wanted.

What if underneath that anger is the deep fear of not being loved? Now how does this person show up in the world when they can now recognize they aren't just angry, they are also sad, fearful and holding a lot of emotional pain. They now can identify with multiple emotions that exist simultaneously and won't be relegated to resting on the surface emotion of anger. Imagine going your whole life thinking you were just angry then to find out you aren't this hard angry person at all, you are just in pain and the anger is an unconscious attempt to bypass the vulnerability of emotional pain. This is how tricky the mind can get, these are the many ways the mind and the ego attempt to protect us. It uses anger to help us feel empowered, in control and dominant, when the truth is underneath that anger is vulnerability, human emotion and even fear.

Once I give my clients the homework assignment of downloading the "Emotional Wheel" now we can have a more in-depth conversation and they can acknowledge, express and examine their emotions on a deeper level because they have a broader emotional vocabulary.

Updated client conversation example:

Me: How did it make you feel that your mom was abusive to you.

Them: Initially I thought I was only angry, now I know I feel neglected, abandoned, unwanted, unworthy, less than and grief.

Now that we've acknowledged the true depth of their emotional pain, we can begin the deep healing and processing the deeply rooted emotions and not just the surface emotions that a person has become use to identifying with. The emotion wheel allows us to all explore the spectrum on emotions. People tend to rush to anger because they aren't clear of what emotions come before anger is even formed. The rush to sadness because they aren't aware of what emotions come before sadness. Many people don't know what they feel because their emotional vocabulary is so limited. The emotional wheel allows us to express the totally of our human expression. It gives us permission to dissect abandonment, before rushing to anger, before rushing to forgiveness. Before we forgive or arrive to understanding anyone, we must allow our full spectrum of emotions to be honored, there is a process to arriving to forgiveness and that path begins with honoring and acknowledging the truth of all emotions that lead to true emotional liberation.

If you sit with anger long enough,

you might find that its real name is

grief

HEALTHY COMMUNICATION

What's the point in having a message, if you don't have the skill or self-awareness to deliver your message properly so it's receivable. It deeply matters how a message is delivered and how you consciously or unconsciously deliver your messages is a clear reflection of your own self-awareness, emotional intelligence, compassion & your ability to adapt.

Telling the truth, communicating clearly or even firmly doesn't requires discernment. There's never a need to be brutally honest, just be honest. You can tell the truth without being blunt and you can honor someone's feelings and your truth simultaneously. Both can exist at the same time to minimize unnecessary argument, emotional pain or bad timing on message delivery.

Most people don't hear what you said, they imagine what you meant. This is where communication breaks down because comprehension is filtered through perception, Fears, trauma, voids, life experiences & beliefs. Have you ever gotten into a disagreement & that person has misinterpreted everything you've said to the point you feel like you're talking to a wall? Some even say" You hear what you want to hear" & that could be true, but what's even more true is people hear what their trauma needs them to hear.

People hear what their voids, fears and insecurities, need them to hear. This is also how many people enter unhealthy toxic relationships and ignore clear red flags. They allowed themselves to hear from their wounds and traumas. Our traumas, fears, wounds and voids shape our perception, they mold our hearing, sight & senses to give us what we need at all times even if it not based in truth or reality.

Everyone that watches the same film doesn't see the same movie.

To be a skilled communicator especially with family members or in romantic relationships you must learn how to deliver your messages based on those persons emotional, psychosomatic and psychological capacity, so they're more likely to receive you & your words. Some people need coddling, nurturing, firm, patient, or even aggressive methods of communication. This doesn't mean walk on eggshells when you communicate this is just a healthy to effectively communicate with someone who receives messages differently than you. one size doesn't fit all & its ok to learn, practice and remain open to other methods of delivery.

Self-care is no longer arguing,

No longer defending yourself and

No longer attempting to prove your point to

people who are committed to misunderstanding you.

No-Buts

The word "BUT" can be detrimental to an apology or a person's attempt to take accountability. But, tends to automatically eradicate and dismiss the apology or attempt to take accountability, leaving the person still feeling unheard.

Apologies & accountability aren't for you, they're for the person you're apologizing to. Apologies are how you emotionally cater to someone that matters to you. Many people need deep intentional acknowledgment of how they feel, what you did, what you could have done better and offering ways that situation will not happen again. Apologies are felt quicker when they are done from the heart and not the mind.

Apologies to someone aren't always your opportunity to get what you feel off of your chest, sometimes you need to make sure the person has heard, felt, acknowledged & trusted the sincerity in your apology before you go on to explaining yourself or sharing your perspectives. Even going as far as asking them,

"are you emotionally open enough to allow me to explain why I did what I did or what my reasoning was so I can offer you better clarity with my apology"?

Asking is a beautiful option because if you're like me, sometimes in the moment I don't want or care to hear perspectives, reasons why, I just want to be seen, heard acknowledged & reassured. A person explaining their reasons why before their apology actually lands in my heart, just sound like excuses especially if I haven't had adequate time to fully feel the closure & sincerity of the apology & accountability. Apologize and hug that person, hold their hand or give them eye to eye contact, make sure they feel your apology has landed before moving forward in conversation.

When you intermingle an apology with "BUT" or attempting to give the person clarity on your perspective or point of view it rushes them out of mending and feeling into their heart by being forced to go into their mind just to understand you. Sometimes people don't need understanding right then and there, they just need to feel heard & reassured.

An apology followed by "BUT" is a pathway to taking two steps backwards in accountability.

Apologizing properly is a love language.

It's a healthy relationship practice to begin asking our partners or loved ones, if a time comes where I have to apologize to take accountability or apologize to you, how can I apologize to you in a way that will make sure you feel heard, feel my sincerity & love? We are all different & need different things to feel loved, seen heard & acknowledged. Just like learning love languages, we must learn people's apology language as well.

Apologizing properly is a love language.

THE GIFT IN, STARTING OVER

A hurdle that typically keeps people from experiencing the life they desire and deserve is their fear, embarrassment, shame, guilt and frustration with the process of starting over.

They feel exhaustion and even defeat just by thinking of what that will look like, feel like and they feel fear coupled with the question of, will starting over will even work again, because it didn't work this time? Many people desire to have a healthy relationship, create a masterpiece, to quit a habit but they're having a really hard time in understanding that starting over may be a huge component that aids in the success of their process. Sometimes we must give ourselves permission to start over, so we don't allow our discouragement, fears or frustrations of the process hinder our evolving.

I often find that relationships and breaking unhealthy habits are the areas people typically want to be successful in but also disregard that creating anything healthy and long lasting in those areas will ultimately require much trial and error, and that is ok. For those who are struggling with ending self-sabotaging behaviors or habits of any kind there's something you should know.

The reason it may be difficult to quit your habit whether it's emotional eating, addiction, drinking, smoking or sex, is because your subconscious mind is programmed to make you continue these behaviors. If your subconscious programming knows that food makes you feel better & loved, it will trigger you to crave specific foods. If your subconscious knows sex, relationships make you feel nurtured, loved & seen even if the relationships are toxic and unhealthy, the subconscious will prompt you to send that text to your ex. If your subconscious knows that drinking alcohol & smoking weed will make you forget about your problems, it will continue to make you crave these things to escape your reality or the emotions you're attempting to numb yourself from feeling.

The bodies job is to keep you alive, which means that it's programmed to keep you comfortable or in familiar places. Even if those familiar places are unhealthy or uncomfortable the familiarity is a sign to body you've already passed your stress test in that area so the familiarity becomes the epitome of the body learning to get comfortable with being uncomfortable in that particular space. This is a learned behavior. The body gets uncomfortable when you attempt to change the status quo. When newness is introduced, when you attempt to start a new diet, but you received so much dopamine from your old unhealthy foods, the body senses your stress and your uncomfortableness in your new behaviors of eating salad only. The body thinks its keeping you safe and comfortable out of harm's way so it will trigger cravings of pizza to help you avoid not getting your hits of dopamine and avoid all of the stressful body transitions that come with starting over or starting something new. To a certain degree until you reprogram the subconscious mind it'll continue to prompt you to run on your old programs and interfere with the new programs you want to start to better yourself.

To end this cycle you have to understand how the body & subconscious mind works. This doesn't mean your subconscious mind is bad, it's just a clear reflection of how you have trained & programmed your subconscious mind. Most people's subconscious mind is programmed in survival mode, trauma responses, defense & coping mechanisms and the average human uses 95% of their subconscious mind & only 5% of their conscience mind. This means that 95% of your thoughts, emotions, cravings, reactions, fears, desires and behaviors are not conscious choices at all, they are all programs you've written from the time you were born to 13 years old that run on auto pilot. Only 5% of everything you think, do feel, say, crave, fear etc is a conscious choice. This is why you can drive your car a few minutes and blank out completely forgetting you're driving, when you come back to consciousness you realize you don't even remember passing certain places. The subconscious is so intelligent it records everything, it remembers everything, including what you ate for breakfast 20 years ago. It knows how to heal you if cancer presents itself. Our subconscious mind is supreme intelligence and it remembers how you coped with trauma at age 9. Maybe you didn't have an outlet to express your feelings, or your parents told you that you are to only speak when spoken to, so the way you nurtured your emotions was to eat when emotions were present. The subconscious remembers you used food as your remedy to feel better when emotional pain was present and now as adult the subconscious instructs you to eat when you feel emotionally distressed not to ruin your life, but because your program remembers what worked in the past and is sending signals to do this so it'll work for you again.

However, this is what survival mode looks like, a person running on old programs that use to work to help them survive but now those programs are aiding in your demise and are hindering your from evolving because you haven't updated them. Even computers and phones get regular updates and they're designed to mimic the human. Many people are running on old subconscious programs and instead of doing what it takes to rewrite those programs, they are attempting to force themselves into submission fighting an uphill battle against 95% of their being. This is why it's so hard to start and start over. The subconscious needs a new program to recognize this is what's best for the body.

Repetition is how you rewrite a subconscious program, doing it, until 95% of your body recognizes it to be the new norm. To end bad habits or unhealthy behaviors/thoughts you first have to get clear on the program. Why did you create it? What did you need it to protect you from? How old where you when you created it? What traumatic or emotionally heavy situations occurred that caused you to write this program? When you know the ins & outs of your program it becomes easy to re-write it to something healthier it becomes easier to interrupt the program before it begins because you know when it attempts to show up.

Starting over doesn't always mean you're doing something wrong. It doesn't mean you're unworthy sometimes it just means there are aspects of your being that are still repeating behaviors you allowed in the past and now it's time to intentionally commit to newness. When I was addicted to alcohol, I attempted to quit every single day, I started over every single morning and every single night I'd make a pact with myself that tomorrow was going to be the day I ended this addictive behavior. It took me years of starting over daily, until I learned my subconscious mind 95% of me was working against me, and I physically couldn't start over and maintain it until I healed that version of myself. My addiction was attached to the pain I felt of being abandoned by my dad. Once I healed that relationship, my subconscious mind didn't need to use alcohol to escape the pain anymore and now there was no need to start over, I just maintained my sobriety now 5 years sober.

Don't give up on yourself, I know it can be difficult, but the process is worth it and you're powerful and equipped with everything you need to heal through this.

Starting Over in Life

Sometimes life will require us to let go of what was and start new. Divorce, death, relationships and friendships may end and require us to find who we are outside of those familiar dynamics and that is ok. We experience people and situations in seasons. Some seasons may be longer than others and some shorter than others. When life has instructed you to start over as painful as this new beginning may be, never forget to congratulate yourself on a job well done. Life inviting us to start over means you've grown and outgrown where you currently are. The invitation to start over is also acknowledgment of how much you've accomplished and how it is now time to step into a new version of yourself and expand your healing and growth.

Starting over in life can be extremely painful and that's ok. Cry, be angry, explore your fears, grieve the old and mourn that version of yourself. You are allowed to feel all of the growing pains that comes with starting over. Sometimes starting over is lesson reminding you that you deserve better for yourself, that It's time to honor yourself better or show up in life better or differently. When life calls you to start new, answer the call.

Starting over is a gift, I don't care if you have to start over every single day for 5 years, don't shame you process you're still exactly where you should be. Trust that and keep evolving. Everything happens when it should and how it should.

Anything not growing is dead.

Healing is not a destination my love,

It is the soul's invitation to fall in love with the journey of life. Ego is in a rush to reach a destination, the soul knows there is nowhere to go, nothing to do and no one to become. Your mission should you choose to accept it is just to be.

WHEN WAS THE LAST TIME YOU CRIED?

Hell is wanting to cry & not even knowing how to.

When was the last time you truly cried? Not just shed a couple of tears but allowed yourself to have and experience a deep cry that was so powerful you lost control. A cry so intense you had to remind yourself to breathe. A cry so worthy, every version of your being got an opportunity to release all of the emotion, pain, energy, disappointment, confusion, heaviness, insecurity and fear that has been pent up for years, possibly since childhood. When was the last time you let go and just allowed yourself to shed and release all you've been holding on to consciously & unconsciously.

I cry like this at least once a week and when I don't I know my body, spirit and my heart has a week's worth of gunk, stagnant energy or emotional residue, stored waiting to be released. A heart full of emotions attached to memories. A spirit full of other people's problems and a body that's working overtime just to keep me alive.

When I cry most times, I'm not sad at all, sometimes it's my knees that need me to shed tears for them for always having the job to stand tall & carry my weight. Sometimes it's my back/spine that needs me to cry for it, always having to move, twist, bend and adapt. Sometimes my liver needs me to cry as it continues to heal from my years of alcohol addiction, repressed emotion and anger. Sometimes my heart needs to release tears as she works through reprogramming extremely strong societal programs, memories of pain, hurt and unworthiness. When My husband rubs my heart, I can instantly feel when I'm holding emotional residue there. Typically, when I get deep tissue back massages, I also have a deep emotional release because emotional residue is stored there as well.

Giving yourself permission to release emotion or cry doesn't always mean something is wrong, you're sad or depressed. Crying doesn't need a name or an explanation, it just needs freedom to come and go freely.

Sometimes the body just needs to release stagnant energy from years ago. Sometimes our bones need to be seen, heard and acknowledged with tears. Crying is such a beautiful way to cleanse the aura, heart and spirit.

Hell is needing to cry & not even knowing how to or where to start.

The next time you have the urge to cry, give yourself permission to let go, let loose and shed parts of yourself you need to release to feel weightless. Don't attempt to dissect and figure out why you're crying, just let yourself heal & find gratitude in your cleaning process.

When you resist crying out of fear of looking weak or your own fear of vulnerability you keep the mind, body and spirit locked in your own self-inflicted emotional prison full of constraints, walls and armor. When you give yourself permission to finally let go and just feel, new worlds within your soul open up and you become closer to returning home to yourself.

True power is

allowing yourself to express vulnerability

without deeming it as a weakness.

So many wish they could cry but their souls are numb.

Hell is needing to cry and not knowing how to.

Be grateful for your tears,

they are a reflection of your emotional freedom.

Do You Have the Capacity?

N ormalize asking people if they have the capacity to hold space for you & your problems before you vent.

People aren't required and they aren't always equipped to hold the weight of your issues just because they are weighing you down. Before you pick up that phone and call or text someone you love to vent, share or dump your emotions or feeling onto them, first ask them

"do you have the capacity to listen to me and hold space for me while I share?"

Do you have the emotional capacity to hear me vent, or tell you something that happened or share an experience?"

Sometimes people have so much going on in their own personal lives they don't have extra room to listen to what you have going on. They may not have the emotional bandwidth to hear more problems and they may not have the emotional stamina to hear your issues without also allowing that energy to affect them as well.

It's extremely selfish and inconsiderate to project and dump your stuff onto other people for the sake of

"if they love you they'll listen & be there for you".

If you loved them, you'd check in with them first to make sure they have emotional and mental space to allow your energy to intertwine with their own. Sometimes people are already overwhelmed, stressed, depressed, sad, emotional or just numb and when you energetically intrude on their energetic field you can add on to the emotional heaviness they may already feel. The average person takes on other people's problems, they think because they love you, they must help fix and emotionally care the way you do. Most people don't even know how to get rid of excess energetic residue. They wind up feeling sad, anxious or depressed not knowing those emotions aren't even theirs it the persons that called and vented without permission that's still stuck to them. Many times, after a person vents and the phone call is over, they feel light and weightless because they got all of their emotions off their chest, but the person listening feels heavy, depleted and anxious because that chaotic energy was transferred onto them.

It can be argued that calling someone, spewing anger, yelling, being manic, anxious, talking fast and venting without asking permission is a form of unconscious and unintentional mental and emotional abuse. There are too many healthy avenues to share problems in a healthy way that also give you tools and resources to help. It's not necessary to call people and intrude on their peaceful spaces without first attempting to be your own listening ear and attempting to transmute your own energy and calm your own storm.

Like my husband says. "We are not a clinics" for people that want to use us as medicine. These are people you must set healthy boundaries with because when they are caught up in their own universe of chaotic energy they don't care or they forget to care about protecting you from feeling the residue caused by their energy. It's ok to protect your energy, set your boundaries and tell people when you do or don't have the capacity to hold space for "Their Sh*t".

ACTING BRAND NEW

When growing, healing & evolving into new versions of yourself, you may not know how to function in your new body yet, with your new perspective of life, with your newfound respect for spirit and your new found love for yourself. Sometimes you may not know how to love healthily as this new version of yourself you're becoming because residue of your old self is still slightly present. Maybe you still carry the confidence of your old self even though you have fully emerged as a new evolved, emotionally and spiritually mature being. This is normal.

When you've evolved into a new version of yourself sometimes you must give yourself permission to experience new things, go new places, love in new ways, learn new things and be open to finding peace in new spaces. Fully embodying the growth and healing you've accomplished can be new uncharted territory and sometimes the shoes don't fit quite yet, they may need some breaking into so you can get use to and familiar with this new version of yourself and to learn yourself in deeper layers.

When you're emerging as a new being in your body, healing from depression, coming out of grief, cultivating healthier perspectives about your trauma, learning healthier ways to transmute your energy of anger and exuding beautiful soul confidence it's important to embody your newness. To acknowledge your purity and treat yourself as if you are a shiny new trophy right out of the box. Be gentle, patient and excited about learning the new functions of yourself. You've done the work to heal, grow and evolve, give yourself permission to live in a way that is new as well and watch everything that surrounds you respond to that fresh outlook you have on your life.

Be patient and kind with yourself, you are in the midst of transformation. You may not always get it right. You may revert back to old ways in some moments. You're still exactly where you're supposed to be. Honor yourself

Go heal in the places that once broke you,

Go dance to the songs you used to cry to.

Be patient and kind with yourself,

you are in the midst of transformation.

Don't Rush to Forgiveness & Don't Build A Life in The Memory of Your Pain

A ny emotion that comes up for you deserves to be honored. Don't RUSH to forgiveness.

You are allowed to honor your personal full spectrum of emotions before having the capacity to forgive or have compassion. You deserve to honor your pain, resentment and anger just as much as you deserve to rise and thrive from it. Because Emotions are our teachers and guides, they are meant to be felt and then released.

The issue is most people are choosing to hold onto the memory of their pain longer than their spirit/soul intended for them too. Some people have done horrible things to you, so whatever you feel is valid, you do not have to rush past those waves of emotions that maybe there to teach you something. Sometimes honoring those emotions looks like holding people accountable, taking your power back and standing up for yourself, even at your lowest and highest frequency you may have to utilize your throat chakra and curse or raise your voice and yell in anger. On the road to healing you may experience this entire spectrum and you are allowed too.

However, do your best to not live there. Encourage yourself to find healthy ways to heal and grow emotionally. Feel what you feel, just don't stay there, don't live there.

Don't build a life in the memory of your pain.

When you choose to heal you choose to take your power back. Maintain the awareness that resentment, anger etc produce toxicity in the body, which manifests as disease and energetic blockages, toxic relationships, hindering your own ability to manifest your desires and you also birth new unnecessary worlds of karma when you choose to hold onto emotional toxicity that no longer has a purpose in your life.

Every time you remember without the intention to heal, you Re-Traumatize yourself. Forgiveness is for you. The biggest act of self-love is forgiving yourself for harboring emotions that keep your soul in a state of hell, daily. You heal not to get to a place of forgiveness for others, they probably don't even care about your forgiveness, but so you can release all of the toxic emotions hindering you from thriving. Honor your emotions & then Take your power back.

Healing Self Betrayal

Self-Betrayal is the source of depression, anxiety, lack of confidence of any kind and anger. Subconsciously people carry every single moment they've ever betrayed themselves. It becomes written in their unconscious mind which is 95% of who they are, their bodies, aura and energetic field. This directly effects their ability to have a honorary and strong relationship with themselves, their bodies and their intuition. Self-betrayal secondarily effects their relationships with others, their ability to feel worthy, motivated and capable. It eats away at the soul when a person chooses to consciously dishonor themselves for any source of instant gratification, be it food, relationships, sex, success, money, lack of integrity or opportunity.

Most times the reason people constantly betray you, or betray your trust is because, you betray you and betray your town rust. You teach people how to treat you and your energy tells people how you expect to be treated, not just your words. So many people betray you because your energy says its normal and acceptable, because you betray yourself often and sends the signal that It's ok for others to do the same.

The genius of the human body is it knows how to read a person's energy to discern if that person feels like a safe environment or not. If 95% of your subconscious mind is your mind, body, aura and energetic field then this means when a person see's you they also see your unhealed trauma, whether they are conscious of it or not their body is taking note of your subtle body energy for safety reasons. You think you're putting your best foot forward, smiling, being pleasant showcasing your beautiful personality or "character" and the person in front of you is downloading the person you really are, not the person you're attempting to be in that moment. People can tell how you feel about yourself; they can sense who you are before you even open your mouth if they're in tune with their being. When you betray yourself, you unconsciously teach others they are allowed to do it as well.

Sometimes the bulk of your healing journey is learning how to show up for yourself, listen and create a relationship with your intuition and forgive yourself. Forgive yourself for the relationships you entered and the many red flags you looked past for the sake of feeling loved. Forgive yourself for the things you did in your past, decisions you made that hurt others, behaviors or habits that made your life a little or a lot harder for yourself. Sometimes honoring yourself looks like forgiving yourself for today. For what you ate today, having compassion for yourself being tired and not finishing everything or anything on the to do list.

Many times, we think holding space for ourselves has to be this huge spectacle and task, but at the basic level it looks like creating a relationship with the depths of your being. Healing our internal dialogue & repairing the way we speak to and treat ourselves. Cultivating a real relationship with our bodies, the portal that was chosen to hold and host our souls. This is the framework for physically showing up in the world as the highest version of yourself & embodying the beautiful being you are. Everything we allow to happen on the outside is a direct reflection of how we feel about ourselves on the inside. The first step you can take towards nurturing the versions of your being that you have dishonored, disregarded, ignored and betrayed is by nurturing those parts of yourself with love, compassion and grace. The bottom line is you'll never fully receive those attributes the way you desire and deserve if you don't have the capacity to display them for yourself.

An Affirmation to come back home to the parts of you that

feel betrayed

Say this....

I Forgive myself.

I deserve to be forgiven

I Am worthy of my own forgiveness.

I acknowledge at times I have not made the best decisions for myself. There were moments that I knew better, I could have done better but didn't believe I deserved better.

Right now I offer myself compassion, patience & understanding

I forgive myself

I forgive myself for the times I said yes when I really wanted to say no

I forgive myself for each promise I've broken to myself

I forgive myself for each time I ignored my intuition & gut feeling

I forgive myself for the times I trusted other peoples advice and not my own souls divine guidance

I have compassion for myself right now

I forgive myself, because I love myself.

I release all judgement for myself for the moments I didn't show up as my best self

I have compassion for myself for the times I put myself in unhealthy, unsafe or uncomfortable situations in hopes I'd receive love from others because I didn't know how to love myself yet

I forgive myself for the times I don't speak nicely to myself or I put more pressure on myself to show up perfect instead of vulnerable and authentic

I deserve grace, love, compassion, patience and self honor.

I vow to continue to show up for myself as best as I can because I Am worthy

Ho'oponopono

Is a traditional Hawaiian practice of reconciliation and forgiveness. The Etymology of this words translates to correction, signifying there is a proper and healthy way to to practice self forgiveness and reconciliation.

Step 1: Say "I'm Sorry"

This apology is for self, others or doesn't have to be for anyone outside of yourself just to remove residue of guilt or shame. It's an invitation and opportunity for repentance.

Step 2: Say "Please Forgive Me"

Ask for forgiveness, not just from someone outside of you but in general from the universe or the God of your own understanding, mean it and repeat it.

Step 3: Say "Thank you"

This thank you can be for yourself forgiveness, the forgiveness of the universe or just acknowledging gratitude for a new opportunity to start new.

Step 4: Say "I Love You"

This can also be step one. This is your reminder that love still lives here, in you, in all things. Say it to yourself, the person you have in mind, God or just the presence of existence.

EVERYBODY CAN'T COME

Losing people in the process of healing is normal. Wanting friends and family to evolve with you or at the very least maintain their positions in your life is normal as well but many times as you heal, grow and evolve so will your aura, energetic field and your frequency. This means people will only be able to relate to you if they have the capacity to match your frequency. Sometimes lovers and friends can only identify with the toxic parts of you because it reflects the toxic parts of them. However, once you start your healing journey this does not mean go back to the people, places and things you had to leave behind or transition away from. Sometimes going backwards can tarnish, Hinder and slow your progression of growth and healing. Sometimes old partners and friends can be triggers for you to revert back to your old ways.

It's important to remember that healing requires a new version of you. So, you are not the same person as you were while you were in that toxic relationship, you've changed, you've grown and it's ok to acknowledge that when you grow and heal the people you once loved, places and things may no longer resonate with your spirit anymore. When your spirit is begging to elevate and let go you should honor that and find healthy ways to release attachment.

Many times, we hold onto people because they are familiar and feel safe to us especially when we begin to experience our own emotionally overwhelming, vulnerable and sometimes scary trauma. It's normal to want to have our loved ones to call when things get difficult or if we get lonely on our road to healing, but the longer we hold on to people, places, things, relationships that have already served their purpose in our lives, when we try to force them to continue to fit into our lives past their expiration date, we cultivate unnecessary karma and make sustaining these relationships even more difficult and unhealthy.

When relationships start to become toxic and unhealthy, that's when you know you have stayed longer than the time frame your soul and GOD intended. When family gets toxic, you are now operating in that system in a way you're not meant to. When healing it's imperative to build your intuitive muscle so you are cognizant of who/what to keep and who/what to let go of.

Once we begin healing we do ourselves a disservice when we go back to the person, places or environments that aided in our brokenness. Healing requires people, environments & things that will continually aid in your process in healthy ways, so stay mindful when going backwards so that you don't allow old, people, ways & habits to jeopardize your process and progress.

When you choose peace and journey into healing, sometimes it comes with a lot of goodbyes.

STAY IN YOUR POWER

One thing about that light baby, once you step into it unapologetically even the people that "think" they don't like you will start to love you, because you subconsciously remind them to also step into their power and to nurture their light.

The years of being humble just to be digestible, accepted and received well others are over. Remember many truths can exist at the same time, that you're humble and the star of the show. Ain't no "Be Humble" over here. It's only "Show up & show out" season. The best thing you can do for others is

cultivate yourself so much that your boldness reminds them of how much they shrink,

your fearlessness reminds them of how much they hide,

your light reminds them of how dim their own

& your authentic self-expression becomes a mirror of how they are afraid to show up beautifully as their fullest self.

Even and especially if people claim or truly feel that they don't like you, remember they are always watching and even on a subconscious level taking notes. When you stop shrinking you open the door for others to begin giving themselves permission to show up big as well. You reflect to them the parts of themselves they are afraid of, insecure or curious about.

When you allow yourself to take up space you begin to see how beautifully your world expands and you become a conduit and teacher to others that secretly wish they could do the same. Take up space love, exude the greatness that you are. Those that mind don't matter and those that matter don't mind. Period.

There's clarity in silence.

I'm Somewhere Between Humble & Hell Nah

Today I saw a quote that said, "Don't be the bigger person today be the person that helps them understand that when you f*ck around, you find out" and a huge part of me laughed and deeply enjoyed this saying. It felt as if the younger versions of myself had confirmation that it was ok to match someone's energy with no intention for self-accountability. While I whole heartedly agree that sometimes certain people have to "f*ck around and find out" the hard way, there's still a level of personal integrity that should be included in that process.

This stood out to me personally because I used to always be the person that would apologize first for the sake of ending conflict and rushing to resolution to avoid the comfortability in conflict. I would absolutely hate when arguments or disagreements would happen, I'd always be the one to apologize, own my part or take accountability first. I used to ask GOD "Why do I always have to be the bigger person?" I couldn't understand why the other person was ok with thriving in tension while I craved a safe, peaceful & positive environment in our relationship/friendship. There was even a time I wished that I could just not care the way they others did or at least not allow the unresolved situation to bother me, but it always did.

It took me a long time to realize being the bigger person, the first to take accountability was my superpower. Even if I was the only person to apologize or acknowledge my part, I still maintained my spiritual integrity and honored my soul. I'm not ok with knowing I could have handled a situation better & not taking accountability, not just in my mind but using my words & telling the person I could have handled that differently I apologize. Don't get me wrong, my ego still to this day has a field day saying "hell nah that b*tch needs to apologize too" lol but what another person chooses to do is none of my business, they still must answer to their soul. Apologizing for my part, taking accountability & acknowledging them owning their part may not be a part of their journey yet, how they choose to honor or dishonor themselves is none of my business.

But my spiritual journey requires self-accountability & deep self honestly even if the other person never chooses to show up the same way for me. The way I choose to honor my soul is different. Spiritual integrity means full self-awareness of my words, behaviors, thoughts & emotions. This is how I choose to show up for me & keep unnecessary heavy baggage from weighing me down. To me, bigger person doesn't mean better person, it doesn't even mean good person, but it does reflect accountability and it has a lot to do with why my spirit is so weightless.

Petty & unforgiving energy doesn't have permission to exist within my beautiful heart. It doesn't hurt me to say I apologize; it empowers me continue elevating & honoring my journey. It feels good & freeing to live within love. Anger, spite & unforgiveness takes up a lot of room, thoughts & emotions. Choosing to show up as the best version of myself is how I remain weightless.

Don't get me wrong sometimes people deserve to f*ck around and find out, just not at the expense of your spiritual integrity. Remember you are not like everyone else. Some people can afford the karmic debt of matching another person's energy. They are ok with engaging with energies and entities that will invade their spirit for the next 2 years just because they chose to feed the ego and starve the soul. Not everyone is on their intentional healing journey so how you choose to respond is important. If it compromises your growth, if it feels like you must take steps back in you progress to embody a person you no longer want to be, give yourself permission to put ego in the back seat and show up in a way that reflects the healing, growth and evolution of your soul. When in war with ego, the loser always wins.

Stop Playing with Your Healing

There is a time to give yourself grace, & then there are times when you need to stop playing with your growth & healing.

Giving yourself grace is an act of self -love and so is intentionality. This is a beautiful and delicate balance of being understanding of how difficult growth & healing is but also playing no games when it comes to our elevation. Duality is understanding that both exist and both are true. We can simultaneously not meet the mark and that still be our best. Sometimes showing up for ourselves doesn't look like getting every single thing done on the to do list. Sometimes it looks like just writing the list. Both truths can exist at the same time that you're doing great, the best you can and still not meeting your personal level of potential because there are solutions you aren't implementing, like healthy routines, spiritual practices and self-care.

If you want to stop drinking, get off your butt and ask for help.

If you want to be a better mother stop allowing other people parent your child and start prioritizing that intimate time with yourself so you can be more present for you baby.

If you want to stop lashing out in anger, seek a therapist to find the solutions.

At some point you have to stop making excuses for yourself and get into the solution.

Sometimes people don't try or don't give their all because they're subconsciously afraid of succeeding, it hurts to let go of their toxic ways & it hurts even more to continue those ways. It may be true that you're lazy, haven't hit rock bottom hard enough to change, evolve grow or heal. You haven't felt enough pain, disappointed, disgust & sadness to choose the best part of yourself yet. It could be very true that you think you're ready to grow and heal but your soul still may have more lessons for you to learn that require you to stay in your lower vibrational frequencies.

The real truth is whether you choose to stay the same, grow or try your best but still miss your mark, you are still exactly where you're supposed to be! Healing while on your spiritual journey is weird, but it's beautiful because you get to play with the balance of being intentional but not taking life so seriously that you forget to experience the experience. Even when you feel stuck & stagnant, please remember most times healing & growth are happening in layers of your being you aren't even aware of. When you become intentional and commit to your healing everything in your life will begin to reflect your commitment to yourself. Love and honor yourself enough to keep doing your best to show up for yourself. Give yourself grace & stay intentional.

WARRIOR'S ETHOS

Do you have a warrior's ethos?

A way to embody your warrior spirit when times get difficult. When you are struggling emotionally. When you're having a tough time getting back on track, re-Aligning With your purpose & goals. Do you have a saying, mantra, affirmation or quote that you developed for yourself to dig you out of your own self-inflicted & self-sabotaging holes? Your warrior ethos is your light that guides your back to yourself. It's your reminder when you forget who you are, what your purpose is and how to return back home to yourself. Your warrior ethos is designed to remind you of your power, your purpose, your importance, your love, your boundaries, your standards, your integrity, your relationship with self, God the universe and your soul. Your warrior ethos is a personal song of power and vulnerability that elevates your energy back into remembrance of self.

Sometimes you misinterpret needing or wanting to find motivation from outside sources like podcasts, books & YouTube videos & sometimes you disregard or you're unaware that the motivation you need & the motivation you deeply yearn for is your own. The motivational messages that are everlasting come from within your own spirit & soul, as these are the inspirational words that you will feel to the depths of your core. Most times people can't "find" motivation because they are waiting for it to come from a source outside of themselves.

When you're not vibrating at your highest frequency, & cannot seem to align your emotions, thoughts & behaviors with what you know your soul's purpose to be, what do you say to yourself to get yourself back in your rhythm? What is your warrior's ethos? What words will remind you of your power, give you the courage to instantly embody your strength, remind you of your purpose & make you feel like you can do & accomplish anything? Having a warrior ethos is like playing a video game, right when you're on your last life, about die in the game, your find a gem that gives you an extra life. Your warrior ethos is a gem you can keep in your back pocket at any time in your journey.

So, if you're in a time of needing to realign with the highest version of yourself, create your own warrior ethos. A mantra, affirmation, quote or saying that empowers you enough to start living the life you deserve. Remember who the f*ck you are.

ASSIGNMENT

Write you "Warrior Ethos" mantra, song, affirmation, poem or letter to yourself.

This can also be a song that is already written, however the intention and energy behind it means a lot more when it comes from you and not someone else.

Write your personal warrior ethos, print it out, hang it in a place you frequent often like your bathroom and read it before you enter or before you leave, each time.

Warrior Ethos Journal Prompts

1. When emotional pain is present how do you find your way back home to your soul?

2. How do you speak to yourself when emotional pain is present?

3. What practices do you utilize to help calm your emotional storm?

4. What thoughts find a home in your mind when you experience difficulty in life?

5. How does your body feel when you react vs respond to life difficulty?

6. Which responses makes you feel anxiety, lack of control, uncontrollable emotions & thoughts?

7. How do you treat & speak to yourself when you make mistakes?

8. How do you feel, treat & speak to yourself when people don't love you, abandon you or don't see you the way you see yourself?

9. Where do you feel DISCOMFORT in your body?

10. What songs help you connect back to your power?

11. What practices help you connect back to your power?

12. What is your warrior ethos mantra, that always helps you find your way back to you?

THE GRIEF OF ENDINGS AND NEW BEGINNINGS

It's ok to give yourself permission to mourn after a tough breakup.

No matter how unhealthy, abusive or toxic a relationship is, it's very normal to grieve an ending. The same as you would if someone passed away, died or transitioned. If your heart was attached to them, it may take work detaching your heart and the first step is allowing yourself to grieve or mourn what is no longer and possibly what could have been. Even if you've transitioned out of the most toxic relationship that doesn't mean your feelings aren't valid. Horrible relationships don't take away from the pain that comes with moving on and they don't mean you aren't allowed to feel emotional pain, even if you're deeply happy the relationship is over.

It also doesn't mean you stop loving a person because things didn't work out. Sometimes you may love and long for them even more after a breakup or transition. & that is ok. This is why it's imperative that before we enter any type of relationship you understand the process of healthy detachment and unhealthy attachment. The phrase "Connected to everything, attached to nothing" describes how we can explore deep connectivity with others without falling into the trap of attachment.

In my past breakups I'd intentionally allow myself to mourn and grieve. I'd give myself to time to feel all my emotions because I knew I'd have to fully detox that person out of my system to move forward in a healthy way. Just like with food, we all know before beginning a healthy diet we must first detox the toxins out of our systems. Most people don't detox because they know it can be painful and uncomfortable, so they tend to go back to the unhealthy foods to just satiate their cravings. The same goes for the ending of a relationship. We must detox those toxic unhealthy emotions out of our bodies and when these moments become difficult, they are not opportunities to go back to our ex but to just stand firm in the detox process.

When I would detox from an ex, I knew detox was taking place the more the person appeared in my dreams. I'd be mindful not to send any I miss you texts because I was aware of that slippery slope. I knew this wasn't an indication to go back to old relationships it was a sign that I was healing and releasing attachment.

Remember grieving, mourning & detoxing doesn't always feel good and moving on from a relationship happens in stages. Many times, you must grieve your unmet expectations, you must mourn your plans that never came to fruition, and you must grieve the idea of how you hoped that relationship would be your happy ending. Sometimes grieving happens in long stages, sometimes short. It's normal to miss them, miss what could have been, be sad your idea of a relationship didn't work out with that person. Feeling this is all a part of the grieving process. These aren't messages to go back, just triggers to help you face the emotions that come with unhealthy attachments in relationships. Stand firm in your evolving.

One thing about me

I'm going to always return home to myself

I'm going to always continue healing.

*I'm going to always remember who the f*ck I am*

QUICK BREATHING MEDITATION FOR LETTING GO

Close your eyes, lay flat on your back, legs and arms stretched out, arms by your side 5 second breath in and 5 second breath out (clear out energy) Take a huge 5 second breath in from your toes to the top of your head. Release the breath for 5 seconds.

The practice of Letting Go

With eyes still closed. Arms to your side, palms open facing the sky. Breath in for 6 seconds, simultaneously closing fist and tightening forearm.

Release breath for 6 seconds simultaneously "Letting Go" releasing tension in forearm, opening fist and resting fingers. Visualizing yourself letting go of what no longer serves you.

Repeat 6 times or until the ancestors tell you that you're done.

A Journey to No Where

You aren't supposed to always have the answer about how to navigate life.

Your job is just to practice finding comfortability in the process of surrendering to the unknown.

This is a time where many people have no idea what they're supposed to do next? They have no idea how to feel about scary transitions, changes, endings and new beginnings. I just want you to know there is freedom when you allow yourself to stop trying to figure it out and control your way into outcomes that make you comfortable. Sometimes your gifts are based on your ability to withstand these uncertain and uncomfortable spaces. The liminal spaces, the middle passage of somewhere & nowhere.

It's ok if you don't know what makes you happy right now, it's ok if you don't know what decisions you're supposed to make in a situation, it's ok if you don't know what you want to do with your life right now in this moment. Society makes us feel as if we must know, have a plan & know for certain how to navigate all situations, all emotions & all of life at all times. Not only is this unrealistic, it defeats the purpose of the human experience.

Even when you go swimming most times the most relaxing part is not when you're swimming super-fast with a destination in mind, it's when you lay back & just float & watch the sky. You get to see how peaceful, calm & perfect everything is. It's feels like freedom when you surrender to the waves, some water may get in your ear & cause a little discomfort but for a few moments you actually become one with the water & your whole being is clear you don't have to fight any uncomfortableness because you've surrendered to your freedom of just floating with no destination or no plan. You're just enjoying what it feels like to be and not do.

If you're in a space where you don't know what to do, think or feel, give yourself permission to lay back & just be. Give yourself permission to float. Surrender to becoming one with life & just watch life. It may take a moment, but you'll see even in the midst of your unknown everything is still perfect. This means no matter what space you're in, in your life, it is already perfect & is unfolding for your greater good whether you believe this or not.

Dear soul.

I am still learning about what you love. I'm going to spend more time nurturing you.

Thank you for loving me.

AFFIRMATIONS FOR WHEN YOU FEEL LOST ON YOUR JOURNEY TO NO WHERE

Today I remember that i am exactly where i should be. I am exactly where my soul has positioned me in my path to healing, growing & evolving. I release the EGOIC idea that i should be doing more or better. I let go of the attachment to self-judgment that says i should be a certain way by now.

I surrender to the truth that there is a divine source guiding Me & i trust that everything i do, say, feel & think is in alignment with the totality of my souls purpose even & especially when i feel as though I'm stuck, taking steps backward, in limbo or in the midst of self-sabotaging behaviors. I choose to trust that all is STILL working in my favor.

I can rest my shoulders, i can choose a worry less life & i can decide how i want to show up in each moment without allowing myself to become victim to & haunted by the thoughts of "WHATS NEXT"

There is nothing to do

there is nowhere to go

there is no one to be

there is nothing to want

All that is real is in my heart. This is a safe space & i give myself permission to not entertain any person, place thing or thought that robs me if my safety.

Feeling lost is the best part of the journey, it's your reminder to RELAX, kick off ya shoes & relax ya feet. Surrender & let go of expectations to Outcomes.

ENJOY not knowing, & dance because you don't have to know ANYTHING. your only job is just to, BE.

GET TO KNOW YOU...

riting Instructions: As your 1st assignment answer all of the questions below. This assignment is just to help you practice tapping into your subconscious emotions through writing & journaling. Please only use pen & paper to write you answers. Remember BE HONEST WITH YOURSELF. There is not judgement.

Most people can't heal because they haven't properly acknowledged, sat with & felt into their life story. When you are clear about your life story, it makes it easier to pin point the ROOT CAUSE of where you behaviors, traumas, wounds & voids stem from. When you are clear where your pain stems from, Healing is around the corner.

1. What kind of relationship did your mother/father have with their parents?
2. Were you wanted at birth?
3. What were the circumstances of your family growing up? Drugs, depression, poverty, violence, lack of communication, was there fun times or laughter, molestation, family dynamic with siblings, mother/father? Describe in detail
4. Did you feel your parents attitude towards you was different than your siblings?
5. Were you ever separated from any important family members like parents?
6. Was there ever fear around this separation?
7. Did you feel responsible?
8. Did you feel like you had to please your parents?
9. What happened if you didn't please your parents?
10. Were you required to take care of your siblings?
11. Where were you parents while you were caretaking?

12. Were you ever required to be there for your parents emotionally? example= take care of your mom after dad abused her
13. Were your parents loving and nurturing?
14. Did your parent's tell you verbally they loved you?
15. Did you feel loved, wanted, seen, acknowledged, heard?
16. How do you wish your parents loved you?
17. How did it feel not being loved in the way you needed as a child?
18. Did you feel alone? if so, how did this effect you growing up?
19. Did you have both parents? if not why & what was your relationship like with both parents.
20. What did you have to do to feel loved or receive attention by your parents? good grades? star athlete? take care of siblings?
21. How would your parents respond if you missed the mark? Would they take their love away?
22. List & explain in detail ALL of the feelings & MEMORIES of guilt, shame, fear, resentment, embarrassment you had as a child? Where did they stem from?
23. Were labeled anything growing up? bad child, good girl, whore, dumb, retarded, slow, disrespectful
24. How did those labels effect you and make you feel?
25. How did your parents speak to you? curse, call you a bitch? mean, firm, disrespectful, dismayingly,
26. How did they way they spoke to you make you feel about them and yourself?
27. Did you resent you parents, siblings, family members or friends? List WHO & explain why
28. Were you teased or bullied in school? How did it make you feel? How did you defend yourself?

29. Did you defend yourself?
30. Did you ever explain to your parents, how they made you feel? if not Why?

THERE'S AN EMOTION ATTACHED TO EVERY MEMORY

Try this exercise:

anytime you witness the mind travel to a past memory, instead of mindlessly reliving & replaying that memory with no end goal, no intention & no direction. Interrupt the pattern of thought and of reliving the past by acknowledging & asking

"why did the mind bring me to this memory?

This an opportunity to feel into what emotions are still attached to that memory of the past that may still need nurturing, acknowledgement & releasing. I must also note that the mind is always going to think so every thought is not meant to attach to or give any power too. However you are clear on the memories that are surfacing that are asking for your more emotional nurturing.

<u>If a frivolous thought surfaces and is attempting to stay say this:</u>

I acknowledge your presence,

I send you love and ease

I release you from my vessel.

Thank you, I love you

<u>Journal what emotions you felt during this past memory</u>:

Example: (my personal journal excerpt written at 3am)

As i attempted to fall asleep I remembered my mom worked nights when i was little, maybe 8years old and i had to sleep at my aunts house overnight. Sometimes I couldn't sleep so I would sneak & call my mom on the hone to tell her i was having a hard time sleeping. She'd tell me to just take a deep & close my eyes. Then I'd go lay down and fall right asleep. Tonight I miss my moms safety. Maybe there's a part of me that feels unsafe, unsure, restless or all of the above. I'm currently working on a lot of things in my life right now and there are many areas I feel unsafe in, uncertain of and would love to be soothed and told it's ok. Ultimately I think I feel fearful of my responsibilities. Maybe even overwhelmed. My mom makes me feel like life can't get me, as if like can't hurt me. My mom makes life feel unreal and powerless when it comes to her power. I think my inner child just wants to be a child again, carefree and my adult self would like to experience what that feel like as well. I think im scared and afraid. I'm not really sure of what, but I can feel fear in my body so that statement feels true to me. I think I'm afraid to keep going. Each time I keep going I'm required to heal more to evolve more and right now I feel like im being asked to do a lot by God. I'm equally annoyed as I am excited lol. I'm equally overwhelmed as I am rested. I think the fear of the unknown is what's lingering in my body right now. A huge part of me wants to curl up in my mommas bed and watch cartoons, while eat cereal while she's at work. I miss the parts of me that were carefree, innocent and lively. Possibly that version of Candyss is attempting to get my attention. Tomorrow I'm going to honor her with cartoons and cereal, maybe even in my mommas bed lol.

I see you young Candyss

I acknowledge you

I hear you

I hold space for you

I cry for you

I understand you

And I am here for you, with you, as you.

I honor you.

Thank you for being here with me right now.

The emotions attached to this memory are: longing for my mom, feeling safety with my mom, uncomfortable in my environment, protection & provision., inner child vs. adult conflict

The bulk of my emotions reflect wanting, needing & feeling safe with my mom and wanting to return back to childhood without adult responsibilities.

<u>The emotion that stood out is the need to feel</u> relief, safe, childlike and protected.

<u>The solution</u>: pray into the body to the 8year old Candyss that is acknowledging that she feels uncomfortable, wants & wishes she had her mom to sooth her to help her feel better.

This is how you rewrite programs, narratives & stories. This is also how you train yourself to not allow the mind to take you to the past without reconciling the memory it's attempting to make you attach to. Instead of attaching to the memory, break the emotions attached to the memory down, process those emotions & acknowledge those emotions then pray into the body. Change that narrative & that story.

CREATE A MORNING & EVENING ROUTINE

R outines create discipline and aid in repairing your relationship with you intuition by learning to trust your own word and promises to self. Routines also give the human mind normalcy, consistency and stability. Many people feel all over the place, chaotic and unstable because they are. When you begin and end your day with intentionality, you are more likely to feel more ease throughout your day, within your emotional abilities and energy.

Only create a routine based on what you know you can honor and meet. Start small and only do what you can commit to. When you attempt to overdo things, you begin to go back on your word, feel to tired to complete your routine and this leads to another self-sabotaging cycle of guilt, shame, discouragement, embarrassment and discouragement. We make sure this doesn't happen by only committing to what we can handle. There is absolutely nothing wrong with starting small. This gives you an opportunity to surrender to the process of healing, growing and evolving and no longer attempting to force yourself to do everything overnight. This also means you will need to plan accordingly wake up times so you are not rushing your process. Stay in flow.

Remember our medicine is in our ease and our flow.

Morning Routine Example:

- Pray into the body before eyes are even open or you touch your phone
- Meditation or sit in silent practice then journal AFTER
- Move your body, gym, yoga, walking, stretching
- External self care shower etc
- Smoothie, fresh pressed juice, fruit
- Night Routine

- Pray into the body
- Meditation or silence to calm body from the day
- Journal to release unnecessary thoughts & emotions from the day
- Stretch to release any residual tension
- Put phone away 30 mins before bed

BOUNDARIES 101

It's imperative to remember boundaries are NOT WALLS. Boundaries are not created to keep people out; they are created to allow people with perimeters that still allow you to feel safe. Boundaries are an act of self-love and each time you disregard your own boundaries you dishonor yourself and DISEMPOWER yourself. Healing the wound of codependency largely depends on you learning how to empower yourself so boundaries are a NON-NEGOTIABLE.

<u>1st Things 1st</u>

Somatic Healing means to identify how your nervous system feels when triggered. Feeling into what messages your body are sending you when uncomfortable. Not ignoring your emotional & even physical sensations happening when you feel fear, not worthy, not wanted or love. A huge part of healing is first identifying the feelings & bodily sensations that surface so you can work through them in real time without emotionally falling back into codependent self-sabotaging behaviors.

<u>Where are you uncomfortableness in your body?</u>

Close your eyes Take 3 huge deep breaths in & deep exhale out Where is the tension, resistance, fear, unworthiness, voids of love located? your throat (frog in throat feeling) your heart (chest) your back, your stomach? Place both hands over the body area that feels the most tension & resistance & take 3 more deep breaths with closed eyes send love to the version of yourself feels fear, unworthiness, unloved, unseen & unacknowledged validate yourself Remind yourself that you're SAFE & Capable of making healthier decisions that honor YOU Remind yourself that your boundaries are how to prove to yourself that you love yourself.

Your boundaries will be tailored to you. Your experiences, your triggers, wounds and ultimately your way of teaching people how you want to be treated, loved and respected. As you heal, grow & evolve your boundaries will change and evolve as well. At this point your focus is to practice giving yourself permission to set boundaries, speak up for yourself, say no & stand firm in it, while not allowing the aftermath of uncomfortable feelings make you feel like a bad, unworthy fearful person.

Boundaries Don't Always Feel GOOD

& That is ok. Sometimes you may feel nauseas before & after setting a boundary because it's new to use your voice. Send love to yourself. Be proud that you chose yourself.

Setting Healthy Boundaries is Trial & Error

& That is ok. As you learn how to set boundaries you learn that they're rooted in you identifying what you need & that will change & evolve over time. There's no right or wrong boundary.

You may have to practice rehearsing your boundaries BEFORE implementing them

& That is ok. Take pen & paper and write out your boundaries. Acknowledge moments you need them, want them & write your boundary for future scenarios this way you know how to respond without attempting to stumble over your words in real time

People May Get Upset About Your New Boundary

& That is ok. This does not mean second guess yourself or change your boundary to appease them. Maintain your boundary. This may in real time affect your self-esteem, create fear or un-comfortability. It's ok & all a part of the process of validating and honoring yourself.

How To Set Healthy Boundaries

1. Get clear on what your boundaries are & why you need them? What spaces within your being will you use your boundaries to protect?
2. Before setting a boundary with others set a boundary with yourself. You must first remain consistent, firm & Intentional about not only setting boundaries but keeping them regardless of how difficult or painful it is to honor them.

3. Set boundaries for others. Be clear with your words. Your requirements. A great example is. This is my boundary you're not allowed to speak to me this way, it hurts my feelings and makes me feel angry and disrespected.
4. Be clear on what the consequences are when a person oversteps your boundaries or intentionally disrespects your boundaries. An example is, if you're not able to respect my boundaries I will not maintain communication with you. (But spice it up in your own way lol)
5. Give yourself permission to set healthy boundaries. This is how you heal your codependency wounds & stop dishonoring yourself by honoring others. You take your power back when you say no, I'm not willing to go this far with you or this is as far as I'm willing to go with you. You strengthen your spirit when you choose to show up for yourself unapologetically.

Be Clear & Firm When setting your boundary be clear & firm on what your boundary is & why? Explain how it makes you feel when that boundary is crossed. Example: Please do not cut me off when I'm expressing myself, it makes me lose my train of thought & it makes me feel as if what i have to say doesn't matter to you & that frustrates me and hurts me feelings.

BOUNDARY: Do not cut me off when speaking

WHY: It makes me lose my train of thought, hurts my feelings, frustrates me, makes me feel as if what i have to say isn't valued

Set Consequences To maintain your boundaries there must be a consequence if someone does not respect, honor or take them seriously. The consequence is how you ultimately honor yourself when someone attempts to dishonor the way you keep yourself safe with boundaries. As you set your boundary make it very clear what your consequence is and why?

EXAMPLE: If you cannot converse with me without cutting me off, I will not continue our conversation until what I have to say is honored, respected and heard.

CONSEQUENCE: Conversation ends when someone cuts you off after you've asked them not too

The Truth is if you are someone who has never set boundaries and you're attempting to finally set boundaries with someone who isn't used to you using your voice they will respond in 1 of 2 ways.

- Be loving, grateful & eager to do whatever it takes to respect your boundary.
- Inquire about where it stems from to gain more understanding and talk through this space with you.
- Ignore your boundary, become upset, play victim & attempt to dismiss your boundary.

If number #1 happens give yourself permission to be vulnerable and express, why you're setting this boundary on a deeper level. Explain how it connects to your childhood or your wounds and that you're actively working on healing that part of yourself and this boundary is to help you in the process.

If number #2 Happens

DO NOT FALL FOR THE EMOTIONAL GUILT TRIP! DO NOT ENGAGE!

Do not engage with their attempts to gaslight you, stand firm in honoring your boundary. Do not argue, do not debate. When or if you feel, yourself being triggered end the conversation and care for yourself with the somatic techniques given in the previous slide.

If you're new to setting boundaries, you MUST maintain them. Sometimes people forget your boundary, so you'll have to use your intuition to determine whether a person is intentionally disregarding your boundary or accidentally forgot. Remember you're training a person on how to treat you differently and in the beginning, it may take time for them to learn (not that much damn time tho lol). Just know that revisiting, re-implementing and restating your boundary is normal.

Boundary Journal Prompts

1. Why do you need boundaries?
2. What is happening as a result of you NOT implementing boundaries?
3. How does NOT having boundaries make you feel?
4. How do people treat you when you don't have boundaries?
5. How do you ALLOW people to treat you when you don't have boundaries?
6. How does it make you feel that you've ALLOWED yourself to be treated this way?
7. What boundaries do you want to implement? List them
8. How do you feel about setting boundaries? are you fearful, anxious, nervous & why?
9. How will setting boundaries enhance your happiness and quality of life & self-worth?
10. How will you respond when your boundaries are questioned or dismissed?
11. How will you respond when someone becomes angry about your boundaries?
12. How will you continue to cultivate your self-worth & honor yourself even when doubt, fear, confusion, or unworthiness tries to surface? What boundaries are you setting with yourself?
13. Why do you need boundaries with yourself?
14. What is the reason you never set boundaries

Journal Prompts to Work Through Shame

1. What Are you ashamed of?
2. How many shameful stories, do you carry?
3. Where do you carry shame in your body?
4. How does shame feel in your body?
5. Have you ever spoken about your shame, out loud?
6. Have you ever told anyone what you are shameful of?
7. When you did speak about something you were ashamed of, how were your received? How did the persons response make you feel?
8. Why do you feel you chose to carry shame instead of self love & compassion & understanding for yourself?
9. Where did you first learn the concept of shame? How did you learn you should be ashamed of something? Who gave you this idea?
10. Tell the story of everything you carry shame for. Pain the picture of how this event manifested as shame.
11. Who would you be if shame didn't have power over you?
12. How freely would you show up in the world if you didn't carry the weight of shame?
13. Was shame given to you? Did anyone teach you how to carry shame?
14. Was shame apart of your childhood? Did anything happen as a child that caused shame to surface?
15. Did your parents teach you about shame?
16. Were your parents judgmental? Did they compare you to other kids?
17. Were you ever touched inappropriately by someone as a child, young adult or adult that caused you to carry shame?

18. Did you ever tell anyone?
19. If not, why not? what was your fear?
20. Write a letter to SHAME. As if it's sitting next to you, explain how shame has affected you, how your life would be if shame weren't present & how your life is because shame is present. Come face to face with shame & OWN YOUR TRUTHS.
21. Write an apology letter to yourself for carrying shame for so long. Apologize for whatever you did that caused shame to surface & FORGIVE YOURSELF! Write a forgiveness letter.

Journal Prompts to Navigate Trauma?

1. How did this trauma make you feel? (scared, vulnerable, abandoned, powerless,
2. How did you cope with this trauma?
3. What are your coping or defense mechanisms? Are they healthy or unhealthy?
4. How does this trauma still effect you today? (*ex. I'm afraid people will leave me like my parent did)
5. What are your emotional triggers?
6. What traumas of the past are your emotional triggers attached to? (when yelled at, i remember my abusive childhood.
7. What age did your emotional trigger occur?
8. What was the situation or hat occurred that caused this trigger to form?
9. How do you respond when you are emotionally triggered?
10. Are you aware in the moment you are triggered or after?
11. Do you have control when you're emotionally triggered?
12. How has lack of control of your trigger affected your life, relationships or work?
13. How do you feel when you react after being triggered?
14. How would you prefer to respond when emotionally triggered?
15. What difficult thoughts or emotions come up most often for you?
16. Describe a choice you regret? What did you learn from it
17. What parts of your daily life cause stress, frustration, or sadness? What can you do to change those experiences?

18. What are three self-defeating thoughts that show up in your self talk? How can you reframe them to encourage yourself instead?

19. What go to coping strategies help you get through moments of emotional or physical pain?

20. Who do you trust with your most painful and upsetting feelings? How can you connect with them when feeling low?

21. What do you fear most? Have your fears changed throughout life?

<u>Letters For You</u>

In letters for yourself you will write a letter to any person who played a painful part in your trauma, your parent, romantic partner, a stranger, friend or even if it was yourself you will write about any situation that brought you deep pain or trauma. This is your opportunity to release the trauma attached to your memories out of your body.

Letters for you, rules.

1. Paint the picture. Describe in detail the situation & how it made you feel. Ask questions? Describe how this situation affected you growing up, how it made you feel about yourself, how it is still affecting you as adult.

2. Don't minimize your experience. This is your opportunity to say exactly how you feel/felt, think and express all your emotions no matter how mean, angry, ugly, nasty, happy, funny, spiteful, sad, embarrassing, depressing or chaotic your emotions may be. You are allowed to experience any emotion while writing your truth. (if you don't say how you truly feel even to yourself, you'll always have a war going on inside yourself.

3. This letter is for you & you only so be honest about your experience, don't write in fear, as if one day someone will magically read your letter. Do not hold back.

4. Each memory or situation requires a separate letter.

Shadow Work

1. Where do i hold my pain & trauma in my body?
2. What experiences make me occupy unauthentic masks?
3. What experiences regress me back to a younger age?
4. What experiences lead me to dissociate & escape from reality?
5. What unhealthy attachments do I need to release?
6. What do I need to forgive myself for?
7. What aspect of myself am I afraid to allow people to see?
8. How many masks do I wear?
9. What are my masks? list them & what purpose they serve
10. Who are you in the public?
11. Who do you revert into when you are alone?
12. What toxic cycles am I choosing to perpetuate? Why?
13. What makes me feel uncomfortable? Why?
14. What am I lying to myself about?
15. What uncomfortable conversation with myself am I avoiding?
16. In what areas of my life Am I struggling the most?
17. Are there any patterns that keep appearing?
18. What emotions am I attempting to avoid?
19. What are some traumatic situations that happened in your childhood & how do they effect you now?
20. Do you hold any grudges, resentments? If so with you & why?

Journal Prompts to Navigate Vulnerability

1. What stops you from expressing vulnerability?
2. Can you be vulnerable with yourself ALONE?
3. When you run from yourself & your emotions where do you hide? Relationships? Sexual exchanges, marijuana? Alcohol? Work? Tv? Travel? Food?
4. Do you express vulnerability when you first feel it? OR do you allow your emotions to build & fester so long that when you do express yourself it's no longer vulnerability it's frustration & anger?
5. Why don't you give yourself permission to express how you feel in the moment?
6. Who do you wish was present to console you when you do finally give yourself permission to cry?
7. Who was NEVER present for you the way you needed when you really needed to cry?
8. Did you parents create safe environments for you to share your emotions or vulnerable feelings?
9. How did your parents receive you when you shared vulnerable things? How did they respond? How did their responses make you feel?
10. How did it make you feel as a child having or not having a safe environment to share your vulnerability with your parents?
11. If you didn't have a safe environment to embody your vulnerability what behaviors did you create to cope?

12. How has not having a safe space to freely show up in your vulnerability affect you as a young child, young adult & fully grown adult? relationships
13. How has your fear, refusal or inability to express vulnerability or your emotions effected your body?
14. Is it possible your pain isn't actually pain, it's just pent up unexpressed emotions, i said words, unfelt vulnerability?
15. What is the fear you have that stops you from showing vulnerability?
16. Are you afraid to look weak?
17. Are you afraid of being shut down? Feelings disregarded? Told you are overreacting? Shamed? Not accepted? Not nurtured? Feel embarrassed?
18. When did you first learn that it wasn't safe to share your emotions?

EXAMPLE:

When i was 4 my mom taught me to say "my feelings were hurt" if someone did something to me. One day my dad yelled at me & i told him he hurt my feelings. He responded "WHAT, i hurt your feelings?" His response was aggressive & cold nowhere near as nurturing & loving as my moms. & that's the day i learned i wasn't safe to express my emotions & i downloaded the program to keep my emotions bottled in to not protect others not upset anyone & so i could continue to receive love.

• Instead of expressing vulnerability what do you do instead?

EXAMPLE:

when your spouse doesn't answer your phone calls, do you say, why tf aren't you answering the phone? You never answer your phone when i call & I'm getting tired of it? You must be doing something wrong because it takes you forever to text back

INSTEAD of saying …I'd like to bring something to your attention; it hurts my feelings when you don't answer my phone calls or text me back.

It triggers insecurity, abandonment & unworthy ness from my past I'm still working on healing & sometimes it makes me feel like you don't care to talk to me like i care to talk to you. How can we find a solution to this?

HOW IS YOUR INTUITIVE HEALTH?

1. Do you feel you have strong connection with your intuition?
2. Do you feel it can be stronger?
3. What do you feel is blocking your from having a strong relationship with your intuition?
4. How many times a week do you dishonor yourself?
5. Say yes when you really want to say no?
6. How often do you plan to do something & don't follow through?
7. How often do you renegotiate with something you truly want to do, change or know you should do?
8. Write about the times you are deeply motivated to do something & when the time comes you change your mind?
9. How does that feel?
10. How does it feel to go back on your word to yourself?
11. How does it feel knowing you are the only one that keeps you in self sabotaging cycles?
12. How does it feel to put others before yourself? Guilt, shame, embarrassment?
13. What stops you from keeping your word to yourself?
14. What are some ways you can begin to honor yourself today?
15. What are small things you can do daily to build your trust with yourself?
16. What is something big you KNOW your intuition is begging you to do?
17. When you do ignore your intuition, what are the reasons why? What are the incentives to disregarding your internal compass? is it in hopes to receive more love? is it out of fear love will be taken away?
18. When did you FIRST learn to ignore your intuition, gut feeling or desires? what age were you?

19. Was your CHOICE ever taken away, to follow your intuition?

20. Has your intuition ever attempted to keep you safe, you ignored it and put yourself in danger?

Intuitive Relationship Repair (Acknowledgement)

In your "Healing Journal" write your life story. This aspect of your intuitive repair is all about ACKNOWLEDGMENT. As you tell your life story deeply acknowledge

- What you experienced
- How you were treated As a child
- What emotional needs didn't your parents meet or nurture?

People ignore their intuition because of emotional trauma, wounds & voids from their past. Your past hurts & pains sometimes makes you cultivate survival skills & behaviors that numb your intuitive voice. By becoming clear & exploring your life story & just acknowledging what you've been through can shed Light on why you do what you do, ignore your intuition or have certain behaviors

APOLOGY

Write an apology letter to yourself for all of the times you've dishonored yourself by ignoring, disregarding & dishonoring your intuition. Make a list of every single moment, memory & situation you can think of & apologize for the situations you allowed yourself to be apart of against your intuitions better judgment.

Forgive Yourself

FORGIVE YOURSELF! Write a letter forgiving yourself for the times your said yes when you should have said no. Forgive yourself for the moments you didn't choose yourself. When you ignored your gut feeling, when you honored everyone else's advice & guidance before your own. When you put yourself in situations that could have potentially harmed you or changed your life. Especially those things actually did happen. NURTURE yourself, hug yourself & give yourself permission to let it go. Practice deep breaths breathing out any shame, guilt or embarrassment.

Give yourself grace. You don't have to hold on to this anymore. You deserve to forgive yourself & move forward

Visualize Your New Relationship With Self

After your apology letter, acknowledge how you'd like your relationship with your intuition to be, look & feel. What type of person will you be when you can trust yourself & your decisions? What types of relationships will you enter? How would you seek advice & guidance once your relationship with your intuition strengthens?

The Solution

However you expect a ROMATIC PARTNER to treat you, do this for yourself, but BETTER. Start practicing keeping your word to yourself, writing out your boundaries, practicing saying no, leaving situations that don't serve your highest good, cleaning up your diet, moving your body. ONLY YOU KNOW what your soul& intuition are calling you to do. Make a list of what your internal voice is guiding you to do & be honest with yourself about what you can commit to now to begin rebuilding your self trust

Back to Confidence

create a list of things your can commit to that will allow you to keep your word to yourself & rebuild trust. Start small. Example. I will journal 2xs a week for 10mins.Only write down what you KNOW you can be consistent with. At the end of each day create a checklist, or make off your calendar of what all you complete. this will give your an opportunity to cultivate PRIDE in your self love accomplishment. Being proud of yours stimulates deep self CONFIDENCE

JOURNAL PROMPTS TO IDENTIFY ADDICTIVE BEHAVIOR

1. Are you addicted to any mind altering substances? Alcohol, drugs, marijuana or food

2. Are you addicted to any unhealthy behaviors? Sex, serial dating, unhealthy thoughts, worrying, binge eating, wasting disorders,

3. Do you have Addictive behavior? If so explain

4. When do you first remember using a substance, food, relationship, sex, gambling etc to make yourself feel good or better?

5. What emotions did these substances help you escape or forget about?

6. What situations did these substances make feel better about?

7. What is your relationship with the word addiction? How does it make you feel?

8. Have you allowed this word to keep you from acknowledging you need help in a specific area?

9. Do your parents or family have a history of addiction of ANY kind?

10. Did their addiction affect you as a child growing up? Example, if you parent was an alcoholic did that make them treat you differently, make them absent or abusive etc?

11. Can you stop using something, or someone that makes you feel good, for long periods of time without CRAVINGS? (9months to 2yrs)

12. Can you stop, for 4years? Of forever

13. When you CRAVE something, what are you doing in those moments?

14. When you crave something what emotions are you feeling in those moments?

15. Do you fee anxiety when you crave something, as if it's hard to stop thinking about or wanting?

16. Do you have to try to convince yourself not to use or do the thing you crave?

17. How do you feel once you've given into the craving? Happy, guilt, shame etc

18. Does the thing you crave add VALUE to your life? Explain

19. Does the thing you crave or could poisonous be addicted to make you feel better or worse about yourself? Explain

20. BEFORE you partake in the behavior, how do you feel emotionally?

21. Do you NEED this thing to sleep, relax, feel loved, excited about life, have fun or calm anxiety?

22. Can you create this emotion on your own ?

23. Does is aid in emotional clarity?

24. What has happened in your past that could make you unconsciously use the things you could be addicted to, to make yourself feel better or to escape your pain?

25. Do you feel you're using outside sources to escape your pain?

26. Do you enjoy your life? Is there any part of it you consciously would like to escape from?

27. Are there any emotions you feel from past & present you would like to escape from?

28. Do you numb yourself with people places or things so you don't have to feel certain emotions or remember certain painful events?

29. Is it possible that you could have blind spots & you're unaware of why you have certain addictive behaviors?

30. If you're operating at your healthiest, happiest, high frequency, full of love self, would you still need or use the thing in question? How would your life be without it? How would you show up in the world without it? How different would it make you as a person?

31. How would you life be if you don't stop using it or doing it? How would it effect your relationships? Your relationship with yourself? Your relationship with the present moment? Your ability to have emotional, physical & spiritual clarity?

PLEASURE

A Journey Into The Pleasure Body

The pleasure body is the activation of all senses that makes the body, mind, heart & spirit experience deep blissful pleasure or ease. The pleasure body is when all meridians & pathways are open & clear for healthy energy to flow fluidly without obstruction producing serotonin, dopamine & oxytocin.

How would your life be if you committed to a full year of not giving in or giving up. To doing that one thing that you know for a fact will change the entire trajectory of your life. What if you give your full undivided attention to this one thing daily for a year just to give yourself a fighting chance, to prove there is nothing wrong with you, that you're more than capable. What if you intentionally give your all to yourself this year. Go all in & max out

Rest, boundaries, sex, dancing, cooking, fasting, responding in healthier ways, laughing, being creative, exploring, napping, asking for what you need, giving yourself permission to receive love, saying no, not being controlled by thoughts or emotions, silence & stillness, moving the body, changing your mind, ending relationships, having faith, crying, all open & nurture the pleasure body

1. How can i experience deep pleasure 24/7
2. What needs to happen in my life, for even the smallest things to feel pleasurable?
3. What emotional debris needs to be cleared out, that's still lingering?
4. What emotional debris am holding on to intentionally that I'm not ready to let go of yet?
5. What behaviors are hindering me from experiencing pleasure?
6. What foods, relationships, thoughts, conversations, people, desires are keeping me from experiencing pleasure?

7. What does a life of pleasure look & feel like to me?
8. Is pleasure sexual?
9. Is pleasure an energy of ease or harmony in all things?
10. Is pleasure deep enjoyment in your moment-to-moment present life?
11. Is pleasure emotional maturity?
12. Is pleasure not being controlled by thoughts?
13. What behaviors or routines can i begin to practice to nurture my pleasure body?
14. What foods can nurture my pleasure body?
15. What activities can nurture my pleasure body?
16. What self-love rituals can nurture sexual pleasure within my body?
17. Does your environment, room, car, purse, kitchen, cabinets, job, nurture the type & level of pleasure you desire?
18. Do your relationships nurture the types of pleasure you'd like to feel?
19. How do you feel your quality of life will be or evolve if you begin to nurture your pleasure body?
20. Do you sabotage your pleasure? Why
21. Do you feel deserving of pleasure?
22. Do you feel safe enough to experience healthy pleasure in your life, mind body & soul?
23. Do you feel safe enough to explore healthy sexual pleasure with a partner?
24. Do you feel safe enough to explore sexual pleasure with yourself & your body?
25. Do you have any resistance towards pleasure?

EXPLORING SEXUAL & NON-SEXUAL INTIMACY WITH SELF

True intimacy begins when you've cleared trauma from the reproductive organs, the body and reconciled your relationship with the wounded version of yourself that has shown up in all sexual experiences. When a person has sex BEFORE & without healing their wounded-ness this trauma bleeds into their sensuality, their sexuality, their ability to be liberated during sex & their ability to truly be apart of their sexual experience without tainted energy. Many people who have deep wounds regarding sex, sexual abuse, molestation, improper childhood education, early sexual experiences, seeing sex at a young age & being confused about it tend to become PERFORMATIVE actors during their sexual experiences. Lastly those who have wounded emotional trauma tend to use sex as a transaction to receive love in return, dishonoring themselves, betraying their bodies & becoming fragmented beings to the point they confuse themselves & can no longer tell or differentiate if they actually enjoy sex, if they're naturally sexual or if this identity was formed to cope with a past of emotional or sexual trauma. The true pathway to liberated sexual experiences is to heal the wounded self with non-sexual intimacy with self.

Journal Prompts to heal the wounded self around intimacy

1. When did you first learn about sex?
2. When did you first see a sexual image?
3. Did you know what the sexual image was?
4. Was there anyone who explained the sexual image you saw?
5. What was your first sexual experience? was it consensual?
6. Have you experienced sexual trauma as an adult or child?
7. How did that make you feel?
8. Do you remember if you were sexually taken advantage of?
9. Did you feel safe enough to tell anyone?
10. Have you been raped, molested or sexually abused?
11. How did that invasion of your body affect you as child?
12. How has that invasion of your body affected you as an adult?
13. What age did you first have sex or your first sexual experience?
14. How did it make you feel? beautiful, confident, self-conscious, afraid, confused? etc
15. Was your sexual activity a secret or hidden?
16. Was there shame around sex? sometimes parents & religion will shame people into not having sex or fear them into going to hell
17. Did any specific small or major situation happen that tainted your sexual experience?
18. Do you use sex to feel loved by your partner?
19. Do you perform during sex even if you don't feel good sensation?
20. Have you ever said yes to sexual experiences when you really wanted to say no?
21. Have you ever had sex with someone who did not deserve to share your space?
22. Have you ever had sex with someone because you felt lonely & needed to feel loved or wanted?

23. Have you ever had sex with someone in hopes they would choose you or stay with you?
24. Have you ever cried or felt uncomfortable during sexual experiences due to unresolved PAST sexual trauma?
25. Have you ever contracted an STD?
26. Do you currently have an STD or incurable disease?
27. How did or does this make you feel?
28. How did you feel when you found out about the disease or the STD?
29. How does it make you feel about yourself?
30. Are you naturally a sexual person?
31. Can you dedicate 2 years to NOT having sexual experiences?
32. What is your sexual & intimate relationship like with yourself?
33. Do you feel comfortable being intimate with yourself?
34. What does being intimate with yourself look & feel like?
35. How often are you intimate with yourself?
36. If you were sexually taken advantage of How did you nurture yourself?
37. If you were sexually taken advantage of did you have anyone, like a parent to comfort you or tell you it wasn't your fault?
38. Did you have anyone explain what sex was to you, how to have sex, how you should be treated during sex?
39. Were you able to tell you parents when you had your first sexual experience?
40. Do you casually have sex as an adult?
41. Do you feel free & liberated during sex?
42. Does sex make you feel an emotional connection?
43. Do you use sex to cope with not feeling loved, wanted, desired or chosen?
44. Do you use sex as an escape from emotional pain?
45. Do you have healthy sexual intimacy with yourself?

46. Have you ever had sex with someone and later regretted it and why?
47. Have you ever given access to your body to someone that took advantage of your trust? how did that make you feel?
48. If you've experienced sexual trauma, rape or molestation how did you heal from this trauma? How has this trauma manifested in your adult life & relationships?
49. Do you have trust issues, abandonment issues, commitment issues, are you emotionally clingy, needy or emotionally fragile when you've had a sexual relationship with someone.
50. Do you experience any sort of fear or un-comfortability surrounding sex?

Healing the Wound

When sexual trauma is present, its DISRESPECTFUL to your wounded being, your inner child, your young adult self, your adult self and your soul when you have sex searching for pleasure and your entire being is still suffering from hidden and stored emotional pain. There is no such thing as pleasure, intimacy or sexual freedom if there's a version of your being that never received nurturing after being taken advantage of, raped, molested, confused, exposed to sex at an early age, shamed for sexual curiosity, feared or guilted around the sex subject. If you've been taken advantage of or you've taken advantage of yourself, abandonment, neglect & betrayal are essences that run through your body and it is your job to transmute, acknowledge, apologize and heal these versions of your being.

<u>Where to begin</u>

After answering each journal prompt question explain in DETAIL how you feel and describe every emotion that surfaces around this topic.

Write a letter (ONLY FOR YOU) detailing every single sexual experience you've had, good & bad. try to see the nuances in how those experiences effected you good or bad. Process the memory.

ACKNOWLEDGMENT-The memories that hold negative, heavy, sad, confusing or traumatic energy SPEND TIME THERE. i personally listed every single sexual partner i ever had a painted the picture of my experience with them, why i had sex with them, what my intention was, why i dishonored myself, why i allowed them to dishonor me, why i said yes when i really wanted to say no? how this made me feel then, how naive i was in search for love and how it makes me feel now that i didn't know any better at the time or how i feel now knowing that i KNEW better at the time and still chose to dishonor myself.

ACKNOWLEDGE- the inner child that no one came to rescue, explained sex in detail, comforted, told it wasn't your fault, the inner child that needed guidance, that never felt loved, wanted, seen, good enough or chosen. Comfort the young adult or adult version of yourself that doesn't know how to sexually connect to anyone nor yourself. Acknowledge the fear, guilt, sadness, grief

APOLOGIZE- to the version of yourself that knew better but still chose to dishonor yourself with unhealthy choices. Apologize to yourself for putting yourself in unhealthy situations because you just wanted to feel loved. EXPLAIN to yourself your WHY? what you were feeling. give yourself a real apology for abandoning yourself the way others have. acknowledge how it makes you feel right now.

VISUALIZATIONS- visualize yourself mending your relationship with yourself, your inner child, young adult self and adult self. see into your body where the trauma is being held, is it in your womb, your hips, your back, neck, heart? & visualize yourself cleaning the emotional clutter and sending an abundance of love to your wounded areas. Visualize yourself mending the relationship with your inner child, holding your inner child's hand. making a promise to yourself to choose to show up for yourself by making the best choices to honor yourself and no longer hurting people the way others have hurt you.

<u>DAILY JOURNAL</u>- daily CHECK IN WITH YOURSELF. check in with the versions of yourself you've mended relationships with and apologized to. Don't leave yourself hanging don't apologize and then disappear.

We are all walking each other home
We are all visitors to this time, this place.
We are just passing through.
Our purpose here is to observe, learn, grow, love.
And then we return back home.
May you rest in peace
May you laugh in love
May you cry in safety
May you return home in confidence.

TAKE YOUR POWER BACK

Now, I'm going to tell you what I wish someone told me
before reading hundreds of unnecessary books.
Put this book down and intentionally begin to read
The book of your own soul.
You have everything you need.
Your soul remembers lifetimes of wisdom.
Trust yourself
Trust your guidance
Trust your memory
Honor your soul level brilliance
Stop giving your power away & tap into your source.
I didn't tell you anything your soul doesn't already know.
Close this book, close your eyes and say
"Thank you for helping me remember
what my souls already knows"

ABOUT THE AUTHOR

Candyss Love is an intuitive guide that guides people in their emotional healing process and gives them tools to transmute their pain into peace. Candyss Love is a retired police officer and military veteran who chose to dedicate her life to helping others. In 2020 amid the pandemic Candyss began guiding and training Licensed Therapists, Psychologist, Counselors & Life Coaches by teaching them methods to guide their clients and themselves intuitively & no longer solely from regurgitated info from book.

Candyss became passionate about integrating emotional healing process and the spirituality of intuition.

She offers A plethora of resources, modalities, tools & support to aid in her clients healing process.

Including one on one intuitive therapy sessions, emotional healing retreats, sound therapy, breath-work sessions & monthly full moon ceremonies. Remember who the f*ck you are is an addition to how Candyss chooses to intentionally add to the collective consciousness.

Website: CandyssLove.com

Instagram: Candyss.Love

Youtube: Candyss Love

TikTok: Candyss.Love